IDEOLOGIES

Politics
in
Action

IDEOLOGIES

Politics
in
Action

MAX J. SKIDMORE

University of Missouri

HARCOURT BRACE JOVANOVICH, PUBLISHERS

San Diego   New York   Chicago   Austin   Washington, D.C.
London   Sydney   Tokyo   Toronto

Dedicated to
the memory of my father
who resisted the bigotry of the ideologue
and to
Betrenia and Jack Bowker
who encouraged me to think.
Never forget that fulfillment and joy in life
require thought.

ISBN 0-15-540579-9
Library of Congress Catalog Card Number: 88-82143
Printed in the United States of America

Preface

   This book presents a new and different approach to the subject of political ideologies. It is intended both to stimulate thought and discussion and to serve as a comprehensive foundation for study. It begins with a review of the various definitions in current use and notes the lack of agreement as to what should be included in the topic.

   In supplying its own definition, *Ideologies: Politics in Action* has adopted a pragmatic approach, recognizing that a definition's most important element is not its philosophical sophistication (however appealing that may be) but rather its ability to clarify the complex subject of politics. The prime consideration is the real world—the political world—and the degree to which one definition, in opposition to another, may assist in providing insights into the way it operates. The assumption here is, therefore, that the study of political ideology is the study of the manner in which ideas are transformed into action. This brings into consideration many things not generally considered as falling within the scope of political ideology and helps as well to clarify other aspects of politics. A further asumption is that at least some degree of historical awareness is essential to the understanding of the present. As a result, this textbook is both historical and comparative.

It is, of course, important to direct attention to commonly recognized political ideologies. Treatments of such topics as democracy, communism, and fascism form a major portion of this book, as indeed they do of all works in the field. This study also treats nationalism as at least the equal of these, and it deals with the major democratic variations that include democratic capitalism and democratic socialism. It does not, however, stop with such accepted emphases.

Religion, for instance, has an obvious influence on politics, but as a rule it has played little if any part in the study of political ideology. This book deals not only with such themes as liberation theology, Christian socialism, Islamic fundamentalism, and such other fundamentalist movements as the rise of the religious right in the United States, but it also deals with the political effects of mainstream religions, both Christian and non-Christian. Its approach permits religious ideologies to be viewed, when warranted, as political ideologies.

Feminism sometimes receives treament in the study of ideologies, but often it does not. Even when considered, however, it rarely receives the kind of treatment that the body of feminist thought warrants, that is, as an outgrowth—in fact a logical extension—of democracy itself. The approach adopted in this study places feminism in proper perspective.

The rise of professionalism within governmental administration has given rise to what I call "managerialism." Although it has striking effects on politics, it has not previously been identified as what it so evidently is, a form of political ideology. In providing that identification, this book suggests a new source of political insights.

Similarly, anarchism is a topic that many studies ignore as irrelevant to the modern situation, disregarding anarchism's historical importance. Consequently, they obscure a potential form of anarchist thought, identified here as "political anarchism." Even though the force that it exerts on contemporary politics may be small, if it exists at all, "political anarchism" does have adherents and may have increasing appeal to certain groups seeking ways to respond to current conditions. Anarchism should therefore be included in any proper study of political ideologies.

There should be little doubt that theories of nonviolence can become explicit political ideologies, although it is rare for them to be included in studies such as this. This book gives them their due and is unique in expanding its consideration to include the effect of violence and its ideological implications. It is the pervasiveness of violence—not only in practice but implicitly and explicitly within ideologies themselves—that has given rise to ideologies of nonviolence in their many variations. A proper understanding of the ultimate effects of violence, and the strengths and limitations of nonviolent responses, is impossible without understanding political ideology, broadly conceived.

Such an understanding requires an examination, not merely of definitions and specific ideologies, but of the broad effects of ideology. This book, for example, points to the political role of economics to call attention to the function and role of ideology in general—its usefulness and its dangers. Above all, it examines and describes the role of the ideologue.

The title of this book is thus a literal reflection of its contents. It deals with ideologies and with politics in action. Observations and discussions, formal and informal, at universities and intellectual centers in the United States and around the world have helped to develop and distill my ideas. These have included over the past decade such places as the Universities of Bombay, Calcutta, and Madras, Osmania University and Jawaharlal Nehru University in New Delhi, and the American Studies Research Centre in Hyderabad (where I was once the director), all in India; Chittagong and Dacca Universities in Bangladesh; Tribhuvan University in Katmandu, Nepal; Shanghai and Peking Universities in China; and various universities in Europe. Friends and colleagues have also, albeit usually unwittingly, provided assistance through stimulating conversations. Because this is an intensely personal work, it is unlikely that any of these would recognize their contributions. And, of course, they bear no responsibility for the treatment or the conclusions; they are solely mine.

I nevertheless owe a great debt to Professors David Noble, John Turner, Mary Turpie, and especially Mulford Q. Sibley, all of the University of Minnesota, who helped point me in the right direction many years ago in graduate school; Eric Bockstael of the Catholic University of Louvain in Belgium, who suggested some useful sources; Denny Pilant, head of the Department of Political Science at Southwest Missouri State University and Marshall Carter Tripp, foreign service officer and my coauthor on two other books (who also suggested useful sources) for enlightening conversations through many years; my aunt, Betrenia Bowker, who beginning in my childhood attempted to make me aware of the effects of ideology; numerous colleagues at the University of Missouri, Kansas City, especially Steven Gilham, Carla Klausner, Harris Mirkin, and Dale Neuman for their helpful suggestions; and my thoughtful editor at Harcourt Brace Jovanovich, Drake Bush, for his sound advice. As always, I appreciate my wife, Charlene, more than I can say. She helped me refine many of my ideas and put up with me through the months of weekends and evenings that were required to write this book.

Max J. Skidmore

Contents

Introduction

"Ideology" has been responsible for mass murder and for the production of works of high culture, for the creation of nation states and for the overthrow of political regimes, for torture and imprisonment and for elaborate protection of human rights. It has been defined in various ways, some contradicting one another, and there is no general agreement as to its precise meaning. Nevertheless, all who study ideology recognize its powerful influence on human affairs.

BACKGROUND

Despite the obvious importance of ideology, it has only recently received the attention it warrants. Niccolo Machiavelli (1469–1527) provided an influential ideology justifying the modern state and the use of power, even ruthless power. Thomas Hobbes (1588–1679) similarly laid an ideological groundwork for the exercise of absolute power to maintain order and the state. The term "ideology," however, did not come into being until after the French Revolution created truly mass politics for the first time. The French philosopher Destutt de Tracy (1754–1836) appears to have coined

1

DESTUTT DE TRACY

. . . as I have often said, logic, as it has always been known, was nothing but the art of drawing legitimate conclusions from recognized principles. It was not therefore what it should have been if it were true logic, or the beginning of everything. It was only an art, it should have been a science. . . . Yet how could this logic be perfected? How could it be completed? How could it be turned into a real science, the first of them all? It is obvious, or I am completely mistaken, that this could only be done by making it consist of the study of our means of knowledge.

From *Elements of Ideology* (1817)

---

the term in the early nineteenth century when he attempted to develop a science of the mind through the study of the development of ideas.

Thomas Jefferson was interested in Tracy's writings and introduced the study of ideology in America. He sought to have it included in the curriculum of the University of Virginia, but interest in the subject vanished with his death.[1] Ideology became an object of study only with the development of communism, Fascism, and Nazism in the twentieth century, and it was not until the years of the Cold War that the subject began to receive widespread attention. It was even later, well into the 1960s in fact, before bibliographic listings on the subject became numerous.

DEFINITIONS

For Karl Marx, ideology was a pattern of illusions resulting from economic relations between classes, or, as he put it, the class struggle. He saw ideology as a pattern of rationalization, deception, and self-deception, preventing a true understanding of social and economic reality. For the sociologist Karl Mannheim,

---

[1] Adrienne Koch, *The Philosophy of Thomas Jefferson* (New York: Columbia University Press, 1943), pp. 56–63.

KARL MARX

The ideas of the ruling class are in every epoch the ruling ideas:
i.e. the class which is the ruling material force of society, is at the
same time its ruling intellectual force. The class which has the means
of material production at its disposal, has control at the same time
over the means of mental production. . . . The division of labour
. . . manifests itself also in the ruling class as the division of mental and material labour, so that inside this class one part appears as
the thinkers of the class (its active, conceptive ideologists, who make
the perfecting of the illusion of the class about itself their chief source
of livelihood), while the others' attitude to these ideas and illusions
is more passive and receptive, because they are in reality the active
members of this class and have less time to make up illusions and
ideas about themselves.

From *The German Ideology* by Marx and Engels (1845)

ideology was the conceptual structure of a social class, the framework through which it views reality. Sigmund Freud described
ideology from another point of view. He believed that it arises
from the repression of psychological urges and provides an organizing framework that, once again, is largely illusion.

Political ideology may be distinguished from mere attitudes,
beliefs, or opinions.[2] Many writers go to great lengths to separate
it from other forms of political thought, such as philosophy and
theory. Political philosophy may be deemed to be more profound
or to speak directly to the individual and call for individual improvement, as opposed to ideology's narrow activist orientation
and its appeal to the group.[3] Ideology is commonly seen as including elements of consensus, a foundation formed of a few specific core beliefs and perhaps a connection with an activist group.[4]

The terms "political philosophy," "political theory," and "political ideology" are frequently most confusing. "Theory" may be

---

[2]L. B. Brown, *Ideology* (Baltimore: Penguin, 1973), p. 15.
[3]Leon P. Baradat, *Political Ideologies,* 2nd ed. (Englewood Cliffs, N.J.: Prentice–
Hall, 1984), p. 9.
[4]Reo M. Christenson, et al., *Ideologies and Modern Politics* (New York: Dodd, Mead,
1971), p. 6.

KARL MANNHEIM

The word "ideology" itself had, to begin with, no inherent ontological significance . . . , since it originally denoted merely the
theory of ideas. The ideologists were . . . the members of a philosophical group in France who . . . rejected metaphysics and sought
to base the cultural sciences on anthropolgical and psychological
foundations.

The modern conception of ideology was born when Napoleon,
finding that this group of philosophers was opposing his imperial
ambitions, contemptuously labelled them "ideologists." Thereby the
word took on a derogatory meaning which, like the word "doctrinaire," it has retained to the present day. However, if the theoretical implications of this contempt are examined, it will be found
that the depreciative attitude involved is, at bottom, of an episte-
mological and ontological nature. What is depreciated is the validity of the adversary's thought because it is regarded as
unrealistic. . . . It is thus clear how the new meaning of the term
ideology bears the imprint of the position and the point of view of
those who coined it, namely, the political men of action.

It is no longer the exclusive privilege of socialist thinkers to
trace bourgeois thought to ideological foundations and thereby to
discredit it. Nowadays groups of every standpoint use this weapon
against all the rest. . . . [A]s soon as all parties are able to analyse
the ideas of their opponents in ideological terms, all elements of
meaning are qualitatively changed and the word ideology acquires
a totally new meaning. . . . [T]he general form of the total conception of ideology is being used by the analyst when he has the courage to subject not just the adversary's point of view but all points
of view, including his own, to the ideological analysis.

From *Ideology and Utopia* (1939)

used so broadly as to include virtually any thought about politics,
or it may be used so narrowly as to apply only to empirical generalizations. "Philosophy" usually implies some attention to values. One may hear "ideology" used as an epithet to signify
dogmatism, as a description of a motivating system of values, or
simply as a loose way of saying "political thought." The important thing in studying ideology is to have a clear and workable

idea of the meaning of the term, rather than to distinguish it precisely from some other form of thought. It will be helpful, in arriving at such an understanding, to consider what others have written on the subject.

Lyman Sargent wrote in 1981 that not all people have ideologies. "We all have beliefs," he said, but added that "unless the beliefs are recognized or acted upon with or without recognition, it is difficult to say that we have an ideology."[5] In the 1987 edition of the same book, however, he approached the matter differently, suggesting that he may have revised his definition. "Whether we are aware of it or not," he then wrote, "most of us are influenced by ideology. Every television program, newspaper, book, or film directly or indirectly, intentionally or unintentionally, presents an ideology. . . . In the development of our own beliefs and attitudes, we are affected by a variety of belief systems—religious and/or political views of the world that are, or are believed to be, internally consistent and consciously held by many people; we call these belief systems ideologies."[6] He now seems to be saying that to be classed as an ideology, a belief system must be "consciously held," even though every word in a printed or visual medium presents a belief system, and that ideology affects "most of us." He no longer indicates specifically whether he still believes it to be true that there may be some people without ideologies.

Andrew Gyorgy and George Blackwood have gone so far as to identify "non-ideologies," which they called those systems built on mystery and myth, rather than on truth.[7] Roy Macridis, on the other hand, wrote that everyone has an ideology, whether recognized or not, and whether admitted or not.[8] Clearly, there is great disagreement on this issue.

This is not to say, however, that there is no agreement on any aspect of ideology. Most writers on the subject identify characteristics they consider integral to all ideologies, and their lists have certain themes in common. Christenson and his colleagues,

[5]Lyman Tower Sargent, *Contemporary Political Ideologies*, 5th ed. (Homewood, Ill.: Dorsey, 1981), pp. 5–6.
[6]Sargent, *Contemporary Political Ideologies*, 7th ed. (Homewood, Ill.: Dorsey, 1987), pp. 1–2.
[7]Andrew Gyorgy and George D. Blackwood, *Ideologies in World Affairs* (Waltham, Mass.: Blaisdell, 1967), p. 2.
[8]Roy C. Macridis, *Contemporary Political Ideologies* (Boston: Little, Brown, 1986), p. 1.

for instance, have written that ideologies are broad in scope (although some more than others), they are systematic patterns of thought, they include both empirical and normative elements, they tend to be absolute and exclusive (purporting to present the entire truth, and the only truth), they do develop but tend to resist change, they are persuasive, and they involve political movements.[9] Watkins has included utopian elements of unrealistic optimism, an extreme view of the possibility of human progress, and great oversimplification.[10] In fact, he has listed oversimplification as the prime characteristic of an ideology. Baradat[11] has said that an ideology presents a view of the present and the future, it is action-oriented, it is directed to the masses, and it usually uses simple terms. Mark has indicated that ideologies have two characteristics. Either implicitly or explicitly, they present a value structure and assert that it, and no other, must be acted upon.[12] Rejai's list includes a view of the world involving both fact and fiction, an appeal to emotion, a conception of the good society, and a plan for action.[13]

Rejai also stressed that simplification, both linguistic and non-linguistic, is essential to the communication of an ideology. Ideologies are built around symbols, including words that capture a complex idea and present it simply, regardless of the distortion involved, and such nonverbal devices as flags, monuments, insignia, music, and holidays. His excellent discussion of the use of symbols documents their importance. They pull ideas together, making them intelligible, and present them instantaneously in a way that arouses emotion.

Considering that there is disagreement about an exact definition of ideology but that certain characteristics of ideologies are generally accepted, it should be evident that it is not important for the student of politics to develop an exclusive definition. The main task is rather to arrive at an understanding of the term that will be sufficiently meaningful to be useful in studying the effects of political ideas. This may lead to efforts to identify specifically political ideologies.

[9]Christenson, p. 9.
[10]Frederick M. Watkins, *The Age of Ideology—Political Thought, 1750 to the Present* (Englewood Cliffs, N.J.: Prentice–Hall, 1964), pp. 7–8.
[11]Baradat, pp. 7–8.
[12]Max Mark, *Modern Ideologies* (New York: St. Martin's Press, 1973), p. 3.
[13]Mostafa Rejai, *Comparative Political Ideologies* (New York: St. Martin's Press, 1984), pp. 4–8.

Most ideologies have political effects in one way or another, but some are explicitly political. There is no need to be precise in identifying these political ideologies, just as there is no need to seek clear distinctions that separate ideology sharply from other forms of political thought. It is enough to be able to discern which ideologies and which systems of political thought have political effects. Thrashing through thickets of definitions in search of semantic subtleties requires considerable energy that could be put to better use.

The most useful definition of political ideology, therefore, should be a rather simple one. First, a political ideology is a reasonably coherent pattern of ideas about politics and government. This means ideas about the purposes of collective life, about the ways to attain social goals, about the relationship between the individual and others, and about how resources are to be developed and distributed. Second, a political ideology succeeds in simplifying these ideas considerably. To do this, it relies heavily on verbal and nonverbal symbols. Finally, a political ideology provides a program, and incites action. This will necessarily involve strong emotional appeals. A one-sentence definition might therefore be: "Political ideology is a form of thought that presents a pattern of complex political ideas simply and in a manner that inspires action to achieve certain goals."

It is doubtful that a society sufficiently cohesive to be worthy of the name could exist without the foundation of a political ideology, thus defined, although it might be unrecognized as such by the members of the society. It is ideology that performs certain functions essential to any political culture.

FUNCTIONS AND DISTINCTIONS

Many of the functions of an ideology are implicit in the definition. Ideology provides cohesion by specifying a view of reality, it offers rules of conduct, it defines roles in society, and it provides identification with the group. An ideology helps evaluate, explain, and provide understanding by asserting answers to basic questions such as these: What is the nature of human beings?, Why are things as they are?, How should they be?, What is within the realm of possibility for human achievement?, What is the nature of society?, What is the appropriate role of the state?, What constitutes the "good" in politics?, What should be the relationship between the individual and the community?, What are the appropriate property arrangements for a society?, and What methods are appropriate to achieve political ends? Moreover, it is ideology that supplies a rationale for existing institutions or for attempts to revise them.

The latter point is essential to the understanding of a political ideology. Every one, and in fact every political action, seeks one of two things: to preserve what exists or to change it. One might infer, therefore, that there are two broad categories of political ideologies: conservative (or status quo) ideologies and ideologies of change. Conservative ideologies seek to conserve current institutions. Ideologies of change seek something different. It is not sufficient, however, to say merely that there are ideologies of change, because the idea of "change" is so broad. Change can be violent or peaceful, sudden or gradual, total or partial. Thus it is necessary also to divide ideologies of change into two categories: reformist ideologies, which seek change essentially within the structure of existing institutions, and revolutionary ideologies, which seek to replace them.

The first step in understanding an ideology is to determine whether it is directed toward change and, if so, what manner of change. This identifies it as one of three types:

- Status quo ideologies, which seek to conserve the existing order
- Reform ideologies, which seek change within the existing order
- Revolutionary ideologies, which seek to replace the existing order

An ideology fits into one of these classifications only in relation to the conditions in which it exists. As an illustration, consider the political ideology to which a nation state adheres, the "official" ideology, as opposed to others that are also likely to be present. It will always support the institutions of that state, however much it may require rationalization and strained interpretations to do so. It therefore would be conservative. The ideology of a dissenting group would justify change, but if that group were to come to power and develop new institutions, its ideology—*even if completely unchanged*—would become conservative and justify the status quo. During the seventeenth century, for example, Calvinism was a powerful revolutionary ideology for Calvinist groups opposing non-Calvinistic regimes. At the same time, Calvinism was a strong conservative, or status quo, ideology in societies where Calvinists had gained control. Marxism presents a modern example. For decades it has been the foremost revolutionary ideology in the world, yet where Marxists are firmly in power—places such as the U.S.S.R., the Eastern European states, and Albania—it is profoundly defensive of the status quo and is therefore conservative.

THE LEFT–RIGHT CONTINUUM

The terms "left" and "right" as applied to political ideologies today are frequently confusing and rarely precise. They originated around 1789, during the time of the French Revolution, and reflected the seating of groups in the National Assembly of the First French Republic. On the left were the radicals, who favored immediate and drastic change. In the center sat the moderates, who supported reform and gradual change. Those who supported the monarchy and resisted any change in its powers or those of the nobility were on the right.

Since that time, writers have applied the terms to ideologies according to their acceptance of change and the degree to which their attitudes toward privilege and power tend to be elitist or egalitarian. They identify ideologies on the left as egalitarian, favorable to change, and inclined to the belief that human nature is good and that corruption results from the effects of institutions. They identify ideologies on the right as elitist, hostile to change, and viewing human beings as selfish, weak, and corrupted by nature.

The further one proceeds along the continuum in either direction, the stronger the tendencies presumably become. There are exceptions, however. Although the extreme left does contain the radicals, those advocating immediate and total change to benefit humanity, and although the attitude toward change does become more resistant as one proceeds right along the continuum, there is a sudden shift at the extreme right. There, one discovers the reactionaries who also advocate change—a different kind. They seek to return to a previously existing state of affairs, real or imagined, and their goal is power rather than change for the benefit of humanity.

Obviously there is much inconsistency in the use of the terms today, and just as obviously they are inadequate to describe modern ideologies with any degree of precision. It is customary to assign the extreme left position to communist and anarchist ideologies, with Fascist and Nazi groups on the extreme right. In between, ranging from left to right, are socialists, liberals, conservatives, and certain right-wing anarchist groups. It is commonplace to observe that, in practice, regardless of the differences in the ideas they espouse, those at the extremes of the continuum tend to behave in a similar fashion. The definitions are vague, and they sometimes confuse political ideas with economic ones, but "left" and "right" can be helpful in classifying ideologies if used with great caution.

EFFECTS

This ability of an ideology to shift its character depending upon the circumstances, without changing internally, suggests the most important reason for studying the phenomenon. By definition, it motivates people to political action. If an ideology can inspire people to action, and if that action can be directed differently according to circumstances, it follows that those who can control the terms of the discussion regarding the ideology can use it to control and manipulate the people.

"Social power rests with those who can control and implement an ideology," wrote L. B. Brown.[14] He noted that those who are marginal or deviant—those who dissent from standard assumptions of a political culture—may face trial, jail, incarceration in a mental hospital, or execution. Brown was certainly correct in writing that this illustrates "the social control that is possible through the sanctions on belief and behavior," or, in other words, the power of the controllers.

In considering the power of a controller, or a "mind manipulator," to use Aldous Huxley's term, one should remember the effect that an ideology has upon its adherents, the most fervent

[14]Brown, pp. 12–13.

of whom become "ideologues," or "True Believers," as Eric Hoffer termed them. "It has always to be remembered that ideologists do not believe what they see, but see only part of the truth. They see all in the way of their belief and see all of what they believe." For them, the world "has no independent existence outside of the practical understanding prescribed. An ideology cannot be challenged by either facts or rival theories."[15] Rejai has similarly pointed out that "all ideologies serve as instruments for the manipulation and control of the people. A country's leaders are always in a position to dupe the masses, particularly in the light of contemporary advances in technologies of communication. The only questions are the regularity, extent, and intensity with which popular manipulation and control are exercised."[16] Although he may have overstated the case somewhat, his point is a good one.

There can be no question about the power of an ideology as a tool for the use of political leaders. Within very broad limits, its effectiveness is limited only by their skill and ingenuity or, perhaps, by the extent of their ruthlessness.

CONCLUSION

The early association of ideology with totalitarian movements probably accounts for the tendency on the part of some to view it solely as an instrument of dictatorial propaganda. A more sophisticated understanding of the term leads to the recognition that ideology is a feature of all societies and has a powerful effect in every one of them. It is this recognition that reveals its pervasive effect and the vital importance of understanding the phenomenon. A thorough awareness of the subtle similarities shared by all political cultures—highly developed and less developed, communist and democratic—as well as the obvious differences among them, is essential if we are to come to a true understanding of other cultures and even of our own. The study of political ideologies is one of the most promising avenues to pursue in attempting to arrive at the insights that are so important in this complex and often dangerous world.

[15] D. J. Manning, *Liberalism* (New York: St. Martin's Press, 1976), pp. 141–42.
[16] Rejai, p. 11.

Democracy

1

*D*emocracy has been such a powerful ideology in recent history that nearly every regime in the world today lays claim, in one way or another, to being "democratic." It is the word "democracy" that virtually everyone honors, not always the principles behind it. Sartori complains that the loose usage damages the original meaning, and that to some extent the situation is deliberate: "Democracy still has foes; but it is now best evaded in its own name and by means of its own name."[1] He discusses the Marxist–Leninist use of the word, and concludes that it has little relevance to notions of political democracy.[2]

MacPherson, on the other hand, has identified three legitimate and distinct forms of democracy, one of which is Marxist. In addition to "liberal democracy," as practiced in the West, he has described two versions of "nonliberal democracy." These are the "communist variant," and the "underdeveloped variant," the relatively classless mass politics in certain Third World countries.[3]

[1] Giovanni Sartori, *The Theory of Democracy Revisited* (Chatham, N.J.: Chatham House, 1987), p. 4.
[2] *Ibid.*, p. 10, 456–76.
[3] C. B. MacPherson, *The Real World of Democracy* (Oxford: Oxford University Press, 1966), passim.

13

Regardless of the merits of this argument, we will not include such considerations in our discussion of democracy. Whatever the democratic elements of these other ideologies may be, they are decidedly subordinate to other considerations.

Despite the worldwide acceptance of the term itself, "democracy" is a relatively recent phenomenon; it is essentially a product of the eighteenth, nineteenth, and twentieth centuries. Moreover, many of the characteristics that we tend to associate with democracy are not necessarily the result of a democratic heritage and became part of the "democratic" tradition through other sources, such as liberalism and constitutionalism, which will be discussed later in this chapter.

The right of the people to participate politically is, of course, at the heart of democracy, as is popular sovereignty. Other things that we take for granted as part of a democratic system are less clear-cut in their origins. Equality, for example, clearly is related to democracy (although not uniquely so)—and political equality is an integral part of democratic theory—but it is also possible for a state to remain democratic in form while systematically excluding a minority from political participation, or from equal protection of the laws. Similarly, although many tend to associate civil liberties with democracy, a democratic society could restrict its own people and stifle their liberties. Even the principle that minorities have a right to attempt to become majorities by persuading others to their cause could be sacrificed to the harsh demands of a majority; this situation could exist under the form of a democracy. We should therefore recognize that the form of government we tend to think of as a "democracy" is a special kind of democracy. It is liberal, which implies concern for the individual, for political equality, and for civil liberties; it is constitutional, which denotes limitations upon the exercise of power, even majority power; and it is democratic, which refers to majority rule and political participation.[4] Hence, that form of government is a liberal, constitutional, democracy.

---

[4] Arend Lijphart has identified a model of democracy different from the majoritarian, which he calls "consociational," or "consensual." This involves a coalition of different interests, each of which is required for policy decisions in a manner similar to that formulated by John C. Calhoun and his "concurrent majority." See any edition of Calhoun's *Disquisition on Government* and his *Discourses on the Constitution;* see also Lijphart, *The Politics of Accommodation: Pluralism and Democracy in the*

This form of government can encompass different legal and economic systems, as well as highly varied organizational structures. It is therefore impossible to provide a description of constitutional democracy that would fit all valid cases, but there are certain conditions that must prevail for constitutional democracy to exist. As Ingersoll puts it, there must be "a clear differentiation between the general and the particular," or "between public life and private."[5] The state must be subject to popular control, yet it must recognize a sphere that falls outside its authority to act. That sphere contains certain individual rights. The extent and definition of those rights may vary, but the principle must be accepted, as must the right of minority opinion to exist, and the right of political minorities to seek to become majorities by peacefully persuading others to their cause.

Such a system both reflects and affects the character of the society in which it exists. It encourages discussion and education, and, to operate properly, it requires political education and the availability of political information. It accepts the possibility that a wide variety of opinions have merit, and it provides for orderly changes of leadership. It permits those who seek power and fail—or those who have power and lose it—to "lose with honor" and to try again should they so choose.[6] Above all, it retains options; that is, it protects the ability of the society to change its collective mind and to proceed in a different direction without resorting to violence in order to overthrow a political system.

THE ROOTS OF DEMOCRACY

Democracy itself has many roots. It is true that the ancient Hindus and Chinese developed some ideas that emphasized the role of the people in governing and perhaps could have evolved into democratic theories. It is also true that one must turn to ancient Greece, especially Athens, to discover the seeds of democratic ideas

---

Netherlands, 2nd ed. (Berkeley: University of California Press, 1968) and *Democracies: Patterns of Majoritarian and Consensus Government in Twenty-One Countries* (New Haven: Yale University Press, 1984); for comments on Lijphart, see Sartori, pp. 238–40.
[5]David E. Ingersoll, *Communism, Fascism, and Democracy* (Columbus, Ohio: Merrill, 1971), p. 135.
[6]Charles Frankel, *The Democratic Prospect* (New York: Harper & Row, 1962).

in the West; the word itself comes from the Greek meaning rule by the people, or *demos*. Nevertheless, enthusiasm for democracy was rare, even among the Greeks. Following the Hellenic period, for considerably more than a millenium it hardly existed. There was, however, much thought throughout the succeeding centuries that eventually contributed to democracy's development.

The Stoics formulated the conceptions of natural law and of worldwide brotherhood, and it was primarily they who introduced Greek thought into the Roman world. The most prominent of the Stoic writers, Cicero, was actually a Roman who had studied in Greece. His *Republic* defined natural law as right reason consonant with nature, and his synthesis of the thought of the late Stoic school heavily influenced the development of Roman law, which still serves as the basis for many of the world's great legal systems. Natural law came to be identified with natural rights, and its basic assumption was that human reason can identify basic principles that must govern lawmaking. This was an obvious step toward the modern ideas of constitutionalism and even of judicial review.

The Greeks conceived of the citizen as one with the state; they saw the state as the expression of the social nature of human beings who could not truly be human without it. Roman thought, on the other hand, emphasized the idea that the individual existed prior to the state, and that the state was the creation of citizens by mutual consent. Many centuries passed before the idea developed that individuals form the state by contract, but there were elements in the Roman system that prepared the way for the eventual acceptance of a doctrine of consent that, when combined with the assumption of natural law, made theories of individual rights possible. The innovative ideas of the Greeks and Romans greatly affected Christianity, the dominant system of thought in the Western world for centuries, and it was Christianity that introduced them into the mainstream of Western political thought.

Christianity contributed its own ideas directly, as well. The Judeo–Christian foundations of Western culture certainly affected the ultimate development of the idea of political equality. "The doctrine of human equality . . . was first taught by the Stoics, but Christianity gave it far more depth and force."[7] Jesus explic-

---

[7] A. D. Lindsay, *The Modern Democratic State* (London: Oxford University Press, 1943), p. 58. Lindsay remarked that "When we think of the differences which Christianity has tolerated in society in the course of its history, we might wonder

itly emphasized the downtrodden, the poor, and the humble in his teachings, and he stressed that all are equal in God's sight. One could argue that some of the same elements are present in a related religious tradition, Islam, but it developed largely in isolation from Western culture, and Islamic political practices and ideologies diverged considerably from those in the West.

In the Middle Ages society was largely static. Social and even geographic immobility were its hallmarks. The works of St. Thomas Aquinas capture the thought of the period and emphasize status and hierarchy. Above all, Thomas emphasized the role of law and stressed that natural law binds both ruler and ruled. His attitude was that the ruler who failed to abide by the law was a tyrant, one who ruled in his own interest rather than for the common good. Nevertheless, there was as yet no idea of individual rights against the state. Even a tyrant was to be obeyed while holding office, unless he commanded actions that violated the will of God. At that point the Church would excommunicate him and remove from his subjects all obligation to obey.

The conciliar movement of the early fifteenth century brought controversy between those who regarded the Pope as supreme, and those who argued that papal power should be shared with some sort of council. Although the question was one of Church governance, the Church was an international authority exercising true political power. Any consideration of power within the Church dealt with the same themes as the exercise of secular power. The struggle therefore had obvious implications for the development of democracy.

Before the development of English liberalism, the Renaissance and the Reformation also had implications for the subsequent emergence of democracy. It was during the Renaissance that Niccolo Machiavelli, more than any other single figure, laid the theoretical groundwork for what came to be the modern nation state. Machiavelli (1469–1527) virtually created the ideology of statehood by directing his writings toward the unification of Italy under a stable regime. In providing justification for a secular state,

---

whether this particular Christian conception of equality is not too other-worldly to be of political importance." He argued, nevertheless, that the existence of the Church as a power structure during the growth of Western civilization "prevented society from becoming totalitarian, prevented the omnicompetent state, and preserved liberty in the only way in which liberty can be preserved, by maintaining in society an organization which could stand up against the state" (see pp. 59–60).

NICCOLO MACHIAVELLI

I say that all men when they are spoken of, and especially princes who are in a higher and more eminent station, are remarkable for some quality or other that makes them either honorable or contemptible. . . . No man, I am sure, will deny but that it would be an admirable thing and highly to be commended to have a prince endued with all the good qualities. . . . but because it is impossible to have, much less to exercise, them all. . . . it is convenient that he be so well instructed as to know how to avoid the scandal of those vices which may deprive him of his state. . . . for if we consider things impartially we shall find some things are virtuous in appearance, and yet, if pursued, would bring certain destruction; while others, seemingly bad, yet, if followed by a prince, procure his peace and security.

From *The Prince* (1513)

Machiavelli helped to create the conditions required for liberal democracy.

Although it is nearly forgotten, the radical Anabaptist movement of the fifteenth and sixteenth centuries should be remembered for its contributions to what came to be democratic ideology. The Anabaptists and the followers of Menno Simons, the Mennonites, were early advocates of the importance of individual conscience and the right of dissent. They were, of course, fiercely repressed and had largely vanished by the seventeenth century, but some of their ideas "were to play vital roles in the rise of seventeenth-century democratic thought."[8]

Perhaps most important, however, was the Reformation. Its two foremost thinkers were Martin Luther (1483–1546) and John Calvin (1509–1564). A convenient point from which to date the beginning of the Reformation is 1517, when Luther nailed his Ninety-five Theses to the door of the church in Wittenberg, Germany. Although Luther was attempting simply to reform the Roman Catholic Church by criticizing corruption and excessive luxury

[8]Mulford Q. Sibley, *Political Ideas and Ideologies* (New York: Harper & Row, 1970), pp. 325–30.

in the papal court and condemning the sale of indulgences, his actions led to a movement that ultimately destroyed Western Europe's Christian unity.

Luther argued for the priesthood of all true believers, which placed the Christian in a position to communicate directly with God with no intermediary. In practice, Lutheranism so strongly supported powerful secular authority that it tended to encourage political passivity on the part of the people and unlimited power for rulers. Despite this, the implications of Luther's thought clearly are inherently individualistic and egalitarian. He emphasized the importance of the individual conscience at the same time that he advocated practices that led to political repression. Luther certainly had no intention of creating a climate that would lead, ultimately, to the notion of individual rights against the state, but he accomplished precisely that. It could not have been otherwise, once he assisted in the destruction of the medieval attitude that assumed little distinction between state and society, or even between public and private, and which therefore recognized very little in the way of individual rights.

Equally important to the development of democratic ideology, albeit also equally ironic, was the thought of John Calvin. Calvin's harsh, autocratic temperament reflected none of the humanitarianism that somewhat softened Luther's authoritarianism, and he taught the need for the most stringent measures from both secular and religious officials. By following the teachings of the Church and performing good works, the Roman Catholic could achieve salvation; the Lutheran could do so through faith. There was in each case at least some potential for the individual to affect his or her destiny. Calvinism completely denied any such potential. Calvin taught that all humanity was so unspeakably evil that no person could achieve, or was worthy of, salvation. God, however, had elected to save a select few, and only these would escape damnation. Despite this, there was reason to live virtuously. A virtuous life might be considered as evidence that one was among those whom God had elected to save.

The Calvinists limited church membership to those deemed to be among the elect. This demanded the closest scrutiny of each person's private life to seek sufficient evidence to support the conclusion that he or she was indeed qualified. Calvinism therefore encouraged an intrusive moralism that virtually eliminated

JOHN CALVIN

[I]f we have respect to the word of God, it will . . . make us subject not only to the authority of those princes who honestly and faithfully perform their duty toward us, but all princes. . . . But rulers, you will say, owe mutual duties to those under them. This I have already confessed. But if from this you conclude that obedience is to be returned to none but just governors, you reason absurdly. . . . [I]f we are cruelly tormented by a savage, if we are rapaciously pillaged by an avaricious or luxurious, if we are neglected by a sluggish, if, in short, we are persecuted for righteousness' sake by an impious and sacrilegious prince, let us first call up the remembrance of our faults, which doubtless the Lord is chastising by such scourges. In this way humility will curb our impatience. And let us reflect that it belongs not to us to cure these evils, that all remains for us is to implore the help of the Lord. . . . But in that obedience which we hold to be due to the commands of rulers, we must always make the exception. . . . If they command anything against Him, let us not pay the least regard to it, nor be moved by all the dignity which they possess as magistrates—a dignity to which no injury is done when it is subordinated to the special and truly supreme power of God.

From *The Institutes of the Christian Religion* (1536)

any thought of privacy. Moreover, it taught the duty of passive obedience to rulers, because rulers held their positions by God's will. Even a tyrant was God's agent, and should be obeyed with no less zeal than that accorded a good ruler. Tyranny was God's punishment upon the people for their sins, and abuse of authority was no excuse for resistance.

Nevertheless, there were hints of radicalism within Calvin's doctrines, although they were largely hidden by the major themes that were authoritarian, if not totalitarian. The Calvinists' highly pessimistic view of human nature led them directly to the conclusion that no person should be trusted with unlimited power. Moreover, if a magistrate were to order an action that was against the will of God, Calvin taught that it was a citizen's duty to disobey. When Calvinists were in power, as in Calvin's Geneva, the clear emphasis of their doctrines was passive obedience. When they were the minority, on the other hand, they tended to seek whatever justifications they could find for disobedience in order to secure converts and preserve their own beliefs. John Knox (1505–1572) in Scotland, for example, developed doctrines of disobedience and resistance that went considerably beyond those of Luther and "even beyond his great mentor Calvin."[9] As a result, later generations seized upon the minor themes that might serve to justify disobedience and magnified them far beyond anything that Calvin would have tolerated.

Calvinism in England became Puritanism and Separatism. Puritanism sought to remove the remnants of Catholicism from the Anglican Church, whereas the Separatists, led by Robert Browne, were those who advocated complete withdrawal from the Church of England. The supporters of the feudal institutions of aristocracy, bishop, and king were generally Anglican. The Puritans were the Presbyterians who worked to substitute the power of elected leaders within the Church for the king's power. The most radical were the Separatists, who were congregationalists; that is, they argued that only a congregation could elect its minister. They faced so much hostility from Puritans as well as Anglicans that many were forced to flee to the Netherlands under the leadership of such men as William Brewster.

The power of Parliament in England grew along with the power of Calvinism. The Puritans, or Presbyterians, came to dominate the Parliament, which engaged in the bitter struggles with the royal forces that began in 1642 and led ultimately to the beheading of Charles I in 1649. From then until the restoration of the monarchy in 1660, the Puritan Oliver Cromwell (1599–1658) and his Parliament ruled England. During this time there arose challenges to the rule of his Presbyterians, an affluent elite. The more radical factions, represented by such leaders as John Lilburne and Richard Overton of the Levellers, sought such things as greatly broadened participation and written constitutions limiting political power. Beyond the Levellers were the Diggers and other groups even more radical.

Much of the Leveller agitation came from within the army. The officers as a rule advocated moderate reform, while the soldiers sought more extreme measures. Both accepted such notions

[9]Sibley, p. 335.

as government based upon consent, the existence of higher law, and the right of private property, but their differences were considerable. Colonel Rainboro in speaking for the soldiers argued that "the poorest he that is in England has a life to live as the richest he . . . I do think that the poorest man in England is not at all bound in a strict sense to that Government that he has not had a voice to put himself under."[10] It would be difficult to provide a better summary of the demands of radical democracy.[11]

Calvinism in colonial America had immediate and long-lasting effects upon governmental institutions, political philosophy, and political ideology. The congregational principle of local control of churches strongly affected the governmental structures that the Calvinists developed in New England. This principle was explicit in the Mayflower Compact and implicit in the institutions of Massachusetts Bay. The idea of compact, or the notion of contract, was equally influential. Both congregational control and the idea of contract are related directly to the idea that the only legitimate laws are those to which the people consent. Of course, "the people," as the early New England Calvinists defined them, included only church members, but the principle was important, and it conditioned political development in the new nation; it also had a dramatic effect upon the growth of democratic theory.

LIBERALISM

Seventeenth-century England saw the beginnings also of the secular individualism that led to liberalism, which is so closely associated with democracy. "Liberalism" did not emerge at one time as a fully developed doctrine, but rather evolved slowly through the years, incorporating many ideas and principles. "As a consequence, histories of 'Liberalism' use varying emphases in describing its characteristic marks, and after reading three or four different

[10] A. T. Mason, *Free Government in the Making*, 3rd ed (New York: Oxford University Press, 1965), p. 13.
[11] One should not interpret this as favoring universal suffrage in the modern sense, despite the conclusions of some writers. C. B. MacPherson has demonstrated that the Leveller demand excluded "servants," or those who worked for wages, and all who accepted charity. See his *The Political Theory of Possessive Individualism: Hobbes to Locke* (London: Oxford University Press, 1962), chapter III. Of course, as one would expect in view of the status of women at the time, the demand excluded them as well.

accounts of the phenomenon one is tempted to ask, 'Will the real Liberalism please stand up?'."[12] Fortunately, a general understanding of liberalism and its effects is what is important, rather than developing a precise definition or participating in disagreements regarding details.

Ideologies are oriented toward action and reaction. In the case of liberalism, there was a reaction against the Church and dogmatic beliefs. "It began with an assertion of the right . . . to use . . . reason to question 'received beliefs.' It ended by asserting the faith that reason can explain everything—or at least that nothing should be accepted as true which cannot be substantiated by reference to natural laws as found out by reason, using the methods of science." Moreover, revolts are *for* something as well as against.[13] "On the side of economic and social arrangements, liberalism was a revolt against that vast network of economic restrictions and privileges which comprised feudalism."[14] It reacted *against* in order to have the freedom *to* engage in something new, to participate in a free market, among other things.

The outcome is the amorphous thing that we call liberalism. It includes many themes, not all of them fitting neatly with one another. All, from Hobbes onward, are related to individualism, but otherwise their differences are great. The natural rights emphases of Locke and Jefferson, the utilitarianism of John Stuart Mill, the harsh doctrines of the Manchester liberals such as Spencer and Sumner, the positive approaches of Green and Dewey, all are part of that great and forceful movement.

In his classic work *The Leviathan* (1651) Thomas Hobbes began with the individual in a state of nature in which the life of the human being was "solitary, poor, nasty, brutish, and short." The essence of liberalism is concern with the individual, and Hobbes (1588–1679) was one of the first writers to suggest liberal principles, which constituted a complete break from medieval traditions. Modern liberalism, with its concern for human rights and civil liberties, is sharply different from the stark authoritarianism that Hobbes considered essential, but both place the individual at the center of concern.

[12] William T. Bluhm, *Ideologies and Attitudes: Modern Political Culture* (Englewood Cliffs, N.J.: Prentice–Hall, 1974), p. 61.
[13] J. Roland Pennock, *Liberal Democracy: Its Merits and Prospects* (New York: Rinehart, 1950), p. 10.
[14] Ibid., p. 11.

THOMAS HOBBES

Nature has made men so equal, in the faculties of the body and mind, as that though there be found one man sometimes manifestly stronger in body, or of quicker mind than another, yet when all is reckoned together, the difference between man and man is not so considerable, as that one man can thereupon claim to himself any benefit to which another may not pretend, as well as he. For as to the strength of body, the weakest has strength enough to kill the strongest, either by secret machination, or by confederacy with others . . . .

Hereby it is manifest that during the time men live without a common power to keep them all in awe, they are in that condition which is called war; and such a war, as is of every man against every man.

In such condition there is no place for industry, because the fruit thereof is uncertain, and consequently no culture of the earth; no navigation, nor use of the commodities that may be imported by sea; no commodious building; no instruments of moving and removing such things as require much force; no knowledge of the face of the earth; no account of time; no arts; no letters; no society; and, which is worst of all, continual fear and danger of violent death; and the life of man, solitary, poor, nasty, brutish, and short.

From *The Leviathan* (1651)

Hobbes believed that human beings created government, and that it therefore was an artificial institution. It was not ordained by God, or required by human nature. Its purpose was to provide the protection for life that was absent in the state of nature, where human passions ruled unrestrained. To escape from the state of nature, human beings contracted with one another as individuals to form a civil society and a government. In order to be effective in protecting life, the government had to possess absolute power. However absolute the power, it came originally from each person and existed to provide protection from violent death. There could be no right of resistance or revolution, because that would infringe upon the government's absolute power. Only one situation could justify an act of resistance by a citizen against the ruler, and that would not occur unless the ruler attempted to take the citizen's life.[15] Rebellion could then take place, because for that citizen the contract would have been broken. Rebellion in any other circumstance would constitute anarchy, which would result in a return to the state of nature, the condition that Hobbes feared most.

Hobbes had considerable influence upon the development both of liberalism and of the nation state, each of which was intimately connected with the evolution of modern democracy. The spirit of his writings, however, is in jarring contrast to mainstream liberalism, and certainly to democracy. It was another Englishman, John Locke (1632–1704), who is most closely associated with the modern democratic temperament, especially his *Second Treatise on Government*, published in 1690. Locke gave credit for many of his ideas to Richard Hooker, who wrote at the close of the previous century and whom he called "the judicious Hooker."

Locke followed Hobbes in assuming a state of nature, but his conception of such a state was considerably more benign than that of Hobbes. It did, nevertheless, contain certain "inconveniences" as he called them. Although he viewed human beings as essentially rational and considered that in the natural state they generally functioned according to a law of nature, there was no recourse other than self-enforcement if one happened to be wronged. Locke again followed Hobbes in assuming that human beings escaped such inconveniences by contracting to form a civil society, and therefore leaving the state of nature. Just as the Lockean state of nature was much more pleasant than that in *The Leviathan*, however, so also was the society that Locke described as following the adoption of the contract considerably more desirable than the harsh authoritarianism that Hobbes thought so essential.

Locke's conception of humanity differed similarly from that of Hobbes. Each built his philosophy upon the individual, but for Hobbes the only meaningful right that each person possessed was the right to life. For Locke, on the other hand, the individual was endowed with many rights, among which were life, liberty, and property. It was the government's duty to protect all of these rights, and the individual therefore had strong claims against the government, including the right of revolution if the government failed

[15]Thomas Hobbes, *Leviathan* (Oxford: Basil Blackwell, 1957), pp. 91, 142 (originally published in 1651).

JOHN LOCKE

Men being . . . by nature all free, equal, and independent, no one can be put out of this estate and subjected to the political power of another without his own consent. The only way whereby any one divests himself of his natural liberty and puts on the bonds of civil society, is by agreeing with other men, to join and unite into a community for their comfortable, safe, and peaceable living, one amongst another, in a secure enjoyment of their properties, and a greater security against any that are not of it. This any number of men may do, because it injures not the freedom of the rest; they are left, as they were, in the liberty of the state of nature.

If man in the state of nature be so free as has been said . . . why will he part with his freedom . . . and subject himself to the dominion and control of any other power? To which it is obvious to answer, that though in the state of nature he hath such a right, yet the enjoyment of it is very uncertain and constantly exposed to the invasion of others. . . . it is not without reason that he seeks out and is willing to join in society with others . . . for the mutual preservation of their lives, liberties and estates, which I call by the general name—property.

The great and chief end, therefore, of men uniting into commonwealths, and putting themselves under government, is the preservation of their property. . . .

From the *Second Treatise of Government* (1690)

in its protective functions. The people could rebel not only to overthrow a tyranny, but even to prevent the development of one. Government and law existed to serve human ends, and the interpretation of those ends was highly individualistic. Government was not a leviathan that dominated citizens, nor, as had been assumed in medieval times, was society an organic institution in which each citizen had a natural function and place directed toward the common good. Government was founded upon contract, and law was valid only by virtue of the consent of the people. The purposes of government and society were to protect natural rights and to permit each citizen to pursue personal goals.

Both Hobbes and Locke placed self-interest at the center of concern. Locke's notion of self-interest, however, was based upon his assumption that human beings are rational, and thus can act according to reason, not merely passion. He viewed this potential for rational action as making possible a human community built upon a foundation broader than simple survival. Self-interest, as Locke defined it, was qualitatively different from the Hobbesian formulation, and included the possibility of seeking personal betterment through cooperative efforts, and even of improving one's own lot by improving that of others. Locke, therefore, raised self-interest above mere selfishness.

Others accepted Locke's theme and built upon it. The classical liberal Adam Smith (1723–1790) joined Locke in assuming property ownership to be a human right and asserted that accumulation was central to human freedom. His treatment of property was perhaps narrower and more materialistic than that of Locke, and the economic preoccupation of his thought has led him generally to be considered as the father of modern economics. His praise for economic competition and for the role of the marketplace as a natural regulator, along with his rejection of governmental interference in the economic sphere, set the tone for the classical economics of the nineteenth century. The dominant theme of the rising capitalism of that century, and of the economic thought that served to underpin it, was Adam Smith's doctrine of laissez-faire, that is, "let them alone," or "let the people do as they wish." An emotional attachment to laissez-faire economics persists, however unrelated to reality it may be in an advanced industrial society requiring extensive regulation and welfare measures.

At the time of Smith's writing, liberalism was a challenge to the status quo. This was especially the case with regard to the liberalism of the American revolutionaries, whose radical individualism so shocked a nervous Europe. Thomas Jefferson's Declaration of Independence in 1776 went beyond Locke to assert that governments existed to preserve life, liberty, and—as opposed merely to property—the pursuit of happiness. Thomas Paine called forcefully for "the rights of man," involving equality, civil liberties, the separation of religion and the state, and political participation. Both he and Jefferson advocated minimal government, without, however, going so far as to support anarchy. The liberal ideology in America was the cement that bound the people together in national unity.

That ideology incorporated the language of liberty and equality, and it led to the elimination of aristocratic titles and to considerably greater social mobility than existed in Europe or Great Britain. The architects of the American system accepted the principles of liberal democracy as they were being discussed in both America and Britain, but they had yet to become comfortable with the word "democracy" itself. Classical democracy, of course, had to do with direct rule by the people, something that the founders never considered and against which most of them reacted with horror. They used the term "republic," which referred to government by elected representatives.

Today the terms "republic" and "democracy" generally are interchangeable and mean representative democracy. Occasionally, Americans on the right object to the current usage. Those who do so generally harbor a suspicion of democracy, representative or not, as providing too great a role for the people in government and wish to avoid the term. They prefer their version of a republic that emphasizes elected representatives and has a minimum of popular participation, confining it almost entirely to elections.

The Declaration of Independence is one of the purest and most radical statements of liberal democracy, but it contains little or nothing to guide the formation of a structure to implement its principles. It was the Constitution that was concerned with the practicalities of governing. In reflecting regional, political, and economic interests, it departed from the radicalism of the Declaration. The American system was and is one of balance, containing both individualistic and majoritarian elements. As established by the Constitution, it reflects the concerns of such statesmen as John Adams and James Madison.

The best source available for insights into the intent of the framers is *The Federalist*, a series of articles that appeared originally as newspaper pieces arguing for the state of New York to ratify the new Constitution. Madison, John Jay, and Alexander Hamilton each contributed essays, with Madison's being the most numerous. The concerns were for protection of the individual while endowing the government with sufficient power to be effective, and ensuring popular sovereignty while dispersing and limiting political power, including—and especially—limiting the power of majorities.

THOMAS JEFFERSON

We hold these truths to be self evident: that all men are created equal; that they are endowed by their Creator with [inherent and]* unalienable rights; that among these are life, liberty, and the pursuit of happiness; that to secure these rights, governments are instituted among men, deriving their just powers from the consent of the governed; that whenever any form of government becomes destructive of these ends, it is the right of the people to alter or to abolish it, and to institute new government, laying its foundation on such principles, and organizing its powers in such form, as to them shall seem most likely to effect their safety and happiness.

From the *Declaration of Independence* (1776)

*In the final draft, Congress substituted "certain" for these words.

Madison expressed great concern over "faction," or powerful special interests, in *The Federalist*'s famous tenth paper. The classical position had been that republics fared best as small states, and that democracies, in which the people ruled directly, had to be so small that all citizens could meet together. Madison reversed the argument and praised what he called an "extended republic," in which an expanse of territory and diversity of population would be barriers to the formation of tyrannical majorities that had developed so frequently throughout history in small republics. Majority rule protected against minority factions, while representative government, along with the wisdom of the representatives, separation of powers, and checks and balances would protect against tyrannous majorities.

The extent to which the Madisonian system of the Constitution reflects liberal democracy depends upon a number of things, including not only the definition of "democracy," but also the definition of "representation." The liberal individualistic element that so many associate with democracy seems clearly to be more a matter of *constitutionalism,* or the acceptance of regular limitations upon power, than of democracy itself. "Democracy" is most closely associated with majoritarianism. *Liberal democracy is*

JAMES MADISON

There are two methods of curing the mischiefs of faction: the one, by removing its causes; the other, by controlling its effects.

There are again two methods of removing the causes of faction: the one, by destroying the liberty which is essential to its existence; the other, by giving to every citizen the same opinions, the same passions, and the same interests.

It could never be more truly said than of the first remedy, that it was worse than the disease. . . .

The second expedient is as impracticable as the first would be unwise. . . .

The latent causes of faction are . . . sown in the nature of man. . . . But the most common and durable source of factions has been the various and unequal distribution of property. . . .

It is in vain to say that enlightened statesmen will be able to adjust these clashing interests, and render them all subservient to the public good. Enlightened statesmen will not always be at the helm. . . .

. . . the *causes* of faction cannot be removed . . . relief is only to be sought in the means of controlling its *effects*.

From *The Federalist*, no. 10 (1787)

therefore constitutional democracy, with the liberal, individualistic element forming the constitutional side of the equation, and majoritarianism forming the democratic side. The two elements not only are different, but at times may come into conflict.

"Representation" can be seen as reflecting the will of the people, which would be majoritarian, or democratic. It also can mean the exercise of individual judgment on the part of the representative, which would be a check upon democracy, defined as majoritarianism. Madison clearly implied that representatives— whether legislators or other officials—would function differently on different issues. Thus, the system could react as the majority demanded, but would be capable also of restraining the majority. The degree to which the Constitution reflects the principles of the Declaration of Independence, therefore, depends both upon one's set of definitions, and upon the manner in which governmental representatives fulfill their functions. Some argue that the system restricts the power of the majority so greatly that it is undemocratic, while others complain that it restricts majorities too little, that it is, in fact, too democratic. There should be some definite agreement, however: the Constitution was uniquely liberal for its time, and the system that it established was considerably more democratic than others then existing.

As the nineteenth century progressed, political ideology reflected not merely the rise of democratic politics, but also of a new economic system. With the growth of capitalism, many writers turned to liberalism as a justification for current conditions, which permitted virtually unlimited accumulation. The British economist David Ricardo (1772–1823) formulated his "Iron Law of Wages" supporting the payment of the lowest possible wage that would induce workers to continue to work, regardless of the misery that this would cause. He argued first, that low wages were necessary to encourage accumulation of the capital that was essential to production and second, that production was necessary to prevent even greater misery.

While economists were adding to the thrust of liberalism, philosophers contributed also, and the English utilitarian school developed. Some of the utilitarians worked from themes outlined by Hobbes, but others, like David Hume (1711–1776), departed from a Hobbesian emphasis upon the egotistic nature of humanity and forcefully rejected social contract theories. Jeremy Bentham (1748–1832) followed Hume in building his thought upon the assumption that human beings sought always to maximize pleasure and minimize pain. Bentham was concerned with utility, as defined by the degree to which anything brought pain or pleasure, either to society or to an individual. He rejected any notion of natural law and argued that the purpose of the state was to provide the greatest good for the greatest number. Government existed, therefore, not to achieve anything so abstract as justice or the "good society," but rather to promote happiness.

It is important to note here that Bentham was receptive to change, and that what he outlined was a positive role for government. It was partly his influence that led to the great wave of reform in England shortly before 1850 that included such things as the secret ballot, expanded representation and education, the improvement of conditions in prisons, and generally a more humane attitude toward the poor, toward prisoners, and toward animals. He sought to place the power of government in the hands of the people to use for their own purposes.

The greatest of the utilitarian philosophers was John Stuart Mill (1806–1873), the son of James Mill (1773–1836), who was also a prominent utilitarian. John Stuart Mill expanded upon Bentham's majoritarianism by providing a justification for minority rights. An action against a minority, he argued, could justify similar action against any segment of society, hence, against all. His most famous and most important work was *On Liberty* (1854), in which he provided a resounding defense for civil liberties, one of the greatest ever written. He argued that to provide individual liberty was the most likely way to permit and encourage the development of happiness, and that the state should protect the exercise of free speech and preserve freedom of thought. Only by so doing, he asserted, can society hope to determine the truth of ideas, a determination that can result most effectively only from the interplay of the thoughts of free individuals who express themselves openly in what might be termed the free marketplace of ideas. Mill developed an optimism regarding the human potential, and came to oppose laissez-faire capitalism (or "Manchester liberalism," as it came to be called) as causing exploitation and the virtual enslavement of workers.

A misuse of the findings of science brought conclusions quite different from those of Mill, and gave economists yet another justification for the concentration of wealth. As the nineteenth century progressed, it became clear that the disparity between rich

---

JOHN STUART MILL

If all mankind minus one were of one opinion, mankind would be no more justified in silencing that one person than he, if he had the power, would be justified in silencing mankind. . . . the peculiar evil of silencing the expression of an opinion is that it is robbing the human race, posterity as well as the existing generation—those who dissent from the opinion, still more than those who hold it. If the opinion is right, they are deprived of the opportunity of exchanging error for truth; if wrong, they lose, what is almost as great a benefit, the clearer perception and livelier impression of truth produced by its collision with error.

From *On Liberty* (1859)

and poor in industrialized nations was growing rapidly. A society that looks to religion as its basis will tend to justify its institutions by religion; one that is scientific will turn for its justifications to science. As the industrial state was developing, Charles Darwin published a scientific theory that many turned to in order to demonstrate the correctness—even the inevitability—of the prevailing institutions, regardless of how those institutions were leading to increased poverty and worsening conditions among the working classes. Biological evolution was the theory, and Darwin's book, published in 1859, was *Origin of Species.*

It was not Darwin, however, who applied his biological theories to society, and it is doubtful that he had any idea that they would be so applied. Rather, it was an English sociologist, Herbert Spencer, who seized upon Darwin's ideas and believed that they supported his own views of social evolution. Before Darwin wrote, Spencer had already coined the phrase "survival of the fittest," and he argued against any interference by the state in the "natural" order of things. All state action, he thought, would assist the unfit and permit them to survive longer than they otherwise would, thereby harming society. He went so far as to argue not only against aid to the poor, but also against public education and even public health laws or regulations. He considered such actions to be "illiberal" and argued that the fit would prevail, regardless, and that those who were unfit not only would not, but should not, survive.[16] Spencer's social Darwinism was especially popular in the United States, where its most prominent advocate was the pioneering sociologist William Graham Sumner (1840–1910) from Yale.

It was another English philosopher, Thomas Hill Green (1836–1882), whose ideas served to move liberalism away from the rugged individualism of the social Darwinists and to work toward the positive liberalism of the twentieth century by building upon the foundation laid by the utilitarians. Green, like Mill, recognized the importance of individual freedom. True freedom, however, was not merely the absence of institutional restraint, as Locke would have it, but rather the ability to act individually to contribute to the good of the whole. Green called for government to protect the needy, to regulate living and working conditions, and

[16]Herbert Spencer, *Social Statics* (New York: D. Appleton, 1864), pp. 79–80, 414–15.

WILLIAM GRAHAM SUMNER

[Socialists] criticize the "system," by which they mean the social world as it is. They do not perceive that the world of human society is what has resulted from thousands of years of life. . . . All through human history some have had good fortune and some ill fortune. . . . Poverty belongs to the struggle for existence, and we are all born into that struggle. . . . The existing "system" is the outcome of the efforts of men for thousands of years to work together, so as to win in the struggle for existence. . . . This is a world in which the rule is, "Root, hog, or die," and it is also a world in which "the longest pole knocks down the most persimmons."

From "Reply to a Socialist" (1904)

generally to take positive action to enhance the lives of the citizens. He provided a solid basis for what came to be the modern welfare state, such as the New Deal which began in the United States in the 1930s.

The American philosopher John Dewey (1859–1952) most fully represented the spirit of modern positive liberalism. He followed Thomas Jefferson in placing his confidence in the capacity of the people and in their right to be treated with equal human dignity. He agreed with Bentham, Mill, and Green regarding human happiness as the prime goal of society, but he argued that the environment influenced what happiness was and that it might vary from one set of circumstances to another. He was a strong advocate of government action to shape the environment in a manner that would not be limited to removing oppression but would establish institutions tailored to promote human happiness. His ideas found acceptance in the United States of the 1930s as Franklin D. Roosevelt inaugurated the New Deal. They were further developed in the Fair Deal of Harry S Truman and especially in the Great Society of Lyndon B. Johnson.

All American presidents from Roosevelt through Jimmy Carter, regardless of varying emphases, accepted the broad responsibility of government to act positively to establish conditions within which human beings would be most likely to achieve their potential and

---

LYNDON B. JOHNSON

. . . [I]n your time we have the opportunity to move not only toward the rich society and the powerful society, but upward to the Great Society.

The Great Society rests on abundance and liberty for all. It demands an end to poverty and racial injustice, to which we are totally committed in our time. But that is just the beginning.

The Great Society is a place where every child can find knowledge to enrich his mind and to enlarge his talents. It is a place where leisure is a welcome chance to build and reflect, not a feared cause of boredom and restlessness. It is a place where the city of man serves not only the needs of the body and the demands of commerce but the desire for beauty and the hunger for community.

From a speech in Ann Arbor, May 22, 1964

---

find happiness in a meaningful way. This is a most diverse list, including Dwight Eisenhower, John Kennedy, Richard Nixon, and Gerald Ford in addition to Truman and Johnson. The one exception is Ronald Reagan, who sought to reverse the acceptance of positive liberalism and to return, under the name of conservatism, to the views of an earlier time.

Liberalism, then, has been closely associated historically with democracy. It is, nevertheless, different from democracy. Liberalism has taken many different forms. It can be hostile to democracy, as seen in the writings of Thomas Hobbes, or thoroughly democratic, as it generally is. It can support the most harsh forms of exploitation, as with the social Darwinists, or advance the most humane values, as it usually does. The liberals of the eighteenth and nineteenth centuries generally counseled against governmental action because they saw government as the greatest threat to human freedom. Beginning in the 1930s, however, and in fact even earlier in the Progressive era, many liberals came to advocate highly active government. Some have interpreted this as a complete reversal and a rejection of earlier liberal principles. This is incorrect. The essence of liberalism is individualism, and the greatest concern of the liberal (at least as liberalism developed after Hobbes) is for individual freedom. This remains the core of liberalism. The difference is in the definition of freedom and in the emergence of other threats to freedom besides those from government.

Earlier, as we have discussed, freedom was interpreted essentially to be the absence of restraint by human institutions, especially governmental institutions. By the time of the New Deal, liberals had begun to argue that freedom involved something more than being left alone; merely to be free from restraint was not enough. For freedom to be meaningful there had to be conditions within which freedom could be exercised. One might technically be free, for example, in the middle of a huge and deadly desert with no companionship, transportation, shelter, food, or water, but there would be no benefit from that freedom. Moreover, government previously had been the sole major threat to freedom, inasmuch as government in the early days of liberalism had been the only institution that possessed concentrated power.

By the twentieth century, however, there were two major developments that could hardly have been foreseen. First, the rise of the corporation permitted power to be concentrated in private hands as well as in the government. Second, technology and industrialism had created vastly more power than had ever before existed. Thus, as the twentieth century progressed, the protection of individual freedom required not only the limitation of governmental power, but the regulation and limitation of concentrated private power as well. Government was the only agency that was both directly responsible to the public and sufficiently powerful to counteract the power that had become concentrated in private hands. Government was also the only agency capable of establishing the conditions that were required for the individual to exercise his or her freedom meaningfully.

Liberals, as a result, turned to government as their agent but remained wary of the government's power to stifle individual freedom. This is evidenced by continued liberal emphasis upon civil liberties as reflected in numerous court decisions expanding the protections of the Bill of Rights and also in laws, such as the Freedom of Information Act, that seek to restrict the power of the government.

Despite surface appearances, therefore, liberals had not changed fundamentally. They retained the principles that—with some notable exceptions—generally motivated liberalism throughout most of its existence. They remained optimistic regarding human nature and the potential of human reason, they stressed human rights, and they were no less individualistic for all their emphasis upon governmental activity. The only change had been a broader and more sophisticated interpretation of freedom and an acceptance of tactics that they previously would have rejected. Their goals, however, were essentially unchanged.

This is not to say that there have not been many liberals who have been guilty of inconsistencies, nor that liberals have always managed to use governmental power without at the same time increasing the likelihood that it will oppress the people. The Social Security Program is an example of the positive liberal's use of government power to enhance the lives of individual citizens. Despite some shortcomings, it has been an enormous success, has been responsible for lifting the elderly as a group out of poverty, and has been (and remains) overwhelmingly popular.

There was some strident criticism when the Act became law in 1935, however, from opponents who charged that identification by number was the first step toward a police state. The Act's liberal supporters assured critics and the general public that the Social Security number would be used only for Social Security purposes and would never be available for other uses by the government. For years the government remained true to its word. Nevertheless, in time, other considerations came to supersede this concern, and finally the number came to be used for nearly all governmental records pertaining to a citizen.

Now, even children must have numbers in order to be identified on their parents' income tax returns as dependents. The Social Security number permits the government to compile vast records on each citizen and greatly enhances its ability to pry into individual privacy. The potential that this has created for regulation of personal conduct is enormous. Another example is the personal income tax, a liberal device that provides the most effective and equitable means for securing necessary revenue. As currently devised, however, it also has the effect of providing a government bureaucracy with extraordinary power over the lives of individual citizens. Thus far there is no solution to such dilemmas.

Populism

One of the first instances of efforts to use government to establish the ends of positive liberalism was the Populist movement in the United States in the 1890s. Populism was strong among small farmers in the South and the Midwest and was a reaction to a definite feeling of having been victimized by special interests. The Populists sought regulation to prevent exploitation by such powerful industries as the railroads and grain elevators, and they called for more mass democracy. Much of the Populist platform, such as direct election of U.S. senators, regulation of interstate commerce, and a progressive income tax, became law after having been accepted by the two major parties. In fact, the Peoples' (or Populist) Party joined with the Democrats in 1896 to support the presidential candidacy of William Jennings Bryan and thereafter ceased to exist as an independent force.

Many Populist principles continued to influence the Progressive movement of the early twentieth century and were even in evidence in later programs, such as Franklin Roosevelt's New Deal, Harry Truman's Fair Deal, and Lyndon Johnson's Great Society. These more modern movements had, however, changed considerably in tone. The Populists had often been dismissed as "hayseed reformers," whereas the Progressives tended to be intellectuals of a higher socioeconomic class and tended therefore to have gained increased "respectability." Moreover, many observers have charged populist movements in general with hostility to foreigners and ethnic and religious minorities. These unsavory themes were lacking from many of the subsequent efforts, as was the strong fear of conspiracy that tended to motivate the Populist party. Such themes returned in the 1960s to be reflected strongly in various movements and especially in the presidential campaigns of Alabama Governor George Wallace.

Today there are elements on both the Left and the Right that appear to be populist in spirit, and quite divergent groups frequently claim the label. They purport to speak for the "little person" as opposed to special interests. Such Populist groups range from supporters of prayer in public schools and advocates of lessening restraints on police behavior to those who see the world as dominated by multinational corporations that foment war for their own selfish purposes. A common thread uniting most Populists is acceptance of conspiracy theories and a belief that elites are manipulating them and depriving them of their rights. Not all, however, are extremists. Many are very much in the political mainstream and work both within and outside of the major parties to achieve reform, and a greater measure of democracy, as they interpret it.

Assessing Liberalism

D. J. Manning has written that "liberalism is virtually unique amongst ideologies in that it is addressed to all men regardless of race, class, religion, nationality or language. It is addressed to every man in the world as an individual and nothing else."[17] Perhaps this is the explanation for its great triumphs. Liberalism joined with democracy to create the modern Western world. In producing constitutional democracy, it abolished slavery, expanded political participation, developed bills of rights and worked for human rights generally, and it led to more humane treatment of animals. It also brought about systems of constitutional government, it lessened religious intolerance and eliminated religious tests for political participation and office holding, it encouraged and greatly expanded education, and it advanced the status of women. Finally, it encouraged the development of an international view that has thus far allowed survival in a world in which technology has made mass annihilation possible. This is an incomplete but most impressive list of accomplishments.

CONSERVATISM

Just as liberalism is not the same as democracy, so is democracy not limited to liberalism. Other currents bear examining. One that must be considered as among those that have produced modern democracy is conservatism. A basic feature of conservatism is suggested by the term itself. Conservatism seeks generally to conserve; it tends to resist change. Conservatives generally view the state or society as an organic whole that consists not only of current inhabitants, but also those of the past and the future. Thus,

---

[17]D. J. Manning, *Liberalism* (New York: St. Martin's Press, 1976), p. 140.

they reject liberal individualism. They tend to have a great respect for authority as essential to the order that they so desire, and they are more likely to stress duties instead of rights. Conservatives reject equality and accept human differences as justification for status and hierarchy. They also have a strong tendency to emphasize religion and its values as a method of social control and frequently to reject the separation of church and state even if they favor tolerance of other religions. Running consistently through their thought is a great skepticism regarding human reason and its ability to better the human condition.

Although conservative movements have occurred at various times in a number of European nations and elsewhere, the classic form of conservatism developed and persisted in Great Britain and found its most able expression in the writings of Edmund Burke (1729–1797), a member of the House of Commons. The beginning point for much liberal thought has been the "state of nature" and the contractual beginnings of state and society. The conservative rejects contractual theories because they assume a specific beginning and assumes instead that society and the state evolved naturally, and gradually. Such an assumption not only emphasizes the role of tradition, but also incorporates the attitude toward

---

EDMUND BURKE

. . . [I]nstead of casting away all our old prejudices, we cherish them to a very considerable degree, and . . . we cherish them because they are prejudices; and the longer they have lasted, and the more generally they have prevailed, the more we cherish them. We are afraid to put men to live and trade each on his own private stock of reason; because we suspect that this stock in each man is small, and that the individuals would do better to avail themselves of the general bank and capital of nations, and of ages. . . . Prejudice . . . engages the mind in a steady course of wisdom and virtue, and does not leave the man hesitating in the moment of decision, sceptical, puzzled, and unresolved. Prejudice renders a man's virtue his habit; and not a series of unconnected acts. Through just prejudice, his duty becomes a part of his nature. . . .

From *Reflections on the Revolution in France* (1790)

change that is central to much of conservatism: change should be only gradual and evolutionary, never sudden or drastic.

For the conservative, an important factor in preserving traditional institutions is sound leadership, and sound leadership implies strong leadership. Some are natural leaders, and the rest should follow. The conservative accepts human inequality and prefers that it be recognized by the formal acceptance of social classes, elites, and hierarchical authority. British conservatives have tempered the potential harshness of their views by accepting social responsibilities that result from an elite position. This has led them to support, and frequently to initiate, social welfare measures and governmental actions to relieve social ills and assist the downtrodden. In contrast to some conservatives elsewhere, British conservatives have been strong supporters of representative government and constitutional limitations.

Accepting welfare measures has not, however, led British conservatives toward liberalism. They reject liberal individualism and egalitarianism, and they retain their view of society as an organic whole that includes—and should include—strict hierarchical arrangements of power. They revere the stabilizing role of religion and are pleased to combine religious and political symbols and functions in government. Above all, they reject the liberal attitude toward innovation and resist change, except when it can be gradual or when it is necessary to avoid greater change to existing institutions. Nevertheless, as mentioned above, conservatives have accepted economic and social reform. Despite their suspicion of majoritarianism, they have accepted popular participation in government. Most important, they have accepted the changes once they have been established and have not attempted to return to the past. Nor have they attempted to suppress their political opponents, however much they lack confidence in liberal solutions to society's ills. Conservatism, at least as it has developed in Great Britain, has therefore evolved into a variant of modern democratic ideology. By far the most thoughtful modern discussions of conservatism are the works of Peter Viereck[18] whose

[18] See, for example, Peter Viereck, *Conservatism: From Burke and John Adams Till Now: A History and an Anthology* (Baton Rouge: Louisiana State University Press, 1985); *Conservatism Revisited and the New Conservatism: What Went Wrong?* (Westport, Conn.: Greenwood Press, 1978); *Meta-Politics: From the Romantics to Hitler*, rev. ed. (Baton Rouge: Louisiana State University Press, 1985); and *The Unadjusted Man: Reflections on the Distinction Between Conserving and Conforming* (Westport, Conn.: Greenwood Press, 1973).

concern is less with the ideology than with the conservative state of mind.

Even outside the democratic tradition, conservatism is not necessarily harsh or unconcerned with individual welfare. The German Empire of the late nineteenth and early twentieth centuries, for example, was a constitutional state, though certainly not democratic. The government operated within understood limits. Furthermore, under the Empire's first Chancellor, the conservative Prince Otto von Bismarck, Germany in the 1880s adopted the world's first elaborate system of social security, preceding the more limited system in the United States by a half century.

America: A Special Case

The dominant mood of the Reagan years was said to be conservative, and many prominent political figures, including Reagan himself, boasted of their conservatism. In a striking reversal of the situation a short time previously, many politicians and other citizens became reluctant to be identified as liberal. Regardless of this, the political policies of the United States and its political rhetoric (ignoring the specific use of the words "conservative" and "liberal") remain explicitly liberal.

Americans still look to the Declaration of Independence, one of the most liberal documents ever written. They continue to praise equality and innovation. They also continue to stress individualism and believe that the proper use of human reason can provide corrections to social ills. At least rhetorically, they continue to emphasize rights and are less comfortable with duties. All these things, and more, are liberal. It is true that there have been some notable American conservative spokesmen, figures such as John C. Calhoun, Henry Adams, Irving Babbit, and Walter Lippmann, but America has never had a lasting conservative political tradition. This is to be expected, in view of the radical doctrines that motivated the founding of the nation. A political heritage emphasizing "life, liberty, and the pursuit of happiness," human reason, and a rejection of tradition has clearly enshrined liberalism.

What, then, is American conservatism? To be sure, there are some elements of the political system that vary from the prevailing liberalism and can be thought of as genuinely conservative. A system of law, however conceived, tends to become a conservative force, if only because it embodies tradition and resists change. The Supreme Court with its appointed justices holding lifetime tenure, the Electoral College, and the role of seniority and the committee system in Congress certainly can be forces for conservatism. On the other hand, regardless of its nondemocratic nature, the Supreme Court is empowered to exercise judicial review on behalf of the citizen against the state, and this hardly can be considered illiberal. Suffice it to say that, although there are some aspects of the system that suggest conservatism, it is best to look at the politicians themselves, rather than the institutions, in order to find answers to the question regarding the nature of American conservatism.

Most of those in America today who purport to espouse the cause of conservatism are not true conservatives; they are liberals who reject the positive liberalism of the New Deal and accept more liberal than conservative principles. Today's conservatives, those to the right of the group known as "moderates" that dwindled sharply during the Reagan years, tend in principle to reject governmental involvement in the economy to promote the welfare of individual citizens. Except for police and military affairs—and here they can be justly accused of inconsistency—"conservatives" oppose big government. They strongly favor individual rights, but their notion of individual rights is likely to be narrow and to refer primarily to economic rights or the freedom to acquire and dispose of income and property with little or no interference.

Many modern conservatives turn for their inspiration to the Austrian-born Friedrich A. von Hayek, who was Professor of Economics at the University of Chicago. *The Road to Serfdom* was his severe criticism of governmental planning as inconsistent with individual liberty. Among his fundamental arguments was that a plan, to be effective, had to be kept in place for a certain length of time. By definition, therefore, it had to be protected from change. This meant that it had to be insulated from political, or democratic, control. Removing governmental policy from the political process would effectively remove the control of the people over their government and would thereby destroy their liberties. Hayek clearly is within the liberal tradition and in fact emphasized this in an article entitled "Why I am not a Conservative."[19]

[19] Friedrich A. von Hayek, "Why I am not a Conservative," in Hayek, *The Constitution of Liberty* (London: Routledge & Kegan Paul, 1960).

Much of the enthusiasm of "conservatives" for Hayek appears to have resulted from his book's title, rather than its contents, because he did concede that there could be a strong case for comprehensive systems of social insurance, including provisions for health care, whenever there were "genuinely insurable risks." He wrote, moreover, that "an extensive system of social services" would be justified, and compatible with competition, if such a system were properly organized.[20] Other economists such as Milton Friedman have followed his lead. Many have accepted Hayek's arguments against government action without allowing for his exceptions when dealing with "genuinely insurable risks," and their writings have been highly influential.

Today's American conservatives speak highly of individual liberties. They praise localism and advocate shifting responsibilities and decisions, wherever possible, to the lowest level of government. They argue for the smallest feasible national government and frequently also for minimal state and local government. They seek the lowest possible taxes at all levels and tend to oppose progressivism in tax rates. They are strong nationalists and stress the virtues of patriotism. Finally, they have been the most forceful advocates of balanced governmental budgets in the United States.

There are numerous inconsistencies within the ideology of modern American conservatism itself and, as is frequently the case across the political spectrum, additional inconsistencies exist between practice and principle. The liberty that conservatives praise tends to be limited to economic liberty, involving low taxation and minimal regulation. Many contemporary conservatives have found the principle of low taxation to be so important that they have permitted it to supersede that of the balanced budget. It is "conservatives" who, in order to keep tax rates low, have proposed and adopted the most unbalanced budgets in U.S. history. They have done this at the same time that they have called for a constitutional amendment to mandate balanced budgets. Some of the inconsistency results from patterns of thought that are essentially liberal, but which also include some actual conservative elements. The conservative elements tend to surface when the conservative turns away from economics.

[20] Hayek, *The Road to Serfdom* (Chicago: University of Chicago Press, 1957), p. 37.

When noneconomic issues of liberty are involved in a conflict between a citizen and the state, for example, the conservative generally will support the power of the state against the liberty of the individual. Similarly, despite their rhetoric of freedom, modern conservatives frequently are truly conservative and overtly anti-individualistic with regard to the traditional values of authority, the family, sexual morality, and religion. Conservatives tend to be uncomfortable with individual nonconformity and wish to enforce outward compliance through the adoption of symbolic measures, such as prayer in the schools, which would extend the power of the government over religion. The opposition to abortion and the emphasis upon increasing the power of the police also reflect a rejection of individualism, as does opposition to the Freedom of Information Act. These positions also violate the principle of limiting the national government and, in fact, would involve considerable extension of federal power.

The answer, then, to the question "What is conservatism in America?," is that it is a mixture of various themes. At best, it is an uneasy mixture. It contains a large measure of liberalism and a small measure of true conservatism. Woven throughout are nationalism, free enterprise, traditional values, and—especially for those further to the right—a resistance to the use of governmental power to alleviate human misery (symbolized by expressions of hostility to the national government). In reality, however, there tends to be an emphasis upon the expansion of that national government. Conservative expansion of national power has ranged from such broad major issues as building up the military or increasing the power of the government when in conflict with an individual, all the way to such details as coercing states to adopt 21 as the minimum drinking age. Moreover, although conservative rhetoric in America tends to oppose executive power, especially at the national level, many conservatives advocate empowering the president to exercise a line-item veto, which they justify as an economy measure. Such authority might or might not have a significant effect upon government spending, but it would be an enormous expansion of the president's power, hence of the power of the branch of government that is potentially the coercive branch.

It is important to recognize that American conservatives and liberals alike share, in general, a basic commitment to constitutional democracy. They work within the system to preserve political competition, no matter which political view tends to be dominant at any given moment. The overwhelming majority both of conservatives and liberals accept traditional American practices and differ largely on matters of emphasis, rather than on fundamentals.

PARTICIPATORY DEMOCRACY

In the 1960s and early 1970s, the New Left movement brought forth demands that democracy be revised to incorporate certain elements of direct democracy. The goal was to provide the citizen with a strong voice in the decisions that affected him or her. This was to be achieved through "participatory democracy," which included, among other things, the development of small political units that would place political power in the hands of the people, instead of elected leaders chosen by extensive units and located far away. It also involved workers' participation in the decisions that affect them in the workplace.[21]

Theories of participatory democracy reflect the influences both of classical liberalism and of Jean Jacques Rousseau (1712–1778), who argued for direct democracy and the supremacy of the "general will" (see pages 57–58). They stress equality and consent, while incorporating strong feelings of individualism. They also are clearly an outgrowth of modern positive liberalism, which emphasizes individual growth and requires an environment that is conducive to the meaningful exercise of freedom.

In view of the concern that many writers and activists displayed for participatory democracy during the heyday of the New Left, it is astonishing that they paid virtually no attention to Thomas Jefferson's proposals for a system of political wards or "elementary republics." Jefferson evidently did not develop this idea until some time after he left the presidency, inasmuch as he appears first to have mentioned it in a letter to John Tyler on May 26,

---

[21] For an interesting and representative selection of writings on the subject, see C. George Benello and Dimitrios Roussoupoulos, eds., *The Case for Participatory Democracy* (New York: Viking, 1971).

1810. He later elaborated upon the theme in several letters, especially those in 1816 to Joseph C. Cabell and Samuel Kercheval. He remained vitally concerned that the republic could not survive as a republic without such a system, and as late as 1824 he was concluding every opinion with the injunction, "divide the counties into wards" (letter to John Cartwright on June 5).

As Jefferson wrote in his July 12 letter to Kercheval, he would "divide the counties into wards of such size as that every citizen can attend, when called on, and act in person." The ward governments would deal with "all things relating to themselves exclusively," including schools, law enforcement, judicial and welfare functions, and the like. Such a scheme, he wrote, would "relieve the county administration of nearly all its business" and would make "every citizen an acting member of the government," thereby encouraging the strongest allegiance to the country and to the republican principle.

Despite Jefferson's sense of urgency regarding his suggestion, it had no effect, and few have even taken note of it. Adrienne Koch did mention ward republics and wrote that they were one of Jefferson's "most significant and original ideas for implementing representative democracy," but she treats the idea only briefly.[22] Hannah Arendt, however, stands almost alone, not only in taking Jefferson's suggestion quite seriously, but in providing a highly perceptive analysis.[23]

Arendt's studies led her to relate Jefferson's ward system to the "feeble germs of a new form of government" that were discernible in "sections of the Parisian Commune and the popular societies during the French Revolution," but she argued that his plan, if implemented, would have "exceeded" them, "by far." She proceeded to say that "both Jefferson's plan and the French *sociétés révolutionnaires* anticipated with an almost weird precision those councils, *soviets* and *Räte*, which were to make their appearance in every genuine revolution throughout the nineteenth and twentieth centuries." Moreover, such developments were spontaneous, and unanticipated by revolutionary leaders, and "like

---

[22] Adrienne Koch, *The Philosophy of Thomas Jefferson* (New York: Columbia University Press, 1943), pp. 162–65.
[23] Hannah Arendt, *On Revolution* (New York: Viking, 1965), pp. 252–59 and 323–24.

Jefferson's proposals, they were utterly neglected by statesmen, historians, political theorists, and, most importantly, by the revolutionary tradition itself." It is equally significant that they have been ignored also by students of political ideologies.

Jefferson's concern was precisely for what we would call participatory democracy. Although the people had acted during the Revolution, they had thereafter permitted public actions to become solely the concern of government. The principle that survived, representative government, was in Jefferson's view inadequate. It was self-government that he sought. He did not intend the "small republic" to strengthen the majority; rather it was "to enhance the power of each citizen."[24] The notion of participatory democracy owes considerably more to Thomas Jefferson, writing more than one and one-half centuries ago, than all but a few have recognized.

FEMINISM

As with most social questions, the fundamental issues of the women's movement are political. The true essence of feminism is not that men and women are identical, or should become so, but rather that the life of each person, man or woman, should be governed insofar as possible by choice, not chance. Thus, it is clearly an expansion of the ideology of liberal democracy.

Although the women's movement is a phenomenon that is widespread throughout the world, it has been most prominent in the United States. This is perhaps appropriate, inasmuch as the democratic ideology in America is one of radical individualism and could be interpreted as leading naturally to an ideology of feminism. Nevertheless, from 1920 when the ratification of the Nineteenth Amendment ensured the right of women to vote, until the feminist movement in the 1960s, the integration of women into America's social and political structure made hardly any progress. There was, in fact, such blatant discrimination against women in employment and other matters that it was creating great indignation among those concerned about equality for all citizens.

[24] Max J. Skidmore, *American Political Thought* (New York: St. Martin's Press, 1978), p. 72.

In June, 1966, a number of interested women met in Washington, D.C. and created the National Organization for Women (NOW). The group's first act was to send telegrams to Equal Employment Opportunity commissioners in the states urging them to move against employment advertisements that discriminated against women. In November of 1967, NOW codified its demands into a "Women's Bill of Rights," seeking a constitutional amendment banning discrimination on the basis of gender, the enforcement of existing laws that banned discrimination in employment, maternity leave rights from employers and in the Social Security Program, tax deductions for home and childcare expenses for working parents, the creation of childcare centers, equal and unsegregated educational opportunities, equal job-training opportunities, and a recognition of the right of women to control their reproductive lives.

The women's movement produced numerous political groups, including Marxist and other socialist groups, anarchists, separatists who shunned a society that included males, and others. The vast majority, however, were moderates whose feminist ideology was simply an extension of American democratic ideology. The climate that they helped to create, and the dedicated efforts of Representative Martha Griffiths of Michigan, brought forth a proposed Twenty-Seventh Amendment to the U.S. Constitution that would have prevented the laws of the United States or any state from discriminating on the basis of sex.

In March of 1972 Congress approved the Equal Rights Amendment with enthusiasm, giving it the required two-thirds vote of each house. It appeared as if there would be no difficulty in securing the approval of the three-fourths of the states necessary for ratification, and in fact the states began quickly to endorse the proposal. Presently, however, the opposition crystalized. Many fundamentalist Christian religious organizations joined forces with groups on the far right, such as the John Birch Society and the Ku Klux Klan, to begin a concerted attack. Some groups, such as the Eagle Forum, emerged specifically to oppose the ERA. The unexpected opposition convinced many legislators in the states that they should not support the amendment, and it died.

Although virtually all studies indicated widespread support for the ERA—and thirty-five states containing more than 70% of the country's population ultimately ratified it—the intensity of that support was not sufficient to counter the fervor of the opposition, which was well organized while supporters tended not to be. The wording of the proposal was clear and simple: "Equality of rights under the law shall not be denied or abridged by the United States or by any State on account of sex." Many opponents asserted that approval of the ERA would outlaw privacy in restrooms, give legal sanction to homosexual marriages, and force all wives to provide half of the family income. Whether or not such inaccurate charges were convincing, they certainly contributed to the climate of controversy that led to the amendment's defeat, thus demonstrating the potential power of a determined and well-organized minority.

The contributions of feminism, however, cannot be judged by the failure of the ERA. Feminist thought has created at least some sensitivity to the issue of discrimination, when previously there was hardly even a recognition that it existed. Moreover, feminist writers have demonstrated that discriminatory thought patterns—even when there is no overt discrimination in practice—cause harm to the whole of society, not merely to those of one sex.

Modern feminist scholars have built upon the pioneering works of such nineteenth-century writers and activists as Frances Wright, Margaret Fuller, Elizabeth Cady Stanton, Lucretia Mott, Susan B. Anthony, and many others. Indeed, Fuller's *Woman in the Nineteenth Century*, written in 1845, remains one of the most insightful studies of the harm that results to all when one segment of society is repressed. As with all great political writing, the best of the feminist studies have implications far beyond considerations of a particular issue.

Virginia Sapiro, for example, has brought the insights of feminism to political science and has succeeded in expanding the reach of liberal democratic thought and ideology.[25] She distinguishes between merely allowing participation and placing a public value on participation. An authoritarian regime may allow participation, but it is essential only to liberal democracy. Although her frame of reference was the position of women in society, her argument that society must place a positive value upon membership if liberation is to be meaningful is equally applicable to racial, ethnic, religious, or linguistic minorities, or to less affluent social classes.

[25] Virginia Sapiro, *The Political Integration of Women* (Urbana: University of Illinois Press, 1983).

MARGARET FULLER

The growth of Man is two-fold, masculine and feminine. . . . [I]f these two developments were in perfect harmony, they would correspond to and fulfill one another. . . . Wherever there was pure love, the natural influences were for the time restored. . . . Wherever religion (I mean the thirst for truth and good, not the love of sect and dogma) had its course, the original design was apprehended in its simplicity. . . . no age was left entirely without a witness of the equality of the sexes in function, duty, and hope. . . . [W]hen there was unwillingness or ignorance which prevented this being acted upon, women had not the less power for their want of light and noble freedom. But it was power which hurt alike them and those against whom they made use of the arms of the servile—cunning, blandishment, and unreasonable emotion. . . . I believe that at present women are the best helpers of one another. . . . We only ask of men to remove arbitrary barriers. . . . [I]f you ask me what office they may fill, I reply—any. I do not care what case you put; let them be sea captains if they will. I do not doubt there are women well fitted for such an office. . . . I have no doubt, however, that a large proportion of women would give themselves to the same employment as now. . . . The difference would be that *all* need not be constrained to employments for which *some* are unfit. . . . I have urged on Woman independence of Man, not because I do not think the sexes mutually needed by one another, but in Woman this fact has led to an excessive devotion, which has cooled love, degraded marriage, and prevented either sex from being what it should be to itself or the other.

From *Woman in the Nineteenth Century* (1845)

Feminism has produced insights into the nature of democracy and the ideology of freedom. Its overall goal is not merely to improve the lot of women, as important as that is, but rather to improve society in general. In this regard, the best of the feminist works rank with the best of the antislavery literature. The issues, if not identical, are quite similar. Democracy will not have achieved what its own logic promises while any part of society remains outside the public sphere. Sapiro is correct in going further still. Women must not only be permitted into the public sphere, but must be integrated into it, while men must also be integrated into what she calls the private sphere of the home and child rearing. She stresses the need for this to be done under conditions of mutual respect and dignity. This not only is consistent with the ideology of democracy, but enlarges it considerably.

DEMOCRATIC IDEOLOGIES IN PERSPECTIVE

The ideologies discussed in this chapter are all related to the broad ideology that originally was a reaction to the feudal past but now has become liberal, constitutional democracy. Each has had its influence. Liberalism, in fact, has become so identified with democracy that it sometimes is difficult to distinguish the democratic from the liberal elements in modern democracy. They are all entwined, but each nonetheless retains certain characteristics that enable it to continue as a narrower entity within a broader framework. Each addresses certain fundamental questions in its own fashion.

Attitude Toward Change

Liberalism initially was a revolutionary ideology, seeking to replace an existing order. As institutions changed to accommodate liberal values, liberalism of course changed also. As one of the bases of liberal democracy, liberalism in liberal democratic states, such as the United States, most of those in Western Europe, and some elsewhere, has become a status quo ideology. It is a special kind of status quo ideology, however. Because a willingness to experiment, to accept change, is part of its essential nature, liberalism always contains within itself something more than a thrust to conserve the existing order. Regardless of the character of the system, liberalism continues to reflect elements of a change-oriented ideology. In a right-wing regime, it would be revolutionary; in liberal democracies, despite its support of the status quo, it remains open to reform. Hence, in a system that institutionalizes mechanisms permitting or even encouraging change, liberalism can at the same time be a status quo and a reform ideology.

The same can be true for that related ideology, populism, although at times it may not be. Populism as such replaces liberalism's emphasis on the individual with an emphasis upon the majority. Its attitude toward change, therefore, is subordinate to the will of the majority. If the people wish change, populism by definition supports change; if they wish to resist change, populism similarly supports that resistance.

Participatory democracy combines liberalism's individualism and populism's majoritarianism. It is intensely liberal in that the major criterion is participation of the individual in decisions that affect him or her. At the same time, it is majoritarian. It emphasizes the will of the people, but emphasizes protection for minority—and when pushed far enough, individual—interests. As an ideology, it, like others, is subject to a variety of interpretations, but when extended to its logical conclusion, it incorporates all the elements of liberal constitutional democracy. It is distinguished by its consistent demand that all those elements be put into actual practice to a greater extent than is the case currently in any political system. Its attitude toward change is therefore receptive; it is at least a reform ideology with elements of the revolutionary, depending upon the character of the regime in which it exists.

Feminism is an example of a comprehensive ideology based upon a narrow subject. Concern for the status of women has led to fully developed political ideologies, the mainstream of which are related to liberal, constitutional democracy or to democratic socialism. There are small offshoots that are on the extreme left, motivated by Marxism-Leninism, or on the far right, such as that represented by "WITCH" (the Women's International Terrorist Conspiracy from Hell) or "SCUM" (the Society for Cutting Up Men). The only feminist ideology of any importance, however, and it is of extraordinary importance, is the one that we have considered in this chapter. It is an outgrowth of liberal, constitutional democracy. In every respect it is simply a logical extension of liberal, constitutional, and democratic principles beyond previous limitations. Under current conditions, its approach toward change makes it a reform ideology.

Conservatism is the one ideology of this chapter that is generally resistant to change. It seeks to conserve the best of the past, rather than to experiment with change in the hope that it might lead to a better future. This is not to say that conservatism opposes all change. Rather, it is an ideology that accepts only gradual, evolutionary change that is based upon, and is an outgrowth of, the past. Even when accepting change, however, its essential attitude remains one of suspicion until the value of a change is proven by time. In general, conservatism accepts change only as a device to guard against more extensive change. Conservatism is clearly a status quo ideology, regardless of the character of the political system. When the status quo is one of liberal, constitutional democracy, conservatism becomes one of its strong supporters. It is in this sense that conservatism fits into this chapter.

Modern democracy as an ideology is therefore a complex amalgam of many themes. Just as conservatism may incorporate even radical institutions after they have stood the test of time, so are democracy's themes highly varied and sometimes seemingly incompatible. It nevertheless has seized hold of human imagination to an extent unparalleled in history. As one of the most revolutionary ideologies in history, hardly any modern political institution fails to reflect at least a bit of its influence in one way or another. Essentially, democracy is receptive to change, and in the form of liberal, constitutional democracy it has succeeded in institutionalizing, as a part of the status quo, a receptivity to change. Historically, this is a remarkable achievement.

Attitude Toward Human Nature

Although there have been contrary themes within liberalism, including the ideas of Hobbes and some of the Utilitarians, its general tendency has been to assume that human nature is essentially good. If human beings are corrupt, it is because of corrupting institutions. The people may be trusted to govern themselves, and even if there are dangers from human imperfections, the dangers from minority government are considerably greater. By and large, populism, participatory democracy, feminism, and liberalism share the same approach to the nature of human beings.

Conservatism, once again, is different. The tendency is for conservatism to accept human beings as selfish, weak, and as being led by pride to dominate others. It is this approach that leads conservatives to stress the importance of institutions as a check upon human fallibility.

Liberal, constitutional democracy as a rule is based upon an optimistic view of human nature. Nevertheless, the constitutional aspect recognizes that human passions, selfishness, and foolishness do exist and assumes that it is important to protect against them. Human nature by and large is good, but not to the extent that it can be relied upon completely without some checks.

Attitude Toward the Potential of Human Reason

With one major exception, all of the strains that go to make up liberal, constitutional democracy are at least somewhat optimistic regarding the potential for human reason to improve society and the human condition. Even Hobbes, with all his fear of human passion and skepticism of reason, assumed that human beings improved their condition through an exercise of reason, the contract that removed them from the state of nature. The major exception is conservatism.

Conservative skepticism of the efficacy of human reason is one explanation for the conservative emphasis upon gradual, evolutionary, change, and upon the maintenance of institutions that have stood the test of time. If an institution has existed for some time, it works. Regardless of how reasonable a new institution may appear, one cannot be certain that it will work unless it is put into practice. To experiment is dangerous, because a failed experiment may make conditions much worse. To the conservative, therefore, it is vastly more prudent to conserve what has proven itself to be workable than to trust reason, however attractive, to devise something different.

Attitude Toward Human Progress

The attitude toward the possibility of human progress is related to the attitude toward the potential of human reason. Conservatives are frankly doubtful that human beings can do much to improve their situation on earth. Their nature is such, their reason so inadequate, that the likelihood of significant progress is small. The other ideologies in this chapter tend to be more optimistic. All accept the possibility of progress, even the likelihood, if human beings exercise reason properly. At the most extreme, some highly optimistic liberals and populists have even come to believe that progress is inevitable.

Attitude Toward the Relationship of the Individual to the Community

Liberalism, populism, participatory democracy, democratic feminism, all place the importance of the individual before that of the community. They assume, in other words, that the community is nothing more than the aggregate of the individuals that comprise it. The conservative emphasis, on the contrary, is on the community. Conservatism assumes that the community has an organic existence of its own, that it is something more than merely a collection of individuals. Such assumptions condition the attitudes that the various ideologies take toward the individual in relation to the community. Those that place the individual as the primary unit of politics are likely to stress individual rights, although they recognize the importance of duties. Those that grant the community an organic existence are more likely to stress duties to the community, although they may recognize the importance of rights. To the one group, rights are inherent in the individual; to the other, the community creates them and grants them to individuals.

The point of greatest agreement between liberalism and democratic conservatism is the institution of private property. The existence of private property historically has been a major component of liberalism. Classical liberals have fiercely protected private property, assuming that its existence is the greatest guarantee of human freedom. Its importance to positive liberals is considerably less, but they too are staunch defenders of the existence of the institution. Conservatives in liberal democracies are some of the most fervent defenders of private property, even though it is inherently a liberal institution that they are conserving.

THE FUNCTIONING OF DEMOCRACY

The popular myth portrays democracy as functioning as mass democracy, with the people determining public policy through elected representatives.Except in the smallest jurisdictions, such as New England Town Meetings, the idea of direct democracy, with the people acting to represent themselves directly, no longer has a place even in the ideology—at least not in the mainstream. This may, however, be simply an instance in which ideology has lagged behind technology. With today's computerized telecommunication, it would be possible, at least technologically, to adapt some form of direct democracy. Whether it would be feasible on other grounds, with the tremendous number of governmental decisions required and the complexity of the issues, is another matter.

The idea of mass democracy, on the other hand, persists. Because of the importance of popular sovereignty to the democratic principle, it is easy to understand why there remains such an attachment to the idea, even though it clearly is inconsistent with the manner in which democracy generally functions. Some American states and local jurisdictions have adopted such devices as the initiative, the referendum, and the recall in an attempt to provide some measure of mass democracy. The initiative permits the people, by petition, to place questions on the ballot for consideration. A referendum provides under certain circumstances for a popular vote on matters passed by a legislative body, and a recall is a negative election, that is, an election held to eject a public official from office when there is sufficient demand to do so. These measures have worked with varying degrees of effectiveness. The policies that have resulted from their use likewise vary considerably in their desirability.

As for mass democracy, despite the appeal of the principle, it rarely exists in practice. In the United States, for example, the people certainly have the power to have some effect upon governmental policies, should they choose to exercise their power, especially at the state and local levels. Just as certainly, though, they more often than not fail to do so. Moreover, the formal institutions of government not only discourage popular control of national policy, but make it almost impossible. The people have no direct control over amendments to the U.S. Constitution, or over the selection of judges. Their choice of a president is mediated through the Electoral College, and—in contrast to the practice under a parliamentary system—elections occur at specified times, regardless of public wishes. In nearly all instances, it is the representatives rather than the people who actually exercise power in systems of representative democracy. The lack of mass democracy is inherently neither good nor bad, and it does not imply that government is unlimited, nor that it fails to respond to public desires.

Some of the popular assumptions regarding mass democracy may well be influenced by attitudes going back as far as the writings of Jean Jacques Rousseau (1712–1778), and the French Revolution of 1789. Rousseau believed strongly in direct democracy and argued forcefully against representative government as likely to distort the "general will." It was the general will that was to be supreme, and Rousseau would not have argued with the contention that the voice of the people is the voice of God. Although Rousseau's theory of the general will is not identical with majoritarianism, it amounts in practice to the same thing.

Rousseau's ideas greatly affected the French Revolution and the direction of democratic evolution on the Continent. His influence in America was considerably less. Nevertheless, his descriptions of mass democracy were so powerful and so emotionally gripping that they may well have encouraged a romantic attachment to the notion, even in the liberal United States, where Lockean ideas were far more influential. As European democracies emerged, most tended to emphasize the majoritarian aspects, in contrast to the individualism so prominent in America. This led to fewer institutional restraints upon democratically elected assemblies in Europe than in America with its Madisonian balance.

It is important to note here that Rousseau's extreme version of unlimited majoritarianism was as much a revolt against autocratic government as was the liberal revolt that stressed constitutional limitations upon political institutions. The greatest difficulty with liberalism is that its strong emphasis upon individualism and its inherently antistatist attitudes, if carried to extremes, can discourage a sense of community and lead to greed and selfishness. The danger with an overemphasis upon majoritarianism is that it can produce a tyranny of the majority that is no less oppressive than the minority tyrannies that both the liberal individualists and the advocates of mass democracy opposed.

Thus, the two democratic extremes contain both common and divergent elements, creating not only tension between them, but also some general agreements. Most democratic systems include reflections of each approach and combine individualistic and majoritarian aspects.[26] The resulting schemes frequently shift with the times from one emphasis to the other. As a rule, they work, although not always smoothly.

---

[26] For an interesting discussion of "majority-rule democrats" and "individual-rights democrats," including (as he describes it) a "very crude summary" of the history of, and arguments for, the position of each, see T. L. Thorson's "Introduction" to his edited collection, *Plato: Totalitarian or Democrat?* (Englewood Cliffs, N.J.: Prentice–Hall, 1963). esp. pp. 4–7.

Perhaps it is the contradictory elements within democracy itself that create different patterns of operation from one system to another and lead even to different interpretations regarding the operation of the same system. Just how does democracy work? Although mass democracy in theory is one possibility, existing conditions render it highly unlikely. At the other extreme is elite democracy.

Theorists of democratic elitism take their cue from the writings of a group of European authors, including Vilfredo Pareto (1848–1923), Gaetano Mosca (1858–1941), Robert Michels (1876–1936), and Giovanni Sartori (1924–   ). Michels, for example, formulated his "Iron Law of Oligarchy," which contends that in any organization, however democratic its form, a few persons inevitably hold the power. Some have concluded from this that democracy not only is impossible, but would also be undesirable because the people in general lack the capacity to govern. This is not to imply that "elitists" necessarily would agree. Sartori, for instance, is a staunch defender of democracy and of broadly based political power. He stresses not only competitive leadership selection, but also the importance of providing power to the people, and enforcing "the *responsiveness* of the leaders to the led."[27] Others, such as Joseph Schumpeter, support an elitist democracy but define away much of the democratic aspect of the system. Schumpeter wrote, for example, that democracy means only that the people may choose which elite will rule them.[28] Jack L. Walker, Peter Bachrach, and others have taken issue with the elitists.[29]

Another form of democratic elitism has been the subject of a vast number of studies, beginning with the arguments of the late sociologist C. Wright Mills pertaining to the operation of American democracy. He wrote not to praise elitism, nor to deny that it existed, but rather to condemn it.[30] He argued that the American system tends to be dominated by a relatively small group, which

[27] Sartori, p. 156.
[28] Joseph Schumpeter, *Capitalism, Socialism, Democracy*, 4th ed. (New York: Harper & Row, 1954), p. 285.
[29] See for example, Jack L. Walker, "A Critique of the Elitist Theory of Democracy," *American Political Science Review*, LX (June, 1966), pp. 285–95 and Peter Bachrach, *The Theory of Democratic Elitism* (Boston: Little, Brown, 1967); see also Sartori's rejoinder, pp. 156–71.
[30] See, for example, C. Wright Mills, *The Power Elite* (New York: Oxford University Press, 1959).

controls the government, industry, the professions, and major interest groups including labor and trade organizations. Group members may move from one segment to another, but they are cohesive and unresponsive to the citizenry, even while controlling the peoples' lives.

"Pluralism" has become a popular explanation that many accept as the best description of modern democratic operation. It falls between the extremes of mass democracy and elitist democracy, and is a theory that sees democratic government as dominated neither by the people as a collective whole, nor by powerful individuals who manipulate society at will. Instead, it replaces the liberal concern for the individual with a concern for interest groups and becomes "interest group democracy."

Pluralism does not mean simply that there is a tolerance for diversity. It describes a situation in which powerful, organized interest groups dominate society, with the government acting essentially as a broker or a referee to facilitate compromise among them. "Government," of course, is not a single force. Different agencies may participate as interest groups themselves, with little or no coordination, and may even work at cross purposes. These groups afford the people access to power through membership. Some therefore argue that they foster popular government, while others respond that they institutionalize elite domination. Some praise pluralism as providing stability and encouraging prosperity. Others accuse it of fostering conformity and materialism and argue that by leaving the individual out of account, it greatly lessens self-government.

Democratic ideology thus accommodates a great variety of *theories*, ranging from those advocated by Rousseau, on the one hand, to the descriptions (and prescriptions) of the democratic elitists on the other. The *practices* prevalent under democratic forms are hardly less varied. The common core, however much it may differ in application, remains the position of the people. Their rights, including political equality, are inherent, not granted by government, and their participation, in one form or another—but including periodic elections with free speech and vigorous opposition—is essential.

Democratic Capitalism

2

Capitalism is as closely associated with liberalism, both historically and in theory, as liberalism is associated with democracy. Many writers on political ideology, in fact, discuss the economic aspects of liberalism rather than devoting specific sections to capitalism.[1] This is understandable, because capitalism, as such, is an economic system rather than a form of politics, and because one would be hard-pressed to draw a clear distinction between capitalism and the economic side of liberalism. Nonetheless, in certain capitalist democracies the economic and political institutions have become so closely related that the phenomenon of "democratic capitalism" has come to be a political ideology as well as an economic one. In such cases the economic ideas of capitalism have come to provide a major justification for democracy, while political ideas serve to justify economic arrangements.

---

[1] See, for example, Roy C. Macridis, *Contemporary Political Ideologies* (Boston: Little, Brown, 1986), Chapter 2, and the discussion of the "economic core of liberalism."

Because of its vital importance to political ideology, it seems appropriate to examine capitalism specifically and in more detail than was done in the discussion of liberalism in the preceding chapter.

As is also true of socialism, captialism is compatible with many different forms of government. There are openly authoritarian political systems such as those in Taiwan and Chile that are capitalistic, as well as democratic systems such as those in Switzerland and the United States. The Republic of South Africa is an example of yet a different capitalistic system, one that functions as authoritarian, but maintains the form of, and professes to be, a democracy. It is evident, therefore, that the form of government does not determine the economic system, nor does the economic system determine the form of government.

There are more capitalist authoritarian systems than democratic ones, despite the historical association between democracy and capitalism. This is true also of socialism, which, like capitalism, developed in close association with democracy. The number of authoritarian socialist systems, including all Marxist-Leninist states and some others as well, far outnumbers socialist democracies such as Sweden's. Our attention, however, will not be directed toward authoritarian systems, but rather toward democratic capitalism, which is the most important, the most political, and the most ideological of all capitalist forms.

A complication in approaching this subject could be the impossibility of arriving at a satisfactory definition. Hardly any two students of capitalism would agree in every respect as to what, exactly, they mean by the term, which was not even in common usage until Marx popularized it. This, of course, is no different from the difficulty that plagues the study of political ideology in general. Rarely, if ever, are there broad agreements as to precise definitions. Fortunately, it is equally rare that precision in definition is necessary, so long as one recognizes the vagueness of terms and the considerable overlap that may exist among definitions. Political ideology is action oriented; it incites to action, it reacts to conditions and to other ideologies, and it inspires—again in reaction—competing ideologies. Its importance is its effects, not its theoretical sophistication.

Capitalism traditionally has referred to an economic system in which individuals or corporations own land and other property;

produce, distribute, and exchange goods; and invest their wealth as they see fit under conditions established essentially by the free and competitive market and with the intent to profit and accumulate wealth. The system is one that results from the aggregate of private economic decisions—from the most tiny and insignificant to ones with enormous effects throughout the system and beyond—rather than from state control. In its classical form it is liberalism, or individualist democracy, applied to economics.

The free and competitive market, however, has rarely, if ever, been completely free and competitive. Even the most capitalist of systems have always had some public investment, ownership, and control of the economy. The early United States is an example. As the new country grew into a democratic capitalist state, it also made huge grants of land to railroads, constructed roads, canals, and other public works, levied high tariffs to protect American industry, and operated a postal system. India has considerable private enterprise along with a large amount of public ownership and a rather tightly-controlled economy. Is India "capitalist," or "socialist"?

The difficulties in drawing such distinctions increase with the tendencies of governments to become more involved in capitalist economies, and the tendencies of socialist states (even in Marxist-Leninist countries) to adopt more free-market mechanisms. Moreover, capitalism, like other ideologies, including its close relative, liberalism, has changed. As noted above, even in simpler times economies did not function completely as the classic capitalist model assumed they did, and the economic reality has become greatly more complicated through the years. The ideology of democratic capitalism has reacted to changing conditions and to competing ideologies to become considerably more sophisticated. It no longer is limited to the rigid classical model.

Some things, however, are not in doubt and remain unchanged. Private property is fundamental to a capitalist system, as are the existence of a free market for the exchange of goods and services and the freedom to pursue profit. The profit motive is the incentive for capitalist economic activity. All models of capitalism since the time of Adam Smith have assumed that the profit motive in operation produces the most efficient economy; it also leads to the lowest prices for goods and the greatest abundance of any system. Capitalism thus seeks progress under the control not of the state, but rather of the marketplace, or as Smith called it, the "invisible hand."

The tenets of democratic capitalism accept economic inequality and assume that the most deserving, in the economic sense, will receive the greatest rewards. They assume, also, that capitalism provides the most democracy, in that private decisions drive the system rather than governmental compulsion, and that such decentralized decisions are a bulwark against tyranny and a protection for liberty. In addition, there has been an emphasis upon the "natural," based upon the assumption that capitalism follows the law of nature, rather than artificial, manmade restrictions. This assumption led to a bias against regulation and against all but the most limited governmental activity.

The elements of a political ideology here are obvious. The reasons economic and political creeds became mixed are equally obvious. Although certainly many factors other than capitalism were at work, capitalist economies have produced the greatest abundance of goods and services in human history. To be sure, early capitalism was responsible for untold depths of poverty at the same time that it was creating huge fortunes. It despoiled the landscape at the same time that it exacted a shocking toll in human misery. Such pernicious side effects generated fervent anticapitalist reactions, such as anarchism, socialism, and Marxism-Leninism. They also inspired the vivid rhetoric and images that continue to motivate much opposition to capitalism, especially in the Third World. As time passed, however, governments in nonsocialist systems moved to smooth off most of capitalism's rough edges and adopted some measures to provide for the general welfare, instead of merely the welfare of the capitalists. In doing so they reacted to the same needs that motivated socialist systems.

The result has been the height of human economic accomplishment. The political result—the enhancement of an expanding democracy—has been equally noteworthy. Modern democratic capitalism certainly has its shortcomings, but they exist largely in comparison with what could be, or should be, not with what has been.

It should nevertheless be apparent that these accomplishments did not come from capitalism in its classical form. On the contrary, they required the development of what is in many respects a different ideology altogether. While classical capitalism provided economic energy, it created great social ills as energetically—and in as cold-hearted a manner—as it created great wealth. The reaction to it was not limited to anarchism and socialism, but included also a new form of capitalism itself, one that retained some basic tenets of the old, such as private property and a predominance of private economic decisions in the marketplace, but that also recognized something new, some measure of social responsibility.

Capitalism brought about abrupt change. When combined with industrialism, it swept through society after society and radically revolutionized the lives of the people. For the first time in history, an overwhelming majority of workers were employed by someone else and worked for wages. This was a striking change in a rather brief period. It is no exaggeration to call it a revolution. However much it was unintended, capitalism in the nineteenth century was a revolutionary ideology. Fortunately, in its later incarnations, it developed many aspects of a reform ideology as well.

CLASSICAL CAPITALISM

Although elements of capitalism had existed in the commercial arrangements of a number of ancient societies, they were largely absent in Medieval Europe. The Church's attitude toward "usury" outlawed the payment of interest among Christians, making the development of a capitalist system highly unlikely. The complicated and rigid institutions of feudalism were equally discouraging. Free enterprise and competitive markets could not develop so long as serfdom and tight economic controls were dominant.

As the Renaissance developed, its new ideas weakened the rigidities of both the Church and the feudal system. Calvinism attacked the Church directly and brought with it an economic emphasis that had not existed during the Middle Ages. Rather than continuing the tendency to diminish the importance of wealth and economic enterprise, Calvinism taught that economic success was an indication that one might belong to the "elect."

At the same time that it stressed the virtues of thrift, hard work, and material success, however, Calvinism condemned luxury and the use of wealth for personal pleasure or for ostentation.

This meant that newly generated wealth, including the introduction of riches from then New World, was allowed to accumulate, and to become investment capital. Wealth was much less likely than previously to be consumed by luxurious lifestyles, or by creating huge monuments, cathedrals, and the like.

The new economic system that developed in reaction to the emerging currents came to be called mercantilism. Countries competed to increase their stores of gold and silver, which they assumed would secure their power. They embarked upon active programs of exploration ad colonization. Colonies might be direct sources of gold and silver. If not, they might contribute indirectly by providing raw materials to be shipped home and manufactured into goods to be sold to other countries. The mercantilist tendency was thus to increase international trade as much as possible, with each country seeking a maximum accumulation of gold and silver at the expense of others. It was also at the expense of the colonies, which were highly restricted. They existed only for the benefit of the colonizing country and could engage only in those economic activities that the home country approved as benefiting itself.

It was this situation that encouraged Adam Smith to produce his classic *Wealth of Nations* in the same year that the thirteen American colonies declared their independence from England: 1776. Smith argued that mercantilist doctrines failed to enrich colonizing countries. On the contrary, a country became wealthy by its production, not by merely accumulating huge quantities of precious metals. He contended that the mercantilist restrictions on trade and economic activity stifled creativity and productivity. By protecting inefficiency, they actually reduced national wealth.

Smith's famous term "laissez-faire" indicated his prescription. An economy would grow and a country would become wealthy if the government were to "let things alone" and permit the ingenuity of the people to produce and create wealth. Competition would be the fundamental principle. Each person or group of persons would compete with others and would have access to resources depending upon the ability to command such access. Inefficient enterprises would perish, while the efficient would prosper. Success would come to those who could produce most efficiently, create goods and services that were in demand, and provide them to consumers at the lowest prices.

ADAM SMITH

The quantity of every commodity which human industry can either purchase or produce naturally regulates itself in every country according to the effectual demand, or according to the demand of those who are willing to pay the whole rent, labour, and profits which must be paid in order to prepare and bring it to market. . . . It is thus that every system which endeavours, either by extraordinary encouragements to draw towards a particular species of industry a greater share of the capital of the society than what would naturally go to it, or, by extraordinary restraints, force from a particular species of industry some share of the capital which would otherwise be employed in it, is in reality subversive of the great purpose which it means to promote. . . .

All systems either of preference or of restraint, therefore, being thus completely taken away, the obvious and simple system of natural liberty establishes itself of its own accord. Every man, as long as he does not violate the laws of justice, is left perfectly free to pursue his own interest his own way, and to bring both his industry and capital into competition with those of any other man, or order of men. . . . The sovereign is completely discharged from a duty . . . for the proper performance of which no human wisdom or knowledge could ever be sufficient; the duty of superintending the industry of private people, and of directing it towards the employments most suitable to the interest of the society.

From *The Wealth of Nations* (1776)

Thus, Smith believed, laissez-faire would permit quality and abundance to remain at the highest levels, while prices to the consumer would be as low as possible. Competition among individuals would result in public benefit and the strength of the economy and the country. The good of society resulted from the pursuit of self-interest, rather than from deliberate attempts to seek the public good through the suppression of selfishness.

The elevation of selfishness to an honored position was something new. Rather than being sinful, as it has been for centuries, it came to be justified as beneficial to society. Laissez-faire had immediate appeal to those who would throw off the shackles of economic restraint, and it became the persistent theme of the emerging economic doctrine of capitalism.

Smith wrote when industrialism was in its infancy and factories were beginning to develop. Enthusiastic supporters saw the potential of the factories for increasing abundance, but not the disruptions that they would cause. Smith's optimism reflected the temper of the time, but such optimism could not be sustained for long when the overall effects of industrialism became apparent.

Not only was there newly created wealth, there were also extremes of newly created poverty. Although there were exceptions—there were some enlightened owners—factories tended to be dim and dirty places, filled with deafening noise, lung-destroying dust, and crippling or deadly machines. These posed definite threats to the general health, the limbs, and the lives of workers, who included men, women, and even small children. Hours were often so long that many workers rarely saw sunlight, except through the filthy windows of the factory. With no social benefits, injuries resulted in immediate dismissal, which meant starvation. The conditions in the workers' living quarters that surrounded the factories were hardly better, with overcrowding and no sanitation.

The writers who followed Adam Smith were therefore considerably less optimistic than he. David Ricardo assumed that the profit motive would compel factory owners to pay the lowest wages possible, keeping pay only high enough to prevent workers from leaving. Ricardo argued that it was essential that wages be kept depressed, despite the admittedly terrible social conditions of the workers, because only then could factory owners accumulate enough capital to maintain production. He believed that if wages were to rise, production would slow to such an extent that the resulting misery would be even greater than that caused by low wages.

Ricardo did not dispute the contention that labor creates value, but he concluded that this did not mean that the workers should retain all of any value that they create. On the contrary, he argued that it was necessary for labor to relinquish much of that value to those who supplied the capital. Only if they did so, would the enterprise be able to attract the additional capital necessary to maintain itself. Although the result that he anticipated was considerably less desirable than that which Adam Smith portrayed,

---

FRANCES WRIGHT

The great principles stamped in America's declaration of independence, are true, are great, are sublime,and are *all her own*. But her usages, her law, her religion, her education, are false, narrow, prejudiced, ignorant, and are the relic of dark ages—the gift and bequeathment of king-governed, priest-ridden nations,whose supremacy, indeed, the people of America have challenged and overthrown, but whose example they are still following.

. . . True, the 4th of July, '76, commenced a new era. . . . True, the sun of promise then rose upon the world. But let us not mistake for the fulness of light what was but its harbinger. Let us not conceive that man in signing the declaration of his rights secured their possession. . . .

That evils exist, none that have eyes, ears, and hearts can dispute. That these evils are on the increase, none who have watched the fluctuations of trade, the sinking price of labour, the growth of pauperism, and the increase of crime, will dispute. . . . [T]he labourer . . . is brought to an untimely grave by those exertions which, while sustaining the life of others, cut short his own. . . .

Such is the information gleaned from the report of the committee lately appointed by the town meeting of the city and county of Philadelphia, and as verbatim reiterated in every populous city throughout the land.

From a speech delivered in Philadelphia, June 2, 1829

Ricardo no less than Smith provided a moral justification for laissez-faire capitalism. His theory came to be called Ricardo's "Iron Law of Wages."

Another English economic writer, the clergyman Thomas Malthus (1766–1834), was even more pessimistic than Ricardo. Malthus observed that food production was limited by the availability of land. Increases in food production would therefore most likely be by arithmetic progression. That is, food production would not be likely to grow more than a given amount, such as a certain number of tons per year. If total food production one year were X tons, it might be $X+1$ the next year, $X+2$ the next, $X+3$ the next, and so on. It could not, however, be X one year, 2X the next, 4X the next, 8X the next, and so on, which would be geometric progression, but population can increase in that manner. His central argument was that maximum food increases can never keep up with maximum population increases.

Malthus carried his argument further. He contended that population increases faster when there is abundance than when there is scarcity. However harsh it seemed, he argued, it was more humane to keep workers as poor as possible in order to prevent catastrophic population increases.[2]

Malthus justified a continuing famine for workers as the only possibility, except for massive epidemics or huge wars, to maintain a balance between population and food supplies. Both he and Ricardo provided moral justifications for the exploitation of workers in order to concentrate wealth in the hands of an elite, regardless of the misery that it caused. They thus served the rising capitalist ideology well. Any ideology requires some kind of moral foundation if it is to develop the force that it requires to move society.

As the nineteenth century advanced, other writers turned to scientific ideas to add to the moral justification for unlimited accumulation. Herbert Spencer coined the phrase "survival of the fittest" and proceeded to misapply Darwinian evolutionary theory to economic matters, followed by his American disciple William Graham Sumner. Nature had decreed that the poor were inferior and would perish, while the most able not only would survive but would improve the human species. Social Darwinism did not explain how so many manifestly "inferior" human beings had managed to emerge in the age of industrialism, inasmuch as evolution had continued since the dawn of time, but it did assert that the capitalist could profit without limit and could do so by plundering others; all this would be done in accordance with the law of nature and would be fully justified morally!

---

[2]One may take some comfort at this point by noting that twentieth-century experience demonstrates that Malthus was not necessarily correct in some of his basic assumptions. Explosive population increases have occurred in Latin America under conditions of scarcity and in India under conditions of extreme deprivation, while population growth tends to remain stable—or even cease—in the developed world. Extraordinary affluence in the United States and Japan, for example, have not caused great population increases. Medical advances such as antibiotics have had some effect. Other factors have had even more influence, and sometimes they work against one another. For example, public health measures such as general sanitation and providing safe drinking water encourage population increase, while contraceptive techniques permit population control.

The popularity of this "social Darwinism" in the United States led to "rugged individualism," which justified the concentration of wealth and condemned any public effort to alleviate social ills. As one might expect, the "Captains of Industry" reigned supreme; some of these were so rapacious as to be called to "Robber Barons." But, despite the appeal of Social Darwinism and laissez-faire capitalism, there were other forces at work.

MODERN CAPITALISM

Along with the rush of unfettered laissez-faire capitalism, other ideas were developing. The capitalist ideology that had initially been so revolutionary had modulated quickly into an ideology of the status quo. At the same time, and long before Marx and Engels developed their bitter attacks on capitalism, capitalist ideas began to generate a reaction, that is, they began to create the nucleus of a reform ideology.

In England as early as 1802, Parliament initiated a series of legislative reforms by forbidding the employment of children—for more than twelve hours a day. Other acts throughout the century provided progressive restrictions upon child labor, mandated safer working conditions in factories, and ultimately promulgated the right of workers to form labor unions. The poet Matthew Arnold (1822–1888) raised his voice against the ills engendered by industrial capitalism, as did essayists such as Thomas Carlyle (1795–1881) and John Ruskin (1819–1900), while Charles Dickens (1812–1870) captured the attention of the public as only a novelist or dramatist can do.

In Germany beginning in 1883, Chancellor Bismarck instituted a number of reforms to alleviate the misery of the workers and prevent the increasing development of socialist agitation. These reforms included government health insurance (not seen in the United States until 1965!) and other forms of social security and retirement income. Great Britain followed early in the twentieth century with various reform measures, including unemployment compensation, health and accident protection, and minimum wage laws.

The United States was considerably slower, yet the Progressive movement of the early twentieth century accelerated the trend toward government regulation that began late in the nineteenth century. Numerous state and federal laws regulated freight rates, working hours, child labor, and the like. The federal government attempted, with varying success, to break up the huge trusts as early as 1890 with the Sherman Antitrust Act and increased its efforts with the Clayton Act of 1916. A group of writers known as the "Muckrakers" called attention around the turn of the century to such things as the abuse of corporate economic power, filth in the meat-packing industry, and the deplorable conditions in urban slums. The response was increased regulation, including the Pure Food and Drug Act, and the adoption of a progressive income tax that was designed to increase the percentage of tax paid as income rises. Progressive taxation remained the fundamental theory of federal tax policy until the strong demand for tax reform and simplification made a revision of the tax code possible in 1986. This "reform" and "simplification" complicated the tax code and virtually eliminated the notion of progressivity, though it did remove some of the tax burden upon those with the lowest incomes.

The greatest reform activity was initiated by the Great Depression, which brought the New Deal (1933–1945) of Franklin D. Roosevelt, followed ultimately by the Great Society (1963–1969) of Lyndon B. Johnson. The New Deal brought the Social Security Act (1935), national protection for collective bargaining, minimum wage legislation, insurance for bank deposits, workmen's compensation, regulation of banks and stock markets, additional protection for workers, and regulations on industry and employers.

The Fair Deal years (1945–1953) of Harry S Truman continued the trend as—to a somewhat lesser extent—did the administrations of Dwight D. Eisenhower (1953–1961) and John F. Kennedy (1961–1963). The Great Society years brought the addition of health care to Social Security, federal assistance to education, and the many programs of the "War on Poverty." The trend continued at a vastly slower rate with the administrations of Richard Nixon, Gerald Ford, and Jimmy Carter (1969–1981), but the ideology of reform capitalism remained substantially the same. With the administration of Ronald Reagan (1981–1989), the official ideology, at least, returned largely to that of laissez-faire capitalism.

It is unlikely, however, that it is possible to return in practice to the capitalism of a simpler time, even if it were desirable to do so. Not even the Reagan administration, however strong its rhetoric, succeeded in doing more than slowing the modern momentum. The fact is that capitalism today is quite different from anything envisioned by the classical theorists.

The American economist Thorstein Veblen (1857–1929) in his *Theory of the Leisure Class* (1899) anticipated that capitalism would come to be dominated by engineers or technicians. In 1932 the Columbia University economists Adoph A. Berle and Gardiner C. Means in *The Modern Corporation and Private Property* pointed out that modern corporations had become a form of nongovernmental socialism. They are huge concentrations of power owned by broad groups of citizens, but those citizens have turned actual control over to a managerial elite.[3] The owners no longer actually control; there are instead professional managers. James Burnham expanded on some of these themes in *The Managerial Revolution* in 1941,[4] but even the role of the manager may no longer be what it seems.

The most interesting elaboration on the changes that have become modern capitalism is in the works of John Kenneth Galbraith. He has pointed out that although the corporate form, with its stockholders and board of directors, remains from earlier times, it no longer reflects corporate reality. Recalling Veblen's themes, he has argued that in the "mature corporation," the official power structure—even including the top managers—does not exercise the true power. That comes from the technostructure, the technical experts of the organization, acting collectively. Top management is not sufficiently close to "the trenches" to be the dominant force.

This results in a dramatic shift from the themes of classical capitalism, which accepted as fundamental that the most important motivation to economic enterprise is to achieve maximum profit. Because the thrust of the organization comes from technical experts, rather than managers or stockholders, however, other considerations enter. "If revenues are above some minimum—they need not be at their maximum for none will know what that is— creditors cannot intervene and stockholders cannot be aroused.[5]

---

[3] See Skidmore. p. 211.
[4] James Burnham, *The Managerial Revolution* (Bloomington: Indiana University Press, 1960); first published in 1941.
[5] See, for example, John Kenneth Galbraith's, *The Affluent Society* (Boston: Houghton Mifflin, 1958), and his *The New Industrial State* (Boston: Houghton Mifflin. 1967); quotation from *Ibid.*, pp. 81–82.

Thus the corporation now seeks a certain minimum level of earnings. Also, because the technostructure is oriented to the production of goods and the creation of demand for those goods, it seeks to increase sales as much as possible. Increased sales lead to corporate growth, which leads to opportunities within the corporation, much as wartime leads to great opportunities for promotion within the military.

At the same time, the corporation may exercise social responsibility. The "goals of the mature corporation will be a reflection of the goals of the members of the technostructure. And the goals of the society will tend to be those of the corporation. If . . . the members of the technostructure set high store by autonomy, and the assured minimum level of earnings by which this is secured, this will be a prime objective of the corporation. The need for such autonomy and the income that sustains it will be conceded or stressed by the society."[6]

This is all quite different from, and vastly more complex than, the assumptions of classical capitalism. Government is now an integral partner in the economy of capitalist countries. Similarly, capitalist ideas have become an integral part of the functioning of politics in capitalist democracies. Thus democratic capitalism has emerged as an ideology of politics, as well as one of economics.

DEMOCRATIC CAPITALISM IN PERSPECTIVE

Essentially, the orientation of democratic capitalism is indistinguishable from that of liberal democracy, with which it is so closely identified.

Attitude Toward Change

As with liberalism, democratic capitalism is based upon change. As indicated above, capitalism originally was a revolutionary ideology, which has gone through both status quo and reform phases. Like liberalism, democratic capitalism tends to be a reform ideology. One essential feature of all forms of capitalism is the element of chance, which presupposes change. Today's winners in the

[6]*Ibid.*, p. 161.

marketplace may be tomorrow's losers. The business cycle—even to the extreme extent of "boom and bust"—is not a malfunction of the system, it *is* the system. However much democratic capitalism may attempt to control economic swings, it cannot eliminate them and remain capitalism. In this very real sense, any form of capitalism incorporates, and in fact institutionalizes, change.

Attitude Toward Human Nature

Capitalism in various forms has incorporated divergent attitudes toward human nature. Human beings are selfish, but they are not only selfish; they act in their own best interest, but they also cooperate for the benefit of others. In order to ensure that the selfish side of their nature does not overwhelm the rest, democratic capitalism accepts the idea that regulation is necessary for the good of all. Classical capitalism, of course, rejected any economic regulation, regardless of the consequences of its lack, assuming that any attempt to regulate economic conduct would simply make matters worse.

Attitude Toward the Potential of Human Reason

Here, democratic capitalism is at one with liberal democracy. Human reason presents the greatest potential for the sound organization of human affairs.

Attitude Toward Human Progress

Democratic capitalism is highly optimistic that human reason has the potential to improve society by adopting the correct institutions and providing sound education.

Attitude Toward the Relationship of the Individual to the Community

Capitalism, like liberalism with which it is so closely associated, is highly individualistic. Its general orientation is to place the importance of the individual before that of the community. Of course, capitalism may exist under an authoritarian structure. In such a case, its individualism is limited to economic activity. Capitalism seeks the economic good of the community through the efforts of individuals working alone or in concert. Even democratic capitalism, which emphasizes more strongly the common good than do other forms of capitalism, remains essentially individualistic. It does, however, recognize the need to temper some forms of individual conduct, including economic conduct.

THE FUNCTIONING OF DEMOCRATIC CAPITALISM

Although there have been many efforts to assist those at lower economic levels, there has never been a serious attempt in the United States to ensure economic equality. To do so would be to violate the basic tenets of capitalism. Wealth, even in the face of reforms, continues to become more and more concentrated. The policies of the Reagan administration encouraged, but did not begin, this tendency.

There is no doubt that any capitalist system favors the wealthy; that, in fact, is precisely what it was designed to do, and no reform even attempts to make it do otherwise. Reform capitalism seeks to preserve the system while protecting those at the bottom. It does not seek to destroy those at the top.

There is also no doubt that modern capitalism functions in an entirely different manner from classical capitalism, and there is little doubt that even classical capitalism in practice was never just what the model presumed it to be. Whatever its function, democratic capitalism has produced powerful economic systems that provide extraordinary affluence to their citizens. The democratic side of the equation has likewise produced impressive political freedoms. Together, the democratic and capitalistic elements have led to such innovations as employee stock ownership plans that achieve, simultaneously, many of the aims of capitalism and socialism, with few if any of the disadvantages of either.

Along with these accomplishments has come alleviation of the worst of the economic miseries, although perhaps in this instance democratic capitalism is not the most successful of all systems. The "trickle down" effect assumes that "a rising tide lifts all boats." There is certainly truth to this assumption that the more powerful the economic system, the more all those involved benefit, even those on the lowest rung of the economic ladder. Modern democratic capitalism generally recognizes, however, that those at the bottom require more assistance than the "rising tide." It has incorporated many elements that early capitalists would not recognize and would have opposed strongly if they did. The evolution from "capitalism" to "democratic capitalism" has brought great improvements, and considerable success, both politically and economically. It has not, however, managed completely to eliminate some fundamental troubles that continue to plague capitalism. Examples of such troubles are unemployment and periodic recessions even including the possibility of severe depressions.

"Capitalism" succeeded politically only by becoming something different. It is too early to tell what will happen in such capitalistic, but nondemocratic, societies as those in Taiwan, South Korea, and Chile. Democratic capitalism has succeeded in a striking manner. To a degree, though, its success was dependent upon its becoming somehow less capitalistic. One should remember always, however, that the labels are unimportant; it is the result that counts.

Democratic
Socialism

3

*T*here are as many definitions of socialism as of democracy,
and they tend to be no less vague. It is true that historically
the programs of economic assistance to needy citizens that characterize the "welfare state" have been associated with socialism.
They may even have developed from the same impulses. Socialism and welfare programs are not, however, the same thing. Welfare programs can exist without socialism, and socialism can exist
with no welfare programs.

Similarly, Marxism should not be considered to be synonymous with socialism. Karl Marx advocated a particular kind of
socialism and had a huge influence upon the development of socialist thought. Much of socialism, however, is not at all Marxist,
and much of what today is called Marxist is quite different from
what Marx envisioned.

Socialism, defined narrowly, is public or governmental ownership of the means of production and distribution. Thus defined,
socialism is essentially an economic rather than a political form
and is compatible with many different governmental systems, just

as democracy is compatible with varied economic systems. Defined more broadly, socialism implies the extension of democracy to include popular participation in economic, as well as political, decisions. The most broad definitions of socialism imply a cooperative way of life that is not limited to economics but involves social and political organization. In fact, these offer a new way of viewing the world and social relationships.

When they are combined with democratic government, the principles of socialism, however narrowly they may be defined, become political. The resulting amalgam of democratic politics and socialist economics has become extremely important in Western Europe and elsewhere. Democratic socialism therefore deserves special scrutiny, even though it clearly is a variant of democracy, as evidenced by its emphasis upon democratic, constitutional procedures. Democratic socialism is, in fact, considerably closer even to liberal democracy than it is to the typical Marxist or Marxist-Leninist regime, which builds its ideology upon the notions of violence and class struggle.

THE SOCIALIST APPROACH

From its beginnings, socialism was motivated by a strong criticism of capitalism. The result was a search for a system that could produce a more equitable distribution of the benefits of industrialism, provide for greater popular participation and increased justice, and at the same time strengthen and stabilize the economy. Socialists believed that such a system would be one that substituted cooperation for competition. Their argument was based upon an expansion of the democratic process to include economic, as well as political, decisions.

Most socialists have been motivated by some of the same considerations as nonsocialist liberal reformers. Both groups have tended to be concerned with the elimination of poverty, ignorance, disease, and various forms of discrimination. Each has contributed considerably to the development of the modern welfare state. The differences between the two groups include the socialists' greater emphasis upon equality and their criticisms of the property arrangements in a capitalist economy.

The modern ideology of socialism emerged after the development of the nation-state. Because the systems that socialism criticizes not only are intimately involved with the system of nation-states but are in fact functions of that system, socialist theorists have had some difficulty in formulating an approach to the nation-state as an entity.

The government of the nation-state undoubtedly can be an agent of injustice and oppression, and the early socialist emphasis upon state ownership, with the attendant bureaucratic growth and increase in centralized state power, brought much opposition to socialism from those concerned with liberty. Many contemporary socialists concede the dangers of governmental power and therefore have abandoned the earlier advocacy of mass nationalization of industries. Their emphasis continues to be public control, but this need not involve state ownership. Rather, there is an increasing tendency to look to cooperatives as the answer.

Cooperatives are groups of private citizens who, for some economic purpose, form a collective enterprise and become its owners. They share in the profits and the labor. There is hardly any limit to the kind of activity that can be the subject of a cooperative. It could produce one or more products and be a manufacturing enterprise. Its purpose might be financial, such as that of a credit union in which the owners pool their money to lend at reasonable rates to individual members with all members profiting from the interest received. There also are cooperatives in which members pool their resources to purchase goods in quantities that make them available at much lower prices. Whatever their purpose, cooperatives may be managed in numerous ways, with the most frequent being a member-elected board to direct the organization.

Many modern socialists view cooperatives as an ideal way to implement public control of some economic activities without the disadvantages of nationalization and state ownership. Moreover, most now take a practical approach that shuns what they see as dogmatism. They may, for example, agree with socialism's critics that public ownership can lead to lack of incentive and lowered productivity, and therefore be highly inefficient, at least under certain circumstances. The response is to reject the idea of mass nationalization or universal public ownership and argue instead for socialization only of those enterprises that lend themselves to collective ownership and management, and then only for a form of socialization appropriate to the activity. For example, cooperatives have worked well for such things as light manufacturing, retail sales, and agriculture. Nationalization, on the other hand, has been successful with utilities, heavy industry, transportation, communication, and other very extensive or naturally monopolistic activities.

Few, if any, socialists today expect or would even advocate a totally socialized economy, leaving such an approach to the communists. The dangers of extreme centralization include cumbersome bureaucracies, inadequate response to changing conditions and to public desires, and probably most important, the obvious threat that extensive government presents to personal liberty. Modern socialism tends to be a mixture of public and private ownership and control that attempts to achieve the benefits that socialism has long sought, without the troublesome side effects against which critics have warned for an equally long time.

Democratic socialism is motivated strongly by humanitarian considerations and grew from efforts to seek a more humane system than that existing during the early days of a capitalism unmodified by welfare measures and governmental regulation. The goal is to provide the best possible life for each individual citizen, and in this regard democratic socialism is closely akin to liberalism. In general, however, socialism's approach to the goal differs sharply from the liberal approach. Socialism tends to stress collective, rather than individual, efforts. Whereas liberalism ordinarily seeks to improve society by improving the lot of the individual, socialism as a rule seeks to improve the lot of the individual by improving society. In economic matters, the socialist tends to consider equality most important, with the liberal assigning that role to economic freedom.

Despite the differences in approach and in economic theories, democratic socialism and liberal, capitalist democracy today have much in common. Each type of system includes public and private ownership, although with more public ownership under socialism and more private ownership under capitalism. Both employ governmental regulation of private economic activities, with capitalism tending to regulate more widely because it has more private activity to regulate and less public enterprise for the government to control directly. All advanced industrial democracies today, whether they are organized along the lines of democratic socialism or liberal, capitalist democracy, provide extensive welfare programs for their citizens. Neither type of system now accepts total economic equality as a goal, and both hope to eliminate poverty. In fact, most modern democratic socialist states have accepted even the continued existence of great personal fortunes. There are certainly differences among these types of systems, and important differences at that, especially in theory and ideology. Even in these respects, however, there are today some similarities. In modern practice, as opposed to in theory and ideology, the similarities are considerably greater than the differences.

EARLY SOCIALIST THEMES

There has been some form of socialistic or communistic organization and thought as long as there has been human society. They are evident, for example, in many early Christian groups and in some ancient empires outside of Western culture. Hobbes and Locke in seventeenth-century England contributed ideas that found their way into socialism. These include the Hobbesian view that human purposes were paramount in society, and that the social collective could control, if not reshape, human nature; also, Locke's justification of revolution, which served both liberals and socialists, and his labor theory of value. Other currents emerged from some of the egalitarian movements of that century, such as the Levellers and the Diggers, from religious movements then and later both in England and on the Continent,[1] and from various utopian writers throughout history.

Modern socialism, however, emerged in the nineteenth century, along with the rise of industrialism and following the turmoil of the French Revolution of 1789. The writings of Jean Jacques Rousseau (see pages 57–58) not only greatly influenced the Revolution, but to some extent also provided inspiration for the

[1]Mulford Q. Sibley, *Political Ideas and Ideologies* (New York: Harper & Row, 1970), pp. 514–15.

emerging ideology of socialism. Rousseau renewed the view of society as an organic whole, rather than merely a collection of individuals. He also opposed extreme disparities in wealth, arguing that they generate inequality of political power among citizens. Socialism adopted these ideas as fundamental. It is ironic that conservatives might also agree with them. Certainly conservatives accept the notion of organic society, and most would accept too the argument that disparities in wealth create disparities in political power. The difference between conservatives and socialists in this regard is that democratic socialists view differences in political power as bad, whereas conservatives not only accept them as inevitable, but believe that they *should* exist.

Rousseau had stressed that society should serve the whole, rather than enforce privilege, and his ideas strongly influenced François-Noel Babeuf (1760–1797). During the French Revolution Babeuf presented an early, and extreme, version of what now would be called socialism. Writing as "Gracchus," he called for complete equality and for the elimination of private property. In 1796, convinced that the principles of the Revolution had been betrayed and that the Directory was moving to the right, he embarked upon a conspiracy to overthrow the revolutionary leaders. He and his "Conspiracy of Equals" were discovered and executed. His death brought a temporary end to violent attempts to establish socialist rule.

UTOPIAN SOCIALISM

The dislocations of the Revolution and the emerging industrialism created enormous poverty and resulted in large numbers of people being thrust to the bottom of the social and economic order. Sincere concern for the "common people" or the "masses" led to what frequently is termed "utopian socialism," a term first applied by Marx and Engels. The Utopians sought a society of equality that would provide prosperity for all, along with a just and humane social order. They criticized capitalism and its effects severely. To demonstrate the practicality of their proposals, they established communities that incorporated their principles.

In France, for instance, Charles Fourier (1772–1837) attempted to achieve a voluntary restructuring of society through his theoretical writings encouraging the creation of communities to serve as examples. Each "phalanx," or "phalanstery," would incorporate a minute division of labor that would involve teams chosen on the basis of worker preferences. Fourier assumed that dividing human beings into twelve categories, each with numerous subdivisions, would reflect all varieties of human nature, and that a group of 800 would constitute a complete community. He did make allowances for error by providing that the number should be doubled. Fourier's approach was not an attempt to achieve complete equality, and his scheme involved a division of profits among the community's members based upon their shares of ownership, which were not necessarily to be equal. Although there were some attempts in France to apply Fourier's ideas, the greatest activity was in the United States, where numerous communities emerged in the nineteenth century, all of them short-lived. Among them was the famous transcendentalist experiment Brook Farm in its latter stages, but only after it had shifted in orientation from the original effort of George Ripley, Margaret Fuller, and others.

In Britain, the wealthy manufacturer Robert Owen (1771–1858) began to analyze the effects of the growth of industrialism. Owen had begun as a child laborer and had risen to become part owner of the largest mills in Scotland, the New Lanark Mills, which he managed. In 1813 he produced a book, *New View of Society,* that examined the disruptions caused by business cycles and by the manufacturing enterprises that brought workers to the growing cities and severed their ties to a traditionally rural environment. Owen turned his attention to practice and attempted to turn New Lanark into a model community.

His initial efforts were limited to reform, such as providing housing and sanitary conditions for the workers, raising their wages, establishing free schools for their children, and in general creating working conditions that were by far the best available. He did not, however, advocate mere handouts to those in need, or the "dole." He also believed that thoughtful and humane reforms could combine with capitalism both to preserve human dignity and to provide better profits to employers. Despite the fact that the mills did prosper under his leadership, there was friction

ROBERT OWEN

Whence . . . have wickedness and misery proceeded? . . . *Solely from the ignorance of our forefathers!* . . .

I have no doubt, my friends, you are at present convinced. . . . Pagans, Jews, Turks, every one of them, millions upon millions almost without end, are wrong. . . . But you will add,—"We are right,—we are the favoured of Heaven,—we are enlightened, and cannot be deceived." . . .

What think you now, my friends, is the reason why you believe and act as you do? . . . It is solely and merely because you were born, and have lived, in this period of the world,—in Europe,—in the island of Great Britain. . . . Without the shadow of a doubt, had every one of you been born in other times or other places, you might have been the very reverse of that which the present time and place have made you. . . .

Will you not, then, have charity for the habits and opinions of all men . . . ?

Direct your serious attention to the cause why men think and act as they do. You will then be neither surprised nor displeased on account of their sentiments or their habits. You will then clearly discover why others are displeased with you,—and pity them. As you proceed in these inquiries, you will find that mankind cannot be improved or rendered reasonable by force and contention; that it is absolutely necessary to support the old systems and institutions under which we now live, until another system and another arrangement of society shall be proved by practice to be essentially superior.

From an address to the inhabitants of New Lanark (1816)

between him and his co-owners over the costs of his reforms. Finally, he was able to gain full control, with new, sympathetic partners who included Jeremy Bentham.[2]

As the years progressed, Owen developed more radical ideas. Not only did he support ownership of industry by workers' cooperatives, but he also adopted other positions that brought him

[2] Albert Fried and Ronald Sanders, eds., *Socialist Thought: A Documentary History* (Garden City, N.Y.: Anchor Books, 1964), p. 151ff.

considerable criticism, including taking up opposition to organized religion. Moreover, he became increasingly frustrated by
his inability to turn the nation in a direction that would establish
workers' cooperatives and would lead to general industrial reform.

In 1824, therefore, he journeyed to New Harmony, Indiana,
where he attempted to put his more radical ideas into practice,
ideas that he had outlined in a pamphlet, *Discourses on a New
System of Society*. He was attracted by the conditions of the frontier
and the early American emphasis upon "the common man." His
reputation as a great philanthropist had preceded him, and he
was well received. In fact, on February 25 and again on March 7,
1825, he spoke in the hall of the U.S. House of Representatives
to a large audience of government officials that included President Monroe.[3]

Owen's experiment was one of many such communitarian reform efforts in the United States during the nineteenth century.[4]
After an initial period that appeared to promise success and inspired many other such Owenite experiments in Indiana, New
York, Ohio, Pennsylvania, and Tennesee, the situation changed,
and it became clear that New Harmony was a failure. By 1830 it
and all its imitators had vanished, and Owen had returned to
Great Britain to continue his efforts at reform. He became instrumental in the formation of British trades unions, which had been
illegal until 1824. Owen's influence continued there for some time
after his death, and for a while others attempted to follow his lead
by, among other things, establishing cooperative communities.

It perhaps is no overstatement to consider Robert Owen the
founder of British socialism. His name is highly prominent also in
the history of non-Marxist and democratic socialism elsewhere,
particularly in America. His sons, William and Robert Dale, maintained their father's interest in reform and remained in the United
States to become citizens. Robert Dale Owen subsequently became a member of the Indiana State Legislature where his accomplishments included success in securing a law on the eve of the
Civil War that added habitual drunkenness as a ground for divorce. The feminist activist Elizabeth Cady Stanton had originally

---

[3] Alice Felt Tyler, *Freedom's Ferment* (New York: Harper Torchbooks, 1962), p. 198.
[4] Ibid., passim.

suggested the idea in New York, and the proposal caused an enormous furor, with Robert Dale Owen being one of the few who came to her support. Even many radical social reformers opposed it,[5] which demonstrates just how far the ideas of feminism and human rights had yet to go at the time. It also demonstrates—because humanitarian concern was the foremost impetus to the socialist movement—the extent to which the ideas of socialists and the spirit of socialism have affected modern social consciousness in the Western world.

The Utopian socialist movement included approaches no less varied than those classed together under the term "democracy." The ideas of Claude Henri, Comte de Saint-Simon (1760–1825) and his followers represent a kind of socialism that is quite different from those of Owen and Fourier. Saint-Simon had fought in the American Revolution and was sympathetic to the Revolution in France. For years, Saint-Simon had placed his faith in science and argued for emphasis to be placed upon scientific, rather than democratic, principles. Late in life, in 1825, his thought took a religious turn. In that year he wrote *Le nouveau christianisme,* in which he advocated a society that would incorporate what he considered to be the principles of Christianity.

Saint-Simon sought the elimination of poverty and the betterment of all social classes. He supported education and argued for social investments that would flow from a new system of central banking. His works display a general spirit of good will and a humane temperament. Apart from these, however, it is only with some difficulty that one can consider them to be socialist. After his death, his ideas became the basis of a powerful religious-political movement, the Saint-Simonians, the leaders of which expanded them far beyond anything that appears in his works.

Saint-Simon's influence joined that of Fourier and Owen in criticizing the effects of liberal capitalism in the early days of industrialism. The Saint-Simonians, however, had no patience with the principle of voluntary change, and worked openly for a society moving toward reform under the dominance of an elite. Their influence was thus less in the direction of democratic socialism than was that of Fourier or Owen. In fact, some elements of Saint-Simonianism would be more similar to Marxism than to demo-

[5] Ibid., p. 460.

cratic socialism, which demonstrates the impossibility of clearly distinguishing the antecedents of each.

THE INFLUENCE OF KARL MARX

Because of the towering influence of Karl Marx (1818–1883) upon socialist thought in general, it is necessary to consider his ideas when examining the background even of democratic socialism. Marx was born in Trier, in what is now the Federal Republic of Germany. At the University of Berlin he studied the ideas of the great philosopher Georg W. F. Hegel, which influenced him significantly. Other major influences were French revolutionary and utopian thought and the writings of the British liberal economists. Marx met Friedrich Engels (1820–1895) in Paris, and the two became lifelong friends and collaborators. In 1847 they coauthored the *Communist Manifesto.* So close was their association, in fact, that much of Marx's work should be considered that of Marx and Engels. For purposes of simplification, however, we will refer to Marx alone.

Marx spent the last several decades of his life in London, essentially in exile from the continent for his radical activities. In 1864 the founding of the International Working Men's Association in London gave him the opportunity once more to participate actively in political matters, and he became heavily involved in this group, known as the First International. In 1867 he published the first volume of *Das Kapital,* his influential and comprehensive treatise on political economy. Engels edited and published the final two volumes, which did not appear until after Marx's death.

Marx had been educated in the Hegelian dialectic, in which history was seen as unfolding in response to conflict among ideas. He retained the notion of the dialectic but said that he turned Hegel "on his feet." Marx concluded that the fundamental element of any society was a substructure consisting of economic relationships, including material "forces of production," and knowledge of how to use the forces of production and exchange within that society. For Marx, ideas were not the motivating factor of history. Rather, ideas were part of the "superstructure" that was determined by the substructure of economic relationships.

KARL MARX

The history of all past society has consisted in the development of class antagonisms, antagonisms that assumed different forms at different epochs. But whatever form they may have taken, one fact is common to all past ages, viz., the exploitation of one part of society by the other. No wonder, then, that the social consciousness of past ages, despite all the multiplicity and variety it displays, moves within certain common forms, or general ideas, which cannot completely vanish except with the total disappearance of class antagonisms.

The Communist revolution is the most radical rupture with traditional property relations; no wonder that its development involves the most radical rupture with traditional ideas.

. . . [T]he first step in the revolution by the working class is to raise the proletariat to the position of ruling class to win the battle of democracy. The proletariat will use its political supremacy to wrest, by degrees, all capital from the bourgeoisie, to centralize all instruments of production in the hands of the State, i.e., of the proletariat organized as a ruling class; and to increase the total productive forces as rapidly as possible. Of course, in the beginning, this cannot be effected except by means of despotic inroads on the rights of property, and on the conditions of bourgeois production. . . .

When, in the course of development, class distinctions have disappeared, and all production has been concentrated in the hands of a vast association of the whole nation, the public power will lose its political character. Political power, properly so called, is merely the organized power of one class for oppressing another.

From *The Communist Manifesto* (1848)

Marx thought of the superstructure as encompassing the state and its dominant ideology, including such things as religion, the arts, law, philosophy, and moral beliefs. The entire superstructure he believed to be a tool of the ruling class to justify and maintain its rule. By class, he meant economic class, which he defined as determined by its relation to the means of production.

It is this notion of economic class, and the conflict between classes, that is the central element of Marxist thought.

What Marx found so attractive in Hegelianism were the ideas of inevitable progress and the process of the dialectic. Hegel viewed history as dynamic. Every situation, which he termed a "thesis," contained within itself tendencies that led to the development of its opposite, or "antithesis." The contradiction between thesis and antithesis led to a resolution, the "synthesis," which in turn became a new thesis. Marx discarded Hegel's notion of the importance of ideas and turned to material conditions. He described his application of the dialectic as "dialectical materialism." Because he believed himself to be studying the material conditions of reality objectively, he called his approach "scientific socialism," to distinguish it from earlier forms, which he termed with some scorn, "utopian socialism." Each historical epoch, feudalism for example, was a thesis containing the beginnings of its antithesis, in this case, capitalism. The synthesis would be communism, in which ultimately there would be no private property, therefore no social class, which meant no ruling class, and of course no more need for that tool of the ruling class, the state, which would "wither away." Exploitation would cease to exist, and the operative principle would be "from each according to his ability, to each according to his need."

Marx accepted an extreme form of the labor theory of value, arguing that only labor creates value. He developed an extension of the theory to explain the phenomenon of profit; profit is "surplus value." Because only labor creates value, he argued, the capitalist pays the worker less than the value that the worker created, keeping the excess, or the "surplus value," as the profit.

There is tremendous controversy regarding Marx's intent or the "proper" interpretation of his thought. The situation became more complicated in the 1930s with the publication of the "early writings" of 1844, the "Paris Manuscripts." These works display a more humanitarian tone than those of later years and center upon the notion of worker "alienation." Marx wrote that capitalism, by forcing the worker to sell his labor, is actually forcing the worker to sell a part of himself. This leads to a separation of the worker from that part of himself. His own labor then becomes an alien force that is his opponent. Most Soviet writers disregard these earlier manuscripts as inconsistent with the later more "scientific" Marx. Many Western writers, on the other hand, argue that one must consider Marx's writings as a whole, and that doing so suggests that Marxism could have developed into a system more akin to democratic socialism than to the highly authoritarian one that the Soviets claim to be the only one possible.

Marx lived in the early years of industrialism and analyzed society in terms of two primary classes. He saw the workers, the "proletariat," as the exploited class. The owners who controlled production were the "bourgeoisie," who lived by profits taken from the workers, the real producers. He gave relatively little attention to the peasants and to the agricultural sector in general, to small shopkeepers and landowners who constituted what he called the "petite bourgeoisie," or to the group he called the "lumpenproletariat," which consisted of social outcasts—the poorest of the poor.

Marx argued generally that violent revolution was inevitable, but that historical conditions had to be appropriate for it to occur. As the proletariat grew, and capital became concentrated into fewer hands, it would ultimately become easier to replace the capitalists. The superstructure functions to maintain the power of the ruling class, but the increase in the proletariat along with the lowering of its earnings would bring dysfunction into the system by reducing the market for the enormous production. The only part of the superstructure that could exercise force is the state, and it would therefore be necessary to use force to bring it down. Revolution would bring down the state and the entire superstructure with it. There would be a period of transition following the revolution before true communism could be achieved and with it the withering of the state. During this period there would exist a "dictatorship of the proletariat," which Marx argued would be necessary to cleanse society of the vestiges of other social classes.

There were few unions when Marx wrote, and those that existed were weak and largely ineffective. There was no universal suffrage. There were no socialist parties; in fact there were hardly any effective political parties at all. It was difficult, therefore, for Marx to envision anything short of violence that could bring about the drastic change that he saw as inevitable. There are suggestions, however, that he admitted the possibility of nonviolent

change, but he considered it to be most unlikely. In 1872, for example, he said in a speech that it might be possible for workers
in certain countries in which there were democratic superstruc-
tures, such as England and the United States, to achieve reform peacefully.[6]

THE DEVELOPMENT OF DEMOCRATIC
SOCIALISM AFTER MARX

After Marx died, his influence grew along with the founding and
expansion of socialist parties throughout Europe and in the United
States. As industrialism burgeoned, creating the enormous bourgeois and proletarian classes that Marx had predicted, so also did
Marxism. The Second International was founded in Paris in 1889,
and a Marxist party soon emerged in virtually every country in
Europe. The world began to feel their effects. The German Socialist Party had emerged as by far the most powerful in the world,
and not only dominated the Second International, but also won
seats in legislative bodies at all levels of government. It was highly
disciplined and well organized, and it controlled huge trade unions.
In the elections of 1912, it received nearly thirty-five percent of
the vote, considerably over four million. Two years later the rather
moderate French Socialist Party polled over one million votes.

Even in the United States, a Socialist party had existed since
1901. The city of Milwaukee had a socialist administration for many
years, and the Socialist party succeeded in 1920 in attracting a
million votes for its presidential candidate, Eugene V. Debs, despite the fact that he was in jail at the time. He had given a speech
in Ohio in 1918 criticizing government policy during the First World
War and thus violated the highly repressive American laws of the
wartime period. In 1918 Victor Berger, the editor of a socialist
newspaper in Milwaukee, won election to the U.S. Congress but
the House of Representatives refused to seat him. The same thing
happened once more in 1920; but in 1922, when he won yet again,
Berger finally was able to take his seat. Similarly, during the "Red

[6]Karl Marx, "Later Political Writings, 1864–82," in *Karl Marx: Selected Writings*,
D. McLellan, ed. (New York: Oxford University Press, 1977), pp. 594–95.

Scare" that followed the War, the New York state legislature excluded five socialists who had been elected.

Despite its official commitment to Marxism at the time, the American Socialist Party was oriented largely toward liberal reform and has remained consistently dedicated to the principles of democratic socialism. Other less moderate and more Marxist parties existed in the United States also, such as the Socialist Labor Party under the leadership of Daniel De Leon and the Industrial Workers of the World (the IWW, or the "Wobblies.)" De Leon, Debs, and William D. "Big Bill" Haywood founded the IWW in 1905, although De Leon and Debs left the organization when "direct actionists" who advocated violence, including sabotage and terrorism, won control.

America's enthusiasm for socialism was never wholehearted and was of limited duration, but it did produce some original contributions to socialist thought. De Leon, for one, attracted attention in Europe, even from some of the most outstanding Marxists. In the utopian tradition, Edward Bellamy's 1888 novel *Looking Backward* is noteworthy. It attracted widespread attention and generated numerous Nationalist Clubs throughout the nation that advocated his brand of socialism, which he termed "nationalism."

Bellamy wrote of a young man of his time who awoke in the year 2000. The new society was an industrial socialism, in which each person worked from the age of twenty-one to forty-five. The pay was equal for all, and the state determined job assignments based upon social need. There was no social class and no poverty. Socialism had been achieved by the increasing tendency toward concentration in industry. When it had progressed to the point at which all producers had merged into one huge monopoly, the state assumed control naturally in a nonviolent revolution. The electorate consisted only of those beyond forty-five, that is, those who had retired, in order to avoid "intrigue" among the workers. Bellamy gave little attention to individual rights and none to the political process. Along with many who have constructed fictional utopias, he assumed simply that in a perfect state there would be too few disagreements regarding policy to warrant politics. Control was in the hands of administrators, who were to be neutral "experts."

One of the great strengths of Bellamy's novel, as with nearly all socialist literature, was his criticism of existing conditions. He equated his society with a coach on a difficult and hilly road:

> The driver was hunger, and permitted no lagging. . . . Despite the difficulty of drawing the coach at all along so hard a road, the top was covered with passengers who never got down, even at the steepest ascents. These seats on top were very breezy and comfortable. Well up out of the dust, their occupants could enjoy the scenery at their leisure, or critically discuss the merits of the straining team. Naturally such places were in great demand and the competition for them was keen, everyone seeking as the first end in life to secure a seat on the coach for himself and to leave it to his child after him. By the rule of the coach a man could leave his seat to whom he wished, but on the other hand there were many accidents by which it might at any time be wholly lost.

Because of the bumpy road, many fell from their seats. They immediately were forced to take a place on the towline. Some compassion did exist, and the riders would frequently call down to the toilers with words of encouragement.[7] It would be difficult to portray the harshness of nineteenth-century capitalism more graphically, and this no doubt contributed to the novel's success.

Bellamy published another novel, *Equality*, in 1897 that attracted much less attention. It presented his views more fully, however, and also in a more doctrinaire fashion. His attitude toward the political process was no different, and he continued to believe that expert administration would be all that would be required in a perfect state.

Another late nineteenth-century phenomenon that emerged in Europe and especially in the United States was Christian socialism (see pp. 228–230). For example, in 1872 an American Congregational minister, Jesse H. Jones, founded the Christian Labor Union. For some three years he published *Equity*, a monthly magazine in which he argued for public ownership of the means of production and distribution. Despite the intense criticism directed toward Jones, in 1876 another minister, Washington Gladden,

---

[7]Edward Bellamy, *Looking Backward: 2000–1887* (Boston: Houghton Mifflin, 1966), pp. 6–7; see also pp. 114–15; first published in 1888.

argued for a limited socialism in his book *Being a Christian*. As an individualist, Gladden rejected communism, but he called for the "socialized individual" who would be led to social responsibility by religious principles. He criticized social Darwinism, which then characterized capitalism, as not natural but rather a crime against nature. His specific proposals included public ownership of utilities, which then was quite radical.

There were numerous voices speaking for Christian socialism at the time. William Dwight Porter Bliss, along with Episcopal Bishop F.D. Huntington of New York, established the Church Association for the Advancement of the Interests of Labor (CAIL) in 1887. Bliss edited the *Encyclopedia of Social Reform* in 1897 and contributed an entry on Christian socialism in Europe and the United States. Francis Bellamy, a cousin of the author, cooperated in the founding of CAIL and in 1895 also helped to form the American Fabian Society. The Christian socialists advocated reform of working conditions to provide more time for workers to spend at home and at church, and they opposed Marxism's dialectical materialism and class conflict. Their goal was a cooperative society with full democracy. George D. Herron, minister of a Congregational Church in Burlington, Iowa, contributed an influential article, "The Message of Jesus to Men of Wealth," calling for love rather than selfishness and criticizing the upper classes who enjoyed the benefits of society without contributing to it. He subsequently joined the Socialist party.

The best known of the Christian socialists is probably Walter Rauschenbusch, also a minister, who argued forcefully in a series of books that capitalist competition was a denial of the spirit of brotherhood. In 1907 his *Christianity and the Social Crisis* condemned the profit motive as selfishness and criticized business as the remaining bastion of autocracy. Rauschenbusch, in common with most of the Christian socialists, did not advocate complete communism but did favor fairly extensive public ownership in order to spread economic benefits more broadly. Their goal was a society in which the humane values of Christianity, as they interpreted them, dominated. They believed that such a society would ensure social justice and abolish unjust privilege.

As the century drew to a close, many of Marx's predictions were proving to be inaccurate. Britain, the United States, and Germany were the most highly industrialized nations on earth.

This made them likely candidates for revolution according to Marxist doctrine, but revolution appeared remote. Despite socialism's gains in the United States, it remained weak, and the elements that exercised any influence at all owed little to Marx.

In Britain, socialism took an almost entirely non-Marxist direction, consisting largely of the Fabians. A group of well-educated young men in their twenties founded the Fabian Society in 1884 out of concern for the social and cultural disruptions of industrialism and a capitalism that was unmodified by social and regulatory legislation. They took the name from the Roman general Fabius, whose defensive tactics defeated Hannibal.

The socialism that the Fabians advocated shunned violence and revolution and was directed toward reform through gradual development of social control of production and distribution, using local cooperatives whenever possible. They became active in such reform movements as those advocating women's rights, tax reform, free public education, and the eight-hour working day.

The Fabians rejected the notion of class struggle, calling instead for cooperation. Not only would there be no dictatorship of the proletariat, the society under Fabian socialism would be middle class. Although they favored the abolition of property, the Fabians remained under the influence of liberalism to a large extent. Many of the reforms that they advocated were those of reform liberalism, and they in fact thought of socialism as a more rational liberalism.[8]

The most prominent of the Fabians were George Bernard Shaw and Sidney and Beatrice Webb. In 1889 Shaw, Graham Wallas, Sidney Webb and others published *Fabian Essays in Socialism* under Shaw's editorship. In 1901 Fabian leaders cooperated with the leaders of the trades unions to create the British Labour Party. Sidney Webb's *Labour and the New Social Order* became the party's 1918 platform and explicitly called for socialism.

REVISIONISM

It appeared as if the democratic structures and processes in the United States and Great Britain were inhibiting the development

[8] George Bernard Shaw, ed., *The Fabian Essays in Socialism* (London: Allen & Unwin, 1958).

of any significant Marxist movement by permitting some measure of popular control or influence without revolution. Germany had been consolidated in 1871 as nondemocratic, and it remained so in the years up to and including the First World War. It was there, in a nondemocratic and highly industrial nation, where Marxism had made its greatest headway.

Yet even in Germany with its powerful Marxist party, not all was well with Marxism. Beginning in the 1880s, the German government had adopted extensive welfare measures, including the world's first system of social security. By improving the lot of the workers, the government had caused its commitment to Marxism to weaken. The Socialist party began to cooperate with other groups seeking reform. Small farmers and socialists, for example, frequently cooperated in matters of mutual interest. Karl Kautsky (1854–1938), the leader and official spokesman of the party, demanded strict adherence to Marxist principles.

In 1896, however, Eduard Bernstein (1850–1932), one of the party's leaders, publicly broke ranks and called for revision of Marxist principles to reflect actual conditions. He pointed out that capitalism, contrary to Marx's predictions, was not on the verge of collapse. In fact, the lot of workers was improving, and the number of capitalists was increasing. Because of the development of the corporation, the ownership of capital was being spread more widely, rather than being restricted. Moreover, Marx had greatly underestimated the extent of democratic reforms and their power to permit parties representing the workers to gain power and to control the state for their ends, as opposed to those of the capitalists. Marx, in other words, had not anticipated the development of the democratic state, nor had he foreseen that the state itself could serve to protect workers and distribute goods more widely.

In 1899 Bernstein published *Evolutionary Socialism*. It was his argument that evolution, not revolution, would result in socialism. It was to be a piecemeal development that would replace capitalism but would avoid violence. He pointed to the lessening of class conflict and the strength of capitalism as evidence that he was correct. Although Kautsky continued to stress that the official position of the party was orthodox Marxism, that ideology had lost its grip upon the minds of the party's members.

The influence of revisionism was tremendous. Marxist parties throughout Western Europe began to abandon their emphasis upon

EDUARD BERNSTEIN

I have now a controversy with socialists who, like me, have sprung from the Marx-Engels school; and I am obliged, if I am to maintain my opinions, to show them the points where the Marx-Engels theory appears to me especially mistaken or to be self-contradictory. . . .

The return to the *Communist Manifesto* points here to a real residue of utopianism in the Marxist system. Marx had accepted the solution of the utopians in essentials, but had recognised their means and proofs as inadequate. He therefore undertook a revision of them, and this with the zeal, the critical acuteness, and love of truth of a scientific genius. He suppressed no important fact, he also forebore belittling artificially the importance of these facts as long as the object of the inquiry had no immediate reference to the final aim of the formula to be proved. . . . But, as Marx approaches a point when that final aim enters seriously into the question, he becomes uncertain and unreliable. . . . [C]ontradictions then appear . . . for instance, in the section on the movement of incomes in modern society. It thus appears that this great scientific spirit was, in the end, a slave to a doctrine. . . .

Nothing confirms me more in this conception than the anxiety with which some persons seek to maintain certain statements in *Kapital*, which are falsified by facts.

From *Evolutionary Socialism* (1899)

the class struggle and instead to stress democratic processes and gradual, parliamentary approaches to change. Such a shift brought considerable success. It not only reduced the hostility of the established order but also managed to be more persuasive in attracting voter support. The idea that workers could achieve protection for their interests within the existing system was vastly more congenial than an insistence upon the inevitability—or the desirability—of violent revolution.

Moreover, the beginning of the First World War had shattered any possibility that might have existed for an international movement that would have brought about worker solidarity without regard to national borders. Most socialists chose to support their nations as they proceeded to war, and the Second International collapsed. Once again Marx was wrong. He had assumed that class interest would lead workers to cooperate with fellow workers across national boundaries against the capitalist class on a worldwide basis. He failed to anticipate the tremendous strength of what has come to be—for better or worse—the most powerful agent today in world affairs: nationalism.

DEMOCRATIC SOCIALISM IN PERSPECTIVE

Democratic socialism is an outgrowth of the same tendencies that produced liberalism, as is democratic capitalism. Each emerged as an economic ideology in reaction to existing political and economic ideologies, and they both developed into full-fledged political ideologies. Capitalism's emphasis on intense individualism brought about its dedication to competition as a way of life. Ironically, it perhaps was the effects of early capitalism's insistence upon unrestrained competition that brought about socialism. To be sure, socialist ideas existed before capitalist industrialism, but the great growth of socialism as an ideology came as a reaction—a reaction to the social and economic disruptions of capitalist policies at the beginning of the industrial age. In rejecting capitalist competition, socialism adopted cooperation as the central principle of its outlook on life.

As the two ideologies have evolved, each has mellowed. Democratic capitalism retains its emphasis upon individual competitiveness and the free market, but it now also recognizes social responsibility and a need to provide at least some regulation in the marketplace. Democratic socialism similarly retains its emphasis upon social cooperation but has come to accept much of the competitive, free-market orientation that motivates its rival ideology. They retain their differences, but there is no longer a line of sharp distinction between them. Each has learned from, and adapted some policies of, the other. As each moves away from extremes, one thing becomes immediately apparent: as the preoccupation with the ideological purity of "socialism" and "capitalism" lessens, the element of "democracy" increases and the situation of the people improves. Ideologues may disagree with this analysis, which simply indicates the potential danger from ideologues.

Attitude Toward Change

Democratic socialism tends to be liberal in its acceptance of change and its lack of reverence for tradition.

Attitude Toward Human Nature

Democratic socialism tends to be highly optimistic in its attitude toward human nature. In emphasizing cooperation, it reflects the belief that human beings are capable of working together for mutual good, and that they can overcome their selfish urges. Probably more than any other ideology, it presupposes the ability of human beings to submerge their individual interests when it is necessary for the good of the whole. Democratic socialism tends to reject the idea that human nature is something static that cannot be developed.

Attitude Toward the Potential of Human Reason

Democratic socialism believes in the potential of human reason. It tends to place more importance upon reason than upon any other factor, including tradition and emotion. Although it may not accept human reason as perfect, socialism accepts it as the only tool available to determine what the outcome is likely to be if society were to adopt a given policy. The proper use of reason is the only thing that can avoid stagnation. Socialism tends to be extremely optimistic regarding the potential of the collective wisdom of the people. Some socialists would even argue that the proper application of reason could perhaps lead human nature itself to improve and develop.

Attitude Toward Human Progress

Democratic socialism is built on the assumption that it is possible to improve the human condition. It sees socialism not only as reflecting that possibility, but in fact demonstrating it. Socialists would argue that socialism is proof that human reason may indeed better the situation of humanity and the world. Of course, socialists differ in the extent of their optimism. At the very least, they would accept an application of human reason as essential for any human progress and would argue that some progress is possible. The most optimistic among them would be "perfectionists" who argue that, with the proper application of human reason, the possibility for progress is virtually limitless.

Attitude Toward the Relationship of the Individual to the Community

It is in its attitude toward the individual/community relationship that socialism, even democratic socialism, differs most from liberalism. The liberal places the individual at the center of concern and contends that only through individualism can the community improve. The democratic socialist places the good of society at the center of concern and believes that only by improving society can the lot of the individual be improved. Each is concerned with the individual and with individual freedom. Each is also concerned with the good of society as a whole and with establishing the best possible conditions for the people, collectively. Each, however, has a different prescription for how to achieve the common goals.

DEMOCRATIC SOCIALISM TODAY

The British Labour Party paved the way, but it had never been Marxist to begin with. The established Marxist parties came to be less and less oriented to orthodox Marxist principles and ultimately most came to abandon them altogether. They became no less socialist, merely more democratic, continuing to seek socialism, but seeking it gradually and democratically. As we have seen, socialist and liberal reformers—and some conservative reformers as well—have managed to create a considerable community of interest, as they have worked together to place a more humane face on the capitalist system that in the nineteenth century had appeared to be so harsh.

Today, socialism in the West is almost entirely revisionist, or completely non-Marxist. The communist parties of France and Italy remain the only significant exceptions, and there have been changes even there. The French Communist Party no longer commands anything approaching its former power, and although the Italian Communist Party remains strong, it has moderated to the extent that it appears content to remain within the structure of democratic parliamentary government.

Socialist parties originally had been parties of the working class. With success, however, came change; socialists in power represented all groups, not merely the workers. As committed democrats, they became a part of the constitutional process and sought policy change through democratic politics rather than through imposition of their views. The realities of governing and the obvious difficulties in dogmatic approaches brought changes in many socialist views as well. Politics involves compromise, and socialists in power accepted this. They demonstrated that the state need not be, as the Marxists assume, merely a tool of the ruling class and that it might be made more responsive to the needs of the whole and be brought, at least to some extent, to serve as an agent of justice in assessing competing demands from various classes and groups. As socialists moderated their positions, they have retained their emphasis upon providing social benefits and eliminating economic hardship, but they have come less and less to advocate mass nationalization and other such policies.

Democratic socialism, as mentioned earlier, is a variant of constitutional democracy. Within the Western democratic mainstream, liberals, conservatives, and socialists share a commitment to constitutional government and democratic principles, to gradual and orderly change, and to the amelioration of conditions for those in need. Thus, both socialist and nonsocialist states have tended to move to the center and to adopt pragmatic solutions rather than to insist upon ideological purity and rigidity.

Marxism-Leninism

4

Except for Marx himself, the most towering figure in the history of Marxism was Vladimir Ilyich Ulyanov, or V.I. Lenin (1870–1924). However intense the discussion may be regarding the nature of Lenin's contribution to Marxism—whether he developed and expanded Marx's thought or distorted and warped it—it is clear that he changed it considerably. It is equally clear that he revitalized it. By the eve of World War I, although socialism had made considerable headway, orthodox Marxism was on its way to extinction. It was Lenin who put it into action and created a situation in which Marxism became one of the most powerful political ideologies in the history of the world.

Marxists who would justify Marxian orthodoxy had much to explain. As Eduard Bernstein had made so clear, many of Marx's predictions appeared simply to have been mistaken. Marx's writings prior to 1850 demonstrate that he obviously considered a proletarian revolution to be near. Not only had this not occurred, except possibly for the brief Paris Commune of 1871, but it appeared to be less and less likely. Lenin took it upon himself to provide the justification.

His 1902 pamphlet *What Is To Be Done?* gave an explanation as to why the spontaneous revolution that Marx had foreseen had not come to pass. The working class by itself, Lenin argued, could develop only "trade-union consciousness," not a true spirit of revolution. They might strike, or otherwise seek to improve their lot, but they required guidance in order to achieve the revolutionary consciousness that would be necessary in order to achieve the communist revolution.

It was here that Lenin outlined the role of the party. The workers must receive leadership from intellectuals who had deep theoretical understanding of Marxism. This would come from a small elite group who would be the communist party. The party would act on behalf of the interests of the workers and speak for them. It actually would substitute itself for the proletariat in fomenting and guiding the revolution under what some have called the "theory of substitution." It would become the "vanguard of the proletariat," and work to develop the revolutionary consciousness that would make revolution inevitable. Party members would do this by "agitation" and propaganda. Agitation referred to working within small groups, distributing leaflets and pamphlets, making speeches, and the like. Propaganda was a broader, more comprehensive activity to spread the doctrine of the party. The two in combination became "agitprop."

In order to accomplish its purposes, the party had to be strict in its membership requirements. It could accept only those who were fully devoted to revolution, those who would place it uppermost in their lives. Moreover, it could accept only those with the mental abilities to understand and the skills to apply Marxist doctrine. This, of necessity, would be a small elite, few if any of whom, because of the need for education, could be drawn from the working class.

The party also had to be organized carefully in order to be effective. For this purpose, Lenin developed the doctrine of "democratic centralism." Under its principles, lower bodies would elect higher ones, and power would flow from the top down. There would be free discussion in party councils, but decisions would be binding upon all, and there could be no dissent once there had been a decision. The lowest level would be the party congress, which would elect the central committee. It was the central committee that would represent the working class and speak for them. The central committee in turn would elect smaller bodies who would carry on the day-to-day work and determine pol-

V.I. LENIN

. . . [T]he organisation of the revolutionaries must consist first and foremost of people who make revolutionary activity their profession. . . . Such an organisation must perforce not to be very extensive and must be as secret as possible. . . . I assert that it is far more difficult to unearth a dozen wise men than a hundred fools. This position I will defend, no matter how much you instigate the masses against me for my "anti-democratic" views, etc. As I have stated repeatedly, by "wise men," in connection with organisation, I mean *professional revolutionaries,* irrespective of whether they have developed from among students or working men.

From *What is to Be Done?* (1902)

. . . [T]he dictatorship of the proletariat, i.e., the organization of the vanguard of the oppressed as the ruling class for the purpose of crushing the oppressors, cannot result merely in an expansion of democracy. *Simultaneously* with an immense expansion of democracy which *for the first time* becomes democracy for the poor, democracy for the people, and not democracy for the rich, the dictatorship of the proletariat imposes a series of restrictions on the freedom of the oppressors, the exploiters, the capitalists. We must crush them in order to free humanity from wage-slavery; their resistance must be broken by force; it is clear that where there is suppression there is also violence, there is no freedom, no democracy. . . . Only in communist society, when the resistance of the capitalists has been completely broken, when the capitalists have disappeared, when there are no classes (i.e., when there is no difference between the members of society as regards their relation to the social means of production), *only then* does "the state . . . cease to exist," and it *"Becomes possible to speak of freedom."*

From *State and Revolution* (1917)

icy between committee meetings. These would include the politburo (political bureau of the central committee) and the secretariat.

In 1917 Lenin added further explanation for the absence of a proletarian revolution in *Imperialism: the Highest Stage of Capitalism.* Imperialism, or colonization, he argued, permitted capitalists to

provide some benefits to the working class by draining the resources of underdeveloped nations and sharing some of the "surplus value" with the proletariat. This served to reduce worker
discontent and postpone the pauperization of the masses that Marx
had predicted. As a result, it also postponed revolution.

Imperialism had, he believed, created a worldwide economy
that may at least temporarily have placated the workers, but which
was nevertheless vulnerable. Lenin likened it to a chain, pointing
out that a chain is only as strong as its weakest link and that
colonial areas were the weak links of capitalism. Capitalist nations
would war among themselves in dispute of the colonial areas.
Moreover, because of imperialism any area in the world could
support a revolution; it would no longer be limited to advanced
industrial societies and should be encouraged everywhere. Lenin's new theory not only helped to explain why revolutions had
not taken place in fulfillment of Marx's predictions but also justified revolution in his native Russia.

Lenin revised Marx's theories with regard to the peasants as
well. Marx had little regard for the peasantry because he considered peasants not to be a true class. They represented a survival of barbarism within civilization. Lenin, on the other hand,
could not accept this view if he were to hope for revolution in
Russia, which was a backward state with little industry, therefore
with only a very small proletariat. He concluded that peasants
could be divided into three classes. The kulaks, or rich peasants,
obviously would side with the bourgeoisie. Those in the middle
might go in either direction, while the poor peasants were "semi-
proletarians," and could join with industrial workers to become
part of the base of a proletarian revolution.

Lenin's new approach to the peasantry combined with his
theory of imperialism to revise Marx in yet another manner. Marx's
philosophy of history had led him to believe strongly that
revolution could not occur until capitalism had developed to
the appropriate stage. Lenin argued that, on the contrary, imperialism had so changed world conditions that it was no longer
necessary to wait for revolution, that history could be accelerated, or telescoped, to achieve the proper stage. Peasants and
workers acting together under the leadership of the party could
force the necessary conditions into place.

Lenin was supported in this view by the brilliant communist theoretician Leon Trotsky (1879–1940), a Russian originally named Lev Davydovich Bronstein. As early as 1906, Trotsky had argued that Russia was in fact likely to have a proletarian revolution, despite the small size of its proletariat. This was because the Tsarist regime was completely corrupt, and the proletariat was concentrated in important locations where it could be well organized. It would be necessary, however, for a Russian revolution to inspire

---

LEON TROTSKY

Leninism is genuine freedom from formalistic prejudices, from moralizing doctrinalism, from all forms of intellectual conservatism attempting to blind the will to revolutionary action. But to believe that Leninism signifies that "anything goes," would be an irremediable mistake. Leninism includes the morality, not formal but genuinely revolutionary, of mass action and the mass party. Nothing is so alien to it as functionary-arrogance and bureaucratic cynicism. A mass party has its own morality, which is the bond of fighters in and for action. Demagogy is irreconcilable with the spirit of a revolutionary party because it is deceitful: by presenting one or another simplified solution of the difficulties of the hour, it inevitably undermines the next future, weakens the party's self-confidence. . . .

Leninism is warlike from head to foot. War is impossible without cunning, without subterfuge, without deception of the enemy. Victorious war cunning is a constituent element of Leninist politics. But at the same time, Leninism is supreme revolutionary honesty toward the party and the working class. It admits of no fiction. . . .

For Russia, [the theory of the permanent revolution] signified: what we need is not the bourgeois republic as a political crowning, nor even the democratic dictatorship of the proletariat and peasantry, but a workers' government supporting itself upon the peasantry and opening up the era of the international socialist revolution.

Thus, the idea of the permanent revolution coincides entirely with the fundamental strategical line of Bolshevism.

From *The New Course* (1924)

and to join with similar revolutions elsewhere in industrial nations if it were to succeed. This became known as Trotsky's theory of "permanent revolution."

No political ideology could long retain mass attraction when its predictions continued to be inaccurate, unless the inconsistency could be explained away. Lenin provided explanations that satisfied many Marxists who had found their commitment to the ideology weakening. Additionally, he added greater appeal to action. His theories and his call for immediate action provided an enormous infusion of energy to Marxism. It is also obvious that he was providing something else—a subtle association of the interests of Marxism with the interests of the Russian nation. The association quickly became less and less subtle, and soon communists came to present them as identical.

THE UNION OF SOVIET SOCIALIST REPUBLICS

In 1903 Lenin's elitist faction won a majority at the second party congress in opposition to those who favored a mass membership party. The Leninists therefore took the name "Bolshevik," or majority, whereas their opponents became known as the "Mensheviks," or the minority. Before the outbreak of the First World War, the groups had split into two separate parties.

In 1917, when a democratic revolution did occur in Russia, Lenin received secret permission from the German government to cross German territory in a sealed train on his way to Russia. On November 6 and 7 of that year, the Bolsheviks seized power and installed Lenin as chairman. By 1918 his dictatorship was secure. He had the able assistance of Trotsky, who became his deputy. Had Lenin not been there to provide his truly charismatic leadership, it is doubtful that Marxism today would be more than a memory. History dictated otherwise.

In order to coordinate the activities of communist parties throughout the world, many of which had emerged in response to the success of the Bolsheviks in Russia, the communist leaders encouraged the formation in 1919 of the Third International, the Comintern. The thirty-five national communist parties that initially made up the Comintern accepted Lenin's "Twenty-one

Conditions"—essentially the same as the requirements for membership among the Bolsheviks—and made their policies subject to the approval of the Comintern's executive committee, which the Soviet party's Central Committee controlled. The Bolsheviks had succeeded in establishing a worldwide network of communist parties subject to the Soviet leaders' direction.

The Third International disbanded in 1943 in deference to the Allied Powers, with whom the Soviet Union was participating in the war against the German Axis. Its successor was the "Cominform," or Communist Information Bureau, which included several European communist parties and existed following the war from 1947 to 1956. The purpose, again, was to further Soviet aims in foreign policy. By this time, however, nationalism had been strengthened in other communist countries, making tight Soviet control more difficult. By 1956 the Comintern no longer appeared to be useful, and it disbanded.

It was widely assumed that Trotsky would succeed Lenin. By the time of Lenin's death in 1924, however, Joseph Stalin (1879–1953) had sufficiently consolidated his support to be able to seize power. Within a few years, by 1929, he had eliminated all opponents, gained total power over the Communist Party (which meant over the Soviet Union), forcibly collectivized all aspects of Soviet life, exterminated the kulaks, and imposed a harsh one-person-rule that ultimately became a "cult of personality." Through the institutionalized use of terror, he established a stifling conformity. Lenin had used the secret police to crush dissent, acting on behalf of the Party. By the middle of the 1930s, Stalin had developed it into a force, subject to him alone, that he used to terrorize even the Party itself. Ultimately Stalin and his rule caused the murders of untold millions of persons, including huge numbers who in no rational way could have been considered his opponents, and some of whom were friends.

In October 1927, Stalin expelled Trotsky and other rivals from the Party, and in early 1929 he exiled him from the Soviet Union. Trotsky's orientation was more theoretically communist and vastly more internationalist than was Stalin's, and he called for immediate revolution worldwide. Stalin opposed this, fearing that it would cause capitalist countries to intervene in the Soviet Union. Stalin's approach was to build "socialism in one country," believing that it was essential to create a strong communist state before

---

JOSEPH STALIN

. . . [An] abyss . . . separates Lenin's theory of the dictatorship of the proletariat from Trotsky's theory of permanent revolution. . . . The opportunists in every land maintain that the proletarian revolution can begin . . . only in countries of advanced industrial development, and that the chances of a victory for socialism in such countries are increased in proportion to the extent of their industrial development. Furthermore, they deny the possibility of a victory for socialism taking place in one country alone, especially if that country be at a stage of backward industrial development. Now Lenin, already during the days of the great war, basing his contention upon the law of irregular development of imperialist States, contraposed this theory of the opportunists by his own theory of the proletarian revolution, which is: That socialism can be victorious in one country alone even when that country is in a condition of backward capitalist development.

From "On the Problems of Leninism" (1924)

---

risking failure by unduly antagonizing other nations, though he did say that there would be a final victory for socialism through worldwide revolution. Trotsky remained highly critical of Soviet policy under Stalin and was murdered in 1940 in Mexico by an ax-wielding assailant, presumably a Stalinist agent.

Although Stalin justified his actions in theoretical terms, as is essential in order to maintain an ideology, one should not examine Stalinist policies in reference to Marxism alone. For centuries there had been conflict in Russia between the "westernizers" and the "slavophiles." The westernizers were those who looked to the West and sought to advance by adapting Western technology and practices. The slavophiles, on the other hand, turned inward and were suspicious of foreign influences. Stalin appears clearly to have been in the tradition of the slavophiles, which greatly affected his approach to Marxism. There had been elements of nationalism in Lenin's doctrines, but Stalin developed them to be explicitly nationalistic. He explained his enhancement of state power—quite contrary to any notion of the state's withering away—by the fact that the Soviet Union was encircled by hostile nations. Any withering would come far in the future, when socialism was achieved worldwide. Stalin's efforts would be devoted to forcing rapid industrialization through a series of five-year plans and developing Soviet might.

Marx had been vague regarding the character of the "dictatorship of the proletariat" and did not suggest that it would be a party dictatorship. Lenin, on the contrary, had justified the Soviet Communist party as the vanguard of the proletariat and moved in the direction of a dictatorship of the Party. Stalin moved still further, and when he had gained complete control of the Party, moved beyond authoritarianism to totalitarianism.

Liberal democratic ideology assumes that the people have rights that are inherent. Government and the state exist to serve the people. Various authoritarian ideologies, on the other hand, assume that whatever rights the people have are granted to them by the government or the state. An authoritarian state could be quite mild, permitting the people to exercise a broad range of civil freedoms, or it could be quite harsh, restricting the activities of the people to an extreme degree. As a rule, an authoritarian government permits great latitude socially, providing that one does not become involved in anything political.

Totalitarianism is authoritarianism carried to its greatest extreme. As the name implies, it is an attempt to achieve total control of every aspect of the lives—and even the innermost thoughts—of the people. Someone once described totalitarianism as "tyranny plus technology," in recognition of the role that technology plays in any state that aspires to be totalitarian. There have been numerous instances throughout history of rulers who would have welcomed totalitarian power, but in general only an extensive and highly advanced technology can provide the ruler with the control that is required to approach totalitarian levels. Totalitarianism, therefore, is largely a twentieth-century phenomenon, the result of applying a combination of technology and mass politics in an attempt to achieve total terror.[1]

There is nothing inherent in Marxist ideology itself that implies totalitarianism, although the theory of the dictatorship of the

---

[1]Hannah Arendt, *The Origins of Totalitarianism* (New York: Harcourt, Brace & World, 1968).

proletariat, like that of any dictatorship, is highly authoritarian. Marxism-Leninism adds to the authoritarianism, but even it does not presuppose totalitarianism. Stalin brought together an unfortunate mix of Marxist theory, traditions of Russian absolutism, and his own personality which was brutal, suspicious, and domineering. The resulting totalitarianism became an exercise of power for the sake of power, such as George Orwell described in his brilliant novel *1984*.

Short of direct physical invasion by drugs or psychosurgery, it is doubtful that any totalitarianism can be perfect, that is, that it can completely stifle dissent and obliterate the individual human personality. Stalin, however, made the attempt and succeeded sufficiently that we may be justified in calling much of his rule totalitarian. His successors, while certainly remaining authoritarian, often harshly authoritarian, have not aspired to the totalitarian ideal.

There are those who allege that the Soviet Union continues to be totalitarian, but they either are confusing the term with "authoritarian" or are speaking from their own ideological point of view that clouds their judgment. They should heed the admonition of Hannah Arendt, whose superb studies of totalitarianism are the best works ever done on the subject. She warned that, because the ability to distinguish totalitarian states from tyrannies and dictatorships is so vital, "we have every reason to use the word 'totalitarian' sparingly and prudently."[2]

There was considerable maneuvering for power following Stalin's death in 1953, but by 1956 Nikita Khrushchev had consolidated his authority and taken the positions of general secretary of the Party and chairman of the Council of Ministers. That year at the Party's Twentieth Congress, he gave a secret speech, quickly leaked to the West, criticizing the cult of personality that surrounded Stalin, and decrying his abuse of power, making "detotalitarianization" official. The Soviets also officially adopted the position of "peaceful coexistence" with other powers.

As of late 1986 and early 1987, Soviet leader Mikhail Gorbachev had adopted a degree of openness unprecedented in the U.S.S.R.—the "Glasnost" policy. The official press had begun for the first time to carry reports of crime, accidents, disasters, and

---

[2] Ibid., part III, pp. ix–x.

other items of news admitting that conditions there were considerably less than perfect. Officials lessened their controls on speech, publication, and the arts. They began also to respond to complaints from citizens and to reply to requests for information. The new openness extended so far as to permit the production and public showing of a motion picture, *Repentance,* that denounced the horrors of the Stalin era. In November of 1987 Secretary Gorbachev vigorously renewed the attack on Stalin and his policies and criticized his predecessor, Leonid Brezhnev, for not having continued "de-Stalinization." Although the official ideology remains in place and the internal controls remain strict, they are not total. Moreover, there is some evidence that they may be progressively weakening, but one should be cautious in making predictions, especially with regard to the Soviets. Trends in the U.S.S.R. are difficult, at best, for outsiders to evaluate. The future of Glasnost is especially uncertain because of apparent strong resistance to change from some segments of the Soviet leadership.

THE PEOPLE'S REPUBLIC OF CHINA

Mao Tse-tung—or Mao Zedong—(1893-1976) was the architect of Chinese communism. His policies, like those of Stalin, reflect more than Marxism. They can be understood only with reference both to Marxism and to Chinese culture. Another factor that must be considered once again is nationalism; in this instance it includes the historical friction that existed between China and Russia. The ultimate break between China and the Soviet Union reflects disputes over territorial borders, ethnic friction, the lack of support for Mao from Stalin in Mao's struggles with Chiang Kai-shek (1886–1975), and other long-standing tensions.

China's relations with the West have historically been such as to cause bitterness on the part of the Chinese. Although there had been contacts earlier, the first significant inroads by Westerners into China began in the sixteenth century, with the influence of traders and missionaries. Initially, Chinese leaders had been almost totally ignorant of the Western world and failed to recognize until too late the power that Western nations could bring to bear upon them. This resulted from traditional Chinese assumptions that China was the center of the world and that lands outside

MAO TSE-TUNG

Our people's government is a government that truly represents the interests of the people and serves the people, yet certain contradictions do exist between the government and the masses. These include contradictions between the interests of the state, collective interests, and individual interests; between democracy and centralism; between those in positions of leadership and the led; and contradictions arising from the bureaucratic practices of certain state functionaries in their relations with the masses. All these are contradictions among the people. . . .

Our state is a state of the people's democratic dictatorship, led by the working class and based on the worker-peasant alliance. . . . Our constitution states that citizens of the People's Republic of China enjoy freedom of speech, of the press, of assembly, of association, of procession, of religious practices, and so on. . . . Our socialist democracy is democracy in the widest sense, such as is not to be found in any capitalist country. . . .

But this freedom is freedom with leadership and this democracy is democracy under centralized guidance, not anarchy. . . .

While we stand for freedom with leadership and democracy under centralized guidance, in no sense do we mean that coercive measures should be taken to settle ideological matters and questions involving the distinction between right and wrong among the people. Any attempt to deal with ideological matters or questions involving right and wrong by administrative orders or coercive measures will be not only ineffective but harmful. . . . Administrative orders issued for the maintenance of social order must be accompanied by persuasion and education, for in many cases administrative orders alone will not work.

From *On the Correct Handling of Contradictions Among the People*
(1957)

were barbarian. The Mandarin word for China, in fact, translates as "center of the world," while the word for the language means "language of the center of the world."

By the nineteenth century there was considerable trade, which the Chinese regarded as a privilege that they could grant or deny. The first great clash came in the Opium War of 1839–1842. Although the Chinese Emperor had banned opium in China as early as 1729, Western nations aided by corrupt officials imported huge quantities of the drug into China as payment in lieu of silver for Chinese goods. By the end of the 1830s, opium addiction, which had previously been uncommon, had spread greatly. Not even an appeal to the conscience of Queen Victoria had any effect, and the Emperor's imperial commissioner at Canton therefore ordered foreigners to turn over all opium to be destroyed. This was done, but the traders refused to pledge that they would bring in no more opium, and war broke out. The superiority of British naval forces led to Chinese surrender and the Treaty of Nanking in 1842, which opened China to the inroads of foreigners and granted extraordinary concessions. This began a series of increasingly intrusive demands from the West that China was virtually powerless to resist. China's humiliation continued well into the twentieth century. To some extent, it continued even to the communist takeover in 1949.

In 1911 Dr. Sun Yat-sen (1866–1925) led a revolution against the corrupt and ineffective Manchu Dynasty. The next year he became president of the new republic, and the emperor, who was the child Pu Yi, abdicated. The new government was, however, too weak to maintain control, and the nation quickly broke into small warring territories under the control of warlords, most of whom previously had been provincial officials.

For more than a decade there was no effective government, but two forces eventually emerged: Sun's Nationalist Party, or Kuomintang, and in 1921, the Communist Party of China (the CPC). At first the groups cooperated, with some CPC members serving also as members of the Kuomintang's Central Executive Committee. Sun welcomed Soviet aid, and there were numerous Soviet advisers working within the Kuomintang on behalf of the CPC. He attempted to control the anticommunist sentiment that was developing, but in March of 1925 Sun died. Following his death, Chiang Kai-shek ultimately brought the Kuomintang under his control.

The cooperation with the CPC came to an end on April 12, 1927, when Chiang, in a surprise move, arrested all Communists wherever he had control and executed their leaders. Years of struggle followed, in which the Kuomintang controlled most of China, but in 1931 the CPC, which by this time was under Mao's leadership, established a Soviet Republic in southern Kiangsi

Province. Pressure from the invading Japanese for a time kept the Kiangsi state safe from Chiang's forces, but in 1934 a truce with the Japanese freed the Kuomintang to begin to bring its superior force to bear on the Communists.

Mao and his army then conducted one of the great feats of military history, the "Long March." Some one hundred thousand strong, they set off over rugged and inhospitable country, with little in the way of supplies, to march 6,000 miles, completely across China. More than two-thirds perished along the way. The Long March symbolized to many Chinese Mao's desire to fight the Japanese instead of fellow Chinese in the Kuomintang, thus securing for the Communists the status of patriots in the eyes of many of their countrymen.

Because of renewed Japanese aggression, there again was some cooperation beginning in 1937. The two groups were uneasy partners, however, and continued to fight one another almost as much as they fought the invaders. This situation continued throughout World War II. Afterwards, Mao's forces clearly were in ascendancy, and Chiang and the Kuomintang armies and supporters fled to Taiwan, a large island east of the Chinese mainland. There they established their capital at Taipei as the Republic of China. Meanwhile, on the first of October 1949, the victorious Mao proclaimed the People's Republic of China from Peking and consolidated the CPC's rule over the whole of the Chinese mainland.

Mao was the first significant non-European Marxist theoretician, and he ranks with the giants of Marxist thought. He was the first to adapt Marxist ideology to Asian conditions. His blending of Chinese and Marxist elements is more innovative than Stalin's Russian contributions to Marxism and even compares favorably with Lenin's development of the ideology.

However harsh Mao's tactics and rule were, he at least had faith in the possibility of rehabilitation. Some of those whom he labelled as "class enemies," such as landlords, were subjected to programs aimed at "reforming" them. This is in marked contrast to Lenin and Stalin, who attempted to eliminate all their opponents ruthlessly. Mao thus exhibited confidence in the power of the mind to overcome objective conditions, deviating not only from Lenin and Stalin but also from Marx.

Arendt has written that Mao's dealing with his opponents by "rectification of thought" was certainly terror, but that it was terror of a different kind from that employed by other totalitarians. "Whatever the results," she said, "it did not decimate the population. It clearly recognized national interest, it permitted the country to develop peacefully, to use the competence of the descendants of the formerly ruling classes, and to uphold academic and professional standards. In brief, it was obvious that Mao Tsetung's 'thought' did not run along the lines laid down by Stalin (or Hitler, for that matter), that he was not a killer by instinct, and that nationalist sentiment, so prominent in all revolutionary upheavals in formerly colonial countries, was strong enough to impose limits upon total domination."[3] One should note that China was never actually colonized, although clearly it had been subject to foreign domination including gross interference in its internal affairs. One should also note that this discussion in no way intends to minimize the brutalities that existed under Mao or the murders that took place in his name.

Mao's greatest departure from previous Marxists is probably his emphasis upon the peasantry. Marx had assumed that peasants had no role to play in the revolution, and that inasmuch as they retained their desire to own land, they could even be an impediment. Lenin, Trotsky, and Stalin, in adapting Marxism to Russian conditions, concluded that some peasants, at least, could cooperate with the proletariat to work for revolution.

It was left to Mao to give the peasants the foremost role as the foundation of the revolution. He had studied the Chinese peasantry and was thoroughly familiar with the manner in which they had been unmercifully exploited. His experience had led him to develop great admiration for their courage and wisdom and for their stoic perserverance. Moreover, as Mao was building his forces, Chiang tended to control urban areas. Because of his position in the countryside, Mao recognized that peasant support, the support of the people, was vital. His army treated the people well, and Mao received their backing.

Consistent with his emphasis upon the peasantry, Mao differed from Lenin in that he built his movement upon mass support, rather than a party of elite membership. He included workers and peasants, but broadened his appeal to elements of other classes as well. His theory even incorporated the middle classes and

[3] Ibid., part III, p. viii.

professionals. In fact the only classes whom he excluded as enemies of the people were the landlords who had so exploited the
peasants and those who sacrificed the interests of China to profit
from dealings with foreigners, such as the Japanese invaders.

In these policies, Mao reflected an intense national pride, which
led him to exalt the whole of China. Similarly, his approach suggests the traditional Chinese attitude toward foreign devils and
barbarians, as well as his resentment of foreign imperialism in his
country. In accepting the continued existence of some of the
bourgeoisie so long as it remained loyal to the regime, he also
demonstrated a pragmatism that was capable of placing practical
considerations ahead of ideology.

There was a strong populist strain in Mao. His admiration for
the peasantry led him to believe that the educated classes could
benefit from exposure to peasant life. He ordered huge numbers
of students, professionals, and others to be "sent down" to farms
or factories to serve as laborers for specified periods. It is this
conviction of the strength of the people as a whole that brought
Mao to his acceptance of more decentralization than most Marxist
leaders and to his formulation of principles for guerrilla warfare,
which is based in the countryside. He accepted violence no less
than did any Marxist revolutionary but stressed that popular support was essential. Human factors, in his mind, were at least as
important as historical currents. Nevertheless, his prescriptions
for state and party organization did not differ significantly from
the Soviet models, and he fully accepted the principle of
democratic centralism.

After Mao's successful revolution, the next few years involved consolidation of his regime during which virtually the entire society was reorganized along communist lines. Nationalization
and collectivization proceeded rapidly. Following the Soviet pattern, the Chinese regime adopted a series of five-year plans. In
1957 Mao delivered his famous speech, "On the Correct Handling
of Contradictions Among the People"; at this time he briefly lib-
eralized conditions, saying "let a hundred flowers bloom." The
"Hundred Flowers" movement led to such criticism of officials
that he called it to a halt and led the nation into the "Great Leap
Forward." This was an attempt to force industrialization using
techniques so decentralized that they even aimed at developing
tiny family-operated units to produce steel. It was a total failure
and ended by 1960.

Highly important to world affairs, including some attitudes in the West toward the character of Marxism-Leninism, was the split in the early 1960s between China and its previous ally, the Soviet Union. Their relations had never been so cordial as they had appeared to many in the West. Nevertheless, Mao considered the Soviet Union's discrediting of Stalin to be a "revisionist" deviation from true Marxism-Leninism and attempted to rehabilitate Stalin's reputation. A factor in this could well have been Mao's sensitivity to his own reputation in view of the cult of personality that he, like Stalin, had encouraged to form around himself. Moreover, China, because of its own status as a Third World country, began to assert itself as the leader of Marxist movements in the Third World, causing further disputes with the U.S.S.R.

As mentioned earlier, many conditions led to the Sino-Soviet break. The most important probably was the simple fact that the world had changed. No longer could the Soviet Union justify its dominance of all world communist movements, but it continued its attempt to exercise control, often to the detriment of the other nations involved. China was simply too large to be dominated when domination meant that its national interests would suffer, particularly in view of China's historical view of the Russian "barbarians."

The Third World issue should not be underestimated. It takes but a short period of residence in a less-developed country to recognize that the Third World directs its resentment not merely at the wealthy United States but at the whole of the industrialized world, including the Soviet Union as well. Moreover, Mao had become not only the leading Marxist theoretician, but the senior Marxist leader. A break was to have been expected. The reason that so few analysts and officials anticipated it reflects more upon their own ideology than upon the quality and amount of information available to them. They tended to be led astray by their assumption that there was in fact (as opposed to in theory) a "monolithic communism" overshadowing national interests.

Beginning in 1966 and continuing for a decade was the most tumultuous period of the regime's existence: the Cultural Revolution. By this time, the aged Mao was failing and had come increasingly under the influence of his wife, Jiang Qing, who contended for power with the moderate and highly regarded Premier Zhou Enlai. She and other top officials, including Mao himself, encouraged young people to attack society's institutions in

order to return to revolutionary values and retain the mass orientation of Maoism.

The rebellious youth came to be known as the Red Guards.
Without restraint or reason, the young thugs pillaged and maimed
Chinese citizens. High status often was no protection. Red Guards
seized Deng Pufang, the son of future Chinese leader Deng
Xiaoping, and threw him from a third-story window. His legs have
remained paralyzed since his injuries. Deng Xiaoping had been in
and out of the Party's inner circles several times. Despite Mao's
ouster of Deng from a position of power, Zhou Enlai—shortly
before his own death—in recognition of Deng's abilities and dedication to progressive policies, succeeded in "rehabilitating" him.
When Zhou died, Mao again suppressed Deng. These situations
surely affected the reaction to "Maoism" after Deng assumed
the leadership.

The best source for insights into daily life in China during the
Cultural Revolution is the memoir by Nien Cheng, who was imprisoned without cause. After seven years in prison during which
her health eroded seriously, she was released in 1973 because she
persistently refused to "confess." She then discovered that the
young fanatics had murdered her daughter Meiping, who had
been a prominent film actress.[4]

With the army's assistance, the Red Guards shook virtually
every aspect of the society in a huge purge that received full publicity. When the leaders determined that it was time to end the
Cultural Revolution, the army turned upon the Red Guards, and
it was over. Hardly any aspect of Chinese life remained un-
touched. The Cultural Revolution certainly demonstrates the
brutality of which Maoism was capable. It nevertheless also demonstrates the differences between Mao's China, in which those
imprisoned could be rehabilitated, and reason at times could prevail, and Stalin's Soviet Union, in which there were hardly any
moderating influences.

Following Mao's death in 1977, more moderate leaders took
charge, blaming many of the excesses upon the "Gang of Four,"
which included Jiang Qing. Mao had been no less guilty than
Stalin of establishing a cult of personality, but the new leaders
embarked upon a pragmatic course. They have established cordial

[4]Nien Cheng, *Life and Death in Shanghai* (New York: Grove Press, 1986).

relations with the West, including even the United States. Under the leadership of Deng Xiaoping (1904–), there came to be a huge exchange of students between China and other countries and many fewer restraints within the nation than previously. The relentless conformity that Mao imposed exists no longer. Symbolic of this is the trend toward replacing the drab uniforms of another era with colorful, fashionable clothing.

At the end of 1986, there was a development that might initially seem trivial but is significant in view of traditional Chinese modesty, Mao's rejection of "degenerate" foreign influences, and the tendency of Marxist-Leninist regimes to be puritanical and prudish in practice. Conditions had so changed that the government not only permitted but encouraged Chinese women to wear bikini swimsuits. Few things could better illustrate the startling new openness of China toward the West and its influences than this. Regardless of the traditionalism that characterizes China, it appears to be moving much faster toward reform than does the Soviet Union.[5]

As one might have expected, there has been a reaction to the new liberalizing tendencies. Some officials have been reassigned or have lost their offices. Renewed criticisms of Western influences have emerged, and officials have suppressed anti-Marxist sentiment. Nevertheless, it appears as if another "cultural revolution" is unlikely. Chinese leaders assure the world that the nation will remain open to the West, and that it will maintain its reforms. The pace of such reforms no doubt will be at a slower rate than in the period of early enthusiasm, but they likely will continue.

The regime now is actively encouraging foreign investments and providing individual economic incentives, by experimenting with limited free-market arrangements. It clearly remains Marxist-Leninist but is considerably less dogmatic than before. The operative principle appears to be that Marxism exists to assist the society in developing as it should, but if a rigid application of Marxism does not accomplish this, it is Marxism that should bend, and not the goal of development.

Deng, possibly because of his own sufferings under the cult of personality that surrounded Mao, appears to be determined to

[5] Earl W. Foell, "Moving Communism's Economic Mountains," *Christian Science Monitor* (November 10, 1987), pp. 3, 5.

prevent the re-emergence of one-person rule; he also appears to be dedicated to continued reform. Although he stepped aside in late 1987 and relinquished his official position as Party leader, Deng retains control of the military and remains enormously influential. His successor as General Secretary of the Party is former Prime Minister Zhao Ziyang, who, despite holding the top position, according to Chinese sources will continue to report to Deng.[6] When he retired officially, Deng required other senior officials to retire, also, and took strict measures to prevent them from interfering with the pace of reform.[7]

Zhao appears to be a pragmatic leader who is under no illusions about the disasters that Mao's later policies caused. Mao had been sheltered from reality by his advisers. For example, he either did not know or refused to believe that huge numbers of peasants had died from starvation during the "Great Leap Forward" of 1958, and he consistently refused to permit grain imports because they would have amounted to "revisionism" and would have "entailed a flirtation with capitalism."[8] Zhao told Harrison Salisbury of the New York Times that "Until his last breath, . . . Mao held to his belief that his view of the world was correct."[9]

One of Zhao's most important responsibilities will be ideological, the interpretation of the doctrines of the Party. "Since Confucian times, Chinese leaders have attempted to legitimize their rule as the upholders of an all-embracing doctrine, whether it be Confucianism or communism," and China's press has described Zhao "as a leader who has established the ideological basis for further economic reform."[10] The Chinese are thus more candid than those in most other societies regarding the importance of political ideology.

[6] Ann Scott Tyson, "China's Zhao Faces Tough Political Maneuvering as Party Chief," Christian Science Monitor (November 6, 1987), p. 12.
[7] Daniel Southerland, "China Imposes New Rules Designed to Block Meddling by Party Elders," Washington Post (November 5, 1987), p. A25.
[8] Harrison E. Salisbury, "Zhao Ziyang, on Mao and China's Future," The New York Times (November 14, 1987), p. 15.
[9] Ibid.
19Daniel Southerland, "China Stresses New Party Chief's Role as Ideological Guide," Washington Post (November 6, 1987), p. A29.

YUGOSLAVIA

After the Soviet leaders consolidated their regime, the U.S.S.R. spread its power throughout Eastern Europe and created systems that mirrored that of the Soviet Union. As time passed, however, the new regimes also evolved and began in varying degrees to reflect their own local conditions. Nowhere is this more evident, or more significant, than in Yugoslavia. Nowhere, also, has communism developed in a more interesting manner.

During the Second World War, the Yugoslavian partisans fiercely resisted the Germans, who had invaded in 1941. Admittedly, there were equally fierce battles among various Yugoslav ethnic groups, which probably were responsible for more Yugoslav deaths than were battles with the Germans. Nevertheless, throughout the war the Yugoslavs maintained strong and effective guerrilla actions that kept the Germans occupied and away from the Russian front. Thus Yugoslav power, not a Soviet invasion, eventually caused the Germans to withdraw. It was the Yugoslav Communist party under the leadership of Josep Broz Tito (1892–1980) that encouraged and coordinated the resistance.

The Party therefore became closely identified with patriotism and national independence, and the people hailed its leaders as heroes. Its popularity so increased during the war that in 1945 when the Germans departed it came easily to power, and Tito was the nation's new prime minister. The Party had unusual advantages. It not only was highly popular but was also well organized nationally and had few opponents. The Germans had shattered most of those affluent groups that might otherwise have offered resistance to the Communists. Those that remained generally had collaborated with the invaders and thus had lost credibility and had become powerless.

Ideologically there were few differences at the end of the war between the Soviet and Yugoslav communists. In fact, Tito and the other leaders were Stalinists who welcomed cooperation with the Soviets. In organization, on the other hand, the Yugoslavian party had developed quite differently from that in the U.S.S.R. For one thing, because it had been impossible during the war to coordinate every aspect of the resistance centrally, there had come to be—certainly by Marxist-Leninist standards—considerable autonomy and freedom of action at the local and regional levels.

Like the CPC in China, the Party grew from the countryside as a guerrilla organization and remained close to the people. Also like the CPC, the Party sought to include the entire society, regardless of class background. Such conditions shaped its development and made the Yugoslavian organization much more open and democratic than its counterpart in the Soviet Union, which was made up of a small elite membership under tight control. There were no "class enemies" as there had been in the U.S.S.R., and the lack of opposition removed any justification for repression or terror based on the Soviet model.

Despite their commitment to Marxism-Leninism, however, Tito and the Yugoslav leaders were staunch nationalists. They also were fully aware that the U.S.S.R. owed them a great deal because of their sustained, dedicated, and effective military activities during the war that prevented the Soviet burden from becoming even greater than it had been. They were therefore in no mood to surrender national autonomy to the Soviets or to permit the U.S.S.R. to dictate policy. In typical fashion, the Soviets attempted to do just that and to treat Yugoslavia as a "satellite" state. Tito then expelled Soviet advisers and proceeded on an independent course. Yugoslavia's strength and national determination, coupled with the terrible losses that the Soviets had suffered during the war, protected against invasion. The threat nevertheless did exist.

Yugoslavia's independence and its unique conditions encouraged communism there to develop a much different character from that in the Soviet Union. As in the U.S.S.R., the state owns most property, but there remains some private ownership of small shops and farms. Consistent with the decentralized nature of the Party as it grew during World War II, there is considerable decentralization in the economy, which involves competition among different enterprises, all publicly owned. Citizens speak openly and may travel outside the country without restriction. Non-party press does exist, and is relatively free—certainly much freer than is the rule outside of Western democracies—although some citizens have been jailed or otherwise punished for their writings.

The most interesting feature of the system is the self-management that it incorporates. A system of workers' councils provides a measure of true democracy within economic enterprises. The workers may participate through the councils in budget and production planning and allocation for each activity, selection of the managers, and in the setting of work conditions. The workers have thus become an official part of the decision structure of the economy in a way not only completely absent from other existing communist systems but largely absent even in Western democracies, except in employee-owned activities. In practice, the system does not work so well as had been hoped. The rate of worker participation is low, and there appears to be little trust in the managers. Nonetheless, a mechanism exists and is in place that creates at least the potential for true worker-management cooperation, however much it may fall short of the ideal.

CUBA

Fidel Castro (1927–) is the architect of communism in Cuba, as well as the national leader. When his guerilla movement overthrew the dictatorship of Fulgencio Batista (1901–1973) in 1959, Castro may already have been a Marxist. He was closely associated with Ernesto "Che" Guevara (1929–1967), who was a committed Marxist revolutionary. It is, however, doubtful that Castro was oriented toward the Soviet Union until hostile American policies under the Eisenhower administration forced him to turn to the Soviets for aid.

By 1961 Castro had declared himself to be a Marxist-Leninist and proceeded to embark upon a program of rapid industrialization. This effort failed, and Castro redirected his nation's efforts toward agricultural production, with mixed success. Like other Marxist-Leninists (and indeed like dictators in general) he deals harshly with dissent. Conditions in Cuban prisons appear often to be especially barbaric. Castro's greatest accomplishment has been in raising the general living standards of the Cuban people, significantly improving education, and lowering illiteracy levels to those of industrial nations. Cuban improvements, though, have not resulted from a successful economy so much as from great amounts of aid from other Marxist-Leninist nations. Whatever success the economy might or might not have had under Castro's policies has been effectively stifled by hostile U.S. actions, including American pressures upon other nations that have severely restricted Cuba's trade.

In his early years in power, Castro adopted a policy of "exporting revolution." He attempted to encourage revolution in other Latin American nations and provided several revolutionary movements with support and training. "Castroism" lost much credibility with other Latin nations when they discovered that Castro had permitted the Soviets to place missiles on Cuban bases; he subsequently directed that they be removed.

As Castro and his regime have matured, he has tended to speak in more statesmanlike fashion, though he certainly has not become passive. It is clear, for example, that he continues to supply troops to the African nation of Angola. It is less clear whether he persists in his attempts to export revolution to other Latin American nations, but many American officials have believed that he does, and that belief was a prime component of U.S. policy toward Latin America during the Reagan administration. Regardless of whether these officials were correct, it is evident that Castro has led his nation's policies to be considerably more moderate than previously. Those observers who fail to recognize this fact share the shortcoming that is so apparent among their predecessors who ignored signals that a break between China and the Soviet Union was possible, even likely; their ideology renders them often incapable of recognizing the obvious.

Castro's regime is different from the typical Marxist-Leninist system in that there appears to be relatively little in the way of party organization. In fact, Cuba in many ways seems more to reflect the personalized rule that has existed in so many Latin American nations than to fit into any other category. Castro's acceptance of Marxism-Leninism thus is only one factor in the character of the Cuban political system. In some ways, he fits rather well into the mold of the Latin caudillo, or "man on horseback."

EUROCOMMUNISM

Beginning in the 1970s, certain changes began to appear in the attitudes and policies of some communist parties within non-Communist Western European nations. These changes have not been uniform from country to country, but where they exist they include similar themes; foremost among them is independence from Soviet policy. "Eurocommunism" is a vague term that refers to these developments.

The impetus for Eurocommunism stems from a number of sources, including a recognition of changing conditions, a strong reaction against Stalinism, and the influence of certain communist intellectuals. Prominent among these is Antonio Gramsci (1891–1937), an Italian Communist who died in prison where he had been sent by the Fascists in 1926. Gramsci wrote critically of Leninism, arguing that communism could result only after receiving the support of the people as a whole; that is, by evolution. An attempt by one class to impose it upon others by violent revolution could only result in a repressive system, as had happened in Stalin's Soviet Union. Gramsci urged that communist parties cooperate fully with other groups. He insisted that full democratic participation was essential, both in the internal workings of parties, and in a true communist state.

Although it would be premature to cite Eurocommunism as marking a definite shift in the character of Marxist-Leninist parties that exist in European democracies, there does appear to be a decided shift away from Soviet domination. This is quite consistent with the strength of nationalism in all nations. There also seem to be tendencies that could lead some of those parties in the direction of democratic socialism.

Because the economic position of the working class in Western democracies has so steadily improved, the workers are considerably less distinct from the bourgeoisie than they once were. There is even overlap between the two groups; for example, in the cases of workers whose income permits investment that could even class them in some instances as capitalists. Many members of the groups that once were the mainstay of communist parties have therefore shifted in their party allegiance or remained in the party while working to moderate Marxist policy.

The result has been an acceptance of reform, rather than revolution, and an attempt to cooperate with other elements of society in order to establish the conditions that will bring about socialism. No longer is seizing power the aim. There is a new expression of willingness to work within the democratic system and not to impose policies upon the rest of society through violence or even a peaceful coup. To illustrate, communist parties in France, Italy, and Spain have explicitly accepted the principles of civil liberties and democratic procedures and promised to maintain them if in office.

These developments present considerable hope to those observers who have commitments to democracy, especially to those who argue that Marxist reform can at the same time accommodate democratic procedures and the democratic spirit. There are, however, reasons for such observers to be cautious in their conclusions. No communist party to date has adopted internal reforms that conform to its expressions of national policy. None, not even the most moderate of them all, the Communist party of Italy, has relinquished democratic centralism. All retain their rigid discipline over members.

So long as a party's internal policies remain Leninist, there is justification for suspicion regarding the character of the rule that it would impose if it were to come to power. It may well be that when a "Eurocommunist" party removes its emphasis upon class conflict, acceptance of violence, and rejection of democratic procedures, it is sincere in its desire to work peacefully with all social elements in a spirit of freedom. It may be, however, that it is simply attempting to appeal to the voters for support. We cannot be sure. Only when such a party abandons its restrictions upon its own members and makes its own internal policies conform to those that it promises to pursue should it gain power, will it have provided any solid assurance.

MARXISM-LENINISM AND OTHER NATIONS

A number of leaders in nations other than those discussed above are Marxists, but many of these are not Communists, or Marxist-Leninist. Robert Mugabe (1924–) of Zimbabwe is one example. Daniel Ortega (1945–) of Nicaragua is another. Salvadore Allende (1908–1973) was yet another.

Allende was democratically elected as president of Chile in 1970, but a right-wing military coup encouraged by the Nixon administration overthrew and apparently murdered him. The result has been a long-term military dictatorship that is highly repressive. Ortega is opposed by right-wing revolutionaries in his country called the "Contras," who have received direct military aid—both open and secret—from the Reagan administration. The re-

REGIS DEBRAY

In Latin America today a political line which, in terms of its consequences, is not susceptible to expression as a precise and consistent military line, cannot be considered revolutionary. Any line that claims to be revolutionary must give a concrete answer to the question: How to overthrow the power of the capitalist state? In other words, how to break its backbone, the army, continuously reinforced by North American military missions? The Cuban Revolution offers an answer to fraternal Latin American countries which has still to be studied in its historical details: by means of the more or less slow building up, through guerrilla warfare carried out in suitably chosen rural zones, of a *mobile strategic force*, nucleus of a people's army and of a future socialist state.

From *Revolution in the Revolution?* (1967)

sult in Nicaragua could well be that Ortega develops close ties with the U.S.S.R. and does indeed become Marxist-Leninist, creating in Nicaragua the communism that the Reagan administration and its supporters sought to prevent.

Such failures of American policy reflect the effects of a rigid political ideology that obscures the nature of leftist regimes and makes them difficult to understand or to be distinguished from one another. Ho Chi Min (1890–1969), the former Vietnam nationalist and leader of North Vietnam, was a committed Communist, but he had made overtures to the West that were rebuffed. No one can say with certainty what the result would have been had officials of the Eisenhower administration been willing at least to talk with Ho, but some of the results of rebuffing him are definite: the Vietnam War, the longest in American history and one of the most bloody; and now a united, and communist, Vietnam to which the U.S. remains hostile.

There is no shortage of communist regimes around the world. Some of them are, or aspire to be, totalitarian. But even among nations that are communist, or Marxist-Leninist, there are differences. Yugoslavia and China, for example, have cordial relations with the West, as do some other states. Ethiopia, Angola, North Korea, and South Yemen all present different pictures. Cambodia, or Democratic Kampuchea, remains communist, but a Vietnamese invasion overthrew the bloodthirsty Pol Pot regime, which on a smaller scale equalled—or perhaps even surpassed—anything that Stalin ever did in terms of terror and brutality. This is an interesting instance in which one Marxist-Leninist regime overthrew another. These are only some of the many examples that illustrate that diversity does exist, even under the name of Marxism-Leninism.

MARXISM-LENINISM IN PERSPECTIVE

Although Marxism-Leninism grew from the same sources as democratic socialism, the result has been vastly different.

Attitude Toward Change

In theory, Marxism-Leninism remains revolutionary, hence, is eager for change. Even though Marxist-Leninist regimes are fierce in their support of the status quo, they profess to work toward the "withering away of the state," which would be a massive—and highly unlikely—change.

Attitude Toward Human Nature

The communist attitude toward human nature is that it hardly exists. That is, it is the product of external conditions and will change as conditions change. The attitude is therefore neither optimistic nor pessimistic toward human nature. Marxism-Leninism perceives human nature as essentially irrelevant and subject to the dictates of the state, speaking for the proletariat.

Attitude Toward the Potential of Human Reason

Marxism and Marxism-Leninism both grant a high position to human reason. They accept reason as the foundation for science and praise science above all else. They assume that their version of socialism is "scientific socialism," and that reason determines its eventual triumph.

Attitude Toward Human Progress

Marxism is extraordinarily optimistic regarding the potential for human progress. In fact, it is utopian in the extreme, envisioning such progress that the state will "wither away." It is no exaggeration to label it "perfectionist." That is, it accepts the possibility—even the inevitability—of ultimate perfection.

Attitude Toward the Relationship of the Individual to the Community

Marxism-Leninism seeks group perfection. The individual is to benefit, but is virtually irrelevant; it is the group that is important. All property belongs to the people; in practice, this means to the state. Except in the most limited sense, Marxism-Leninism rejects the notion of private property. Despite this, many Marxist-Leninist states are moving to accept some free-market mechanisms, providing economic incentive, profit, and some small degree of private property. Without question, however, the strong emphasis has been, and remains, duties, rather than rights.

PROSPECTS FOR THE FUTURE

There are signs of progress in China and the Soviet Union and in the phenomenon of Eurocommunism. Certainly, diversity can exist even within the embrace of Marxism-Leninism. It is premature to be highly optimistic regarding the evolution of democratic institutions within Marxism-Leninism, though one should not dismiss the promising signs, under the assumption that nothing can improve. It does seem apparent, however, that improvement will depend upon the degree to which Marxism-Leninism becomes less committed to the principles of Marxism-Leninism. In this, as in most ideologies, progress depends upon the degree to which the ideology becomes less ideological.

Anarchism

5

O ne of the greatest difficulties in considering anarchism is in defining just what it means. "Anarchy" comes from the Greek and means "no leader," or loosely, "no government." The word itself was current during the French Revolution to describe those revolutionaries who insisted on certain reforms. It was not until 1840, however, when Pierre Joseph Proudhon first applied it to what we now call anarchism that it took on today's meaning.

Some people use the word to mean disorder, or complete chaos: "Your proposal would lead to just plain anarchy!" This phrase, or something like it, is fairly common. To those who accept such a definition, it would make no sense to study anarchism as a system, because they understand it to mean the complete lack of a system.

There are, however, explicit political ideologies of anarchism, many of which have been associated with socialism. Because of the wide variety of anarchist thought it would be inaccurate and misleading to generalize too freely regarding the beliefs of anarchists. It is safe to say, however, that anarchists reject the authority of one person over another and as a result generally reject the state as being the embodiment of such illegitimate authority. Above all, they stress that human actions should be voluntary, never compelled.

PIERRE JOSEPH PROUDHON

. . . [N]o government, no public economy, no administration, is possible, which is based upon property.

Communism seeks *equality* and *law*. Property, born of the sovereignty of the reason and the sense of personal merit, wishes above all things *independence* and *proportionality*.

But communism, mistaking uniformity for law, and levelism for equality, becomes tyrannical and unjust. Property, by its despotism and encroachments, soon proves itself oppressive and antisocial.

The objects of communism and property are good—their results are bad. And why? Because both are exclusive, and each disregards two elements of society. Communism rejects independence and proportionality; property does not satisfy equality and law.

Now . . . imagine a society based upon these four principles,—equality, law, independence, and proportionality,—we find . . . [a] third form of society, the synthesis of communism and property, we will call *liberty*.

From *What is Property?: First Memoir* (1840)

Far from advocating disorder, anarchists tend to see the state as creating it and their own proposals as ultimately providing order. In general, they react against bourgeois democracy, as do Marxists, but they react also against authoritarianism, whether it comes from socialism or from impersonal bureaucracies. Anarchists argue that for the state to add control of the economy to the powers that it already possesses, as socialists and communists would have it do, would simply strengthen the state and thereby increase injustice. As a rule, anarchists have opposed participation in any activities of government, refusing to vote, hold office, or otherwise admit the state's legitimacy. They have tended to work within unions and other labor groups in attempts to spread their viewpoint.

Few anarchists believe in the isolated individual who has little if any relation with others. The ideas of anarchism hardly ever stop with advocating complete liberty, but proceed to assume that human nature, if uncorrupted by institutions, is cooperative.

Human beings under anarchism will naturally operate a society in which they cooperate with one another for the common good. Moreover, the society under anarchism would be dynamic, not static. It would grow, change, and evolve to accommodate new developments and to meet human needs.

Throughout history there have been anarchist ideas in the sense of opposing the exercise of authority and considering the state's use of authority to be illegitimate. In some of the fragments that remain to us of the writings of the Greek Stoic Zeno (342–267 B.C.), there are discussions of a free community in which there is no government and in which humanity's natural reason is sufficient to lead to cooperation. There are instances of similar ideas throughout the Middle Ages and on into the late eighteenth century when the English writer William Godwin (1756–1836) published voluminous works advocating anarchism (though not, of course, under that name). In 1793 Godwin asserted in his *Enquiry Concerning Political Justice* that laws were not the wisdom of previous generations, as conservatives argued. Instead, they were the result of the passions of those generations. Therefore, it would be better to eliminate laws and courts and permit reason to prevail. Government, in fact, was unnecessary and should also be eliminated. Small cooperative communities should replace it and should regulate all property.

For obvious reasons societies generally do everything possible to eliminate such ideas. Even in individualist democracies, it tends to be a damning indictment to say that someone "has no respect for authority." This is not to say that there has been nothing more than beliefs to cause fear of anarchism. In the late nineteenth and early twentieth centuries there were numerous anarchists who advocated and practiced violent terrorism in order to bring down the state that they loathed. In 1894 anarchists became the first group to be denied the right to enter the United States based solely upon their political beliefs.

THE ROLE OF PIERRE JOSEPH PROUDHON ·

The brilliant and largely self-taught French writer Pierre Joseph Proudhon (1809–1865) is a monumental figure in the history of anarchism. He not only influenced the development of anarchist thought indelibly but also inspired the thought even of his opponents. Marx attacked him bitterly, and he responded in kind, rejecting communism or any form of state-oriented socialism. He accepted the need for revolution, but more cautiously than his fellows. He strongly opposed any institutionalization of violence and justified violence only as spontaneously demonstrated by groups of workers. At one time, quite contrary to his principles, Proudhon served in Parliament. Despite this, he recommended that citizens refrain from casting votes, believing that this ultimately would weaken the state.

Proudhon was strident and outspoken, even attacking the Church. This resulted in trouble with the French authorities and ultimately brought him a three-year term in prison. Nevertheless, he remained free from the hate and bitterness that motivated so many who were attacking the established powers.

Some administration would remain necessary even in a society under anarchism, Proudhon recognized, and he outlined a plan of operation. There would be a federation of voluntary associations to produce goods; these associations should be as small as possible in order to allow the members to maintain control. They would also be highly decentralized. This federation of associations would replace the state, which, in Proudhon's view, existed essentially to defend the property arrangements that he opposed.

Proudhon's famous comment that "property is theft!" should not be understood as opposition to all ownership. He opposed existing property arrangements but favored providing citizens with the control over their homes, land, tools, and other property that was essential for them to work and maintain their families. Proudhon believed that this sort of control over property was essential for a citizen's protection. He did advocate common ownership, by those who use them, of certain things such as large machines operating in factories.

Proudhon's primary concerns were economic, not political, arrangements. He suggested the creation of a national bank that would make money available at no interest. All exchange would then be on the basis of work certificates reflecting units of work performed. Equal exchange would be the commercial principle— an item that required a worker one hour to produce would be "sold" for a certificate reflecting one hour of work time. He even created a bank that he intended to operate upon the principles that he outlined, but had no success whatever. The idea of equal exchange did not originate with Proudhon. A few examples of small stores that put the principle into practice had existed previously in England and the United States. The American anarchist Josiah Warren (1798–1874) opened his "Equity Store," or "Time Store," in 1827 in Cincinnati and later opened an "Equity Village" in New York state, which lasted until 1865.

Contracts, Proudhon maintained, would govern relations between the associations, or producing units. He thus placed an enormous emphasis upon contract. This distinguishes him from most other anarchists, as does his stress upon family life. He considered the family to be the matrix within which personal autonomy develops, whereas most anarchists thought of it as the kind of coercive relationship that they strongly rejected.

COMMUNIST ANARCHISM

In the modern world, the anarchist thought that has existed generally originated from reaction to the same conditions that caused the development of socialist ideas. A recognition of injustice and economic deprivation led both anarchists and socialists to suggest new schemes that would provide a just and humane social and economic order. For communist anarchists, the goal is the same as the ultimate goal that Karl Marx described: a communist society in which there is no state. Such anarchists, however, would not trust the state to wither away, and they oppose any scheme that would permit it to exist, even if only as a transition such as the Marxists envision.

The two greatest figures in the tradition of communist anarchy are both Russian: Mikhail Bakunin (1814–1876) and Petr Kropotkin (1842–1921). Bakunin was more an activist than a systematic thinker, and there are numerous contradictions in his thought. Essentially, he saw humankind as having developed by fear, which he believed was the reason for the acceptance of religion and the state, each of which he rejected totally. Science, he thought, would create the knowledge that could free human beings from their fear and lead them to accept anarchy and throw off authority. They then would realize their ability to cooperate for mutual benefit.

Bakunin readily accepted the need for violence, stealth, deceit, treachery, and betrayal in destroying the state and establishing anarchism. He therefore was the forerunner of the Nihilists, a group of violent Russian terrorists who rejected all established values. He accepted a federative organization of associations, following Proudhon, but not the continuance of private property that Proudhon would have permitted.

Marx, of course, proposed to make use of the state following the revolution. In addition, the centralization inherent in Marxist doctrine was directly opposite to Bakunin's emphasis upon decentralization. For these and other reasons, he bitterly opposed Marx, and Marxist communism. Bakunin and his followers engaged in a fierce struggle with the Marxists over the control of the International Workingmen's Association. Although the Marxists were victorious and expelled the Bakuninites, the battle ultimately led to the International's demise.

Kropotkin was a geographer and naturalist who believed from his observations of plant and animal life that cooperation, rather than competition, was the law of nature. He concluded from this that science justified his conception of anarchism; it did not, as Marx insisted, justify Marxist socialism. Kropotkin advocated anarchism in its most classic form. He believed that government was not essential to a good and orderly society, quite the contrary. The good life could exist only when human beings were free from government. Free agreements, alone, could produce stability and harmony. Coercion is the greatest evil. A federation of small and entirely voluntary communes would deal with social needs. Those at the local level would elect delegates to the next highest level, and so on. Each delegate would be only a delegate, an ambassador, who would be bound by the instructions of those who did the choosing.

Violence was an issue at the time, and many anarchists advocated random acts of terror in order to bring on greater instability and hasten the end of the state. Kropotkin at one time accepted the use of violence as necessary for its overthrow but warned strongly against individual acts of terrorism as useless and counterproductive. Subsequently, he came to believe that the revolution would be nonviolent, and that mass violence was incompatible with anarchist principles and aims. Kropotkin supported

PETR KROPOTKIN

It is especially in the domain of ethics that the dominating importance of the mutual-aid principle appears in full. . . . . whatever the opinions as to the first origin of the mutual-aid feeling or instinct may be—whether a biological or a supernatural cause is ascribed to it—we must trace its existence as far back as to the lowest stages of the animal world; and from these stages we can follow its uninterrupted evolution, in opposition to a number of contrary agencies, through all degrees of human development, up to the present times. Even the new religions which were born from time to time . . . have only reaffirmed that same principle.

. . . In the practice of mutual aid, which we can retrace to the earliest beginnings of evolution, we thus find the positive and undoubted origin of our ethical conceptions; and we can affirm that in the ethical progress of man, mutual support—not mutual struggle—has had the leading part. In its wide extension, even at the present time, we also see the best guarantee of a still loftier evolution of our race.

From *Mutual Aid* (1890–1895)

the Allies in the First World War as representing the least evil alternative. For this he received considerable criticism from other anarchists who adhered to the principle of nonparticipation in any activities of the state.

Kropotkin came into conflict with Tsarist authorities who condemned him to imprisonment. He escaped and fled from Russia, remaining outside the country until the 1917 Revolution. The Revolution encouraged him, and he returned with great enthusiasm. He strongly opposed the Bolshevik takeover and condemned Lenin and his tactics. Lenin feigned cooperation with Kropotkin and his associates, indicating that he wished to work with them. The friendly attitude of the Bolsheviks lasted only until they had solidified their power, at which time they turned ruthlessly upon all other groups. In 1918 Trotsky ordered troops to fire on anarchist headquarters in Moscow, and the Bolsheviks proceeded to arrest and eliminate the anarchist leaders. Although Kropotkin escaped arrest because of his great prestige and support, he died in disillusionment within a few years.

CRITICISMS OF ANARCHISM

Anarchosyndicalism is a movement that attempts to apply anarchist principles to industrial society. Its key principle is worker
control of industry, with a national economy based upon a federation of industrial associations. The anarchosyndicalist goal is
markedly similar to the state of communism that Marx envisioned
following the withering away of the state, and is also much like
Bellamy's fictional industrial democracy in his socialistic utopian
novel *Looking Backward.* The movement was strong in France and
the United States in the early years of the twentieth century,
reaching its peak in France in the years just before World War I
and in the United States from around 1915 to the middle 1920s.

Initially anarchosyndicalism grew from the French trade union
movement, and its most prominent French exponent was Georges
Sorel (1847–1941). Sorel, like other anarchists, rejected the state
and all its agents, including political parties and legislatures. He
accepted unions as the agents of revolutionary change. In his 1906
Reflections on Violence, he identified what he believed would be the
inspiration for the revolution. Reason, he argued, would be inadequate to inspire workers to make the struggle that would be
required to achieve their full potential. A "great myth" that would
transcend reason would be necessary.

The myth that presumably would cause workers to throw off
the shackles of their background and conditioning would be the
myth of the general strike. Unions would be the agents of direct
action and would call the strike. Virtually all work would cease,
thus bringing down the state. It is irrelevant whether the strike
truly is general. The important point is that the workers must
believe that it will be, and that it will be effective. Sorel does not
pretend that the myth is a description of reality, rather that it is a
reflection of worker determination to act.

Following the direct action of the workers through their unions,
the state would collapse or wither away. The unions then would
proceed to take charge and become the managers. They would be
organized into loose federations, which would perform the few
administrative tasks that would remain. There would be no need
for a political process, inasmuch as the new society would be one
in which there would be little ground for disagreement.

In America a similar but independent anarchosyndicalist
movement emerged at roughly the same time as that in France.

This was the IWW, the Industrial Workers of the World. American unions at the time tended to be limited to the more skilled workers, and the IWW was founded in 1908 in an effort to encourage industrial as opposed to craft unions; that is, one union to represent an entire industry, instead of a separate union for each category of worker. IWW members frequently were those whom the established unions would not accept.

The IWW was dedicated to the use of the strike as a political weapon, a weapon to revolutionize society. The established unions tended to be quite conservative in their approach, viewing strikes merely as tools to achieve particular goals in the workplace. The IWW, or the "Wobblies," advocated the use of the general strike, as did their French counterparts, and hoped to achieve "one big union" that ultimately could replace the state. The union then would be the social, political, and economic organization and would channel the decisions of the workers into administrative action insofar as any was required.

The anarchosyndicalist unions tended to stress absolute equality for their members. They also spurned any kind of bureaucratic organization. This considerably lessened their efficiency, which placed them at a disadvantage in competition with other unions. As the movement dwindled, some modern anarchist groups occasionally have continued to espouse anarchosyndicalist principles. Often, however, they now view unions as too entwined with management and with the state and its institutions to serve as any kind of revolutionary vehicle. Those who take such a position are likely to oppose unionism as being in the long run detrimental to the workers.

CHRISTIAN ANARCHISM

Many Christian thinkers throughout the ages have taken an anarchist position regarding the state and participation in its affairs. This may result from an attempt to avoid the things of this world, or it may stem from a belief that certain institutions are corrupt. The great Russian novelist Count Leo Tolstoy (1828–1910) is somewhat representative of this latter group.

Following his conversion to a private and intellectual form of Christianity based entirely on the ethics of Jesus, Tolstoy renounced his property, adopted the dress of a peasant, and rejected the state. His studies convinced him that property ownership institutionalized selfishness and injustice and that the state was the creation of force and was the embodiment of evil in the world. He said that organized government was more dangerous to the human personality than robbers could be. He denounced the Church, because of its suppression of reason, and the legal system—especially the laws governing property. He considered both to be agents of injustice.

Tolstoy's immense prestige makes his arguments especially important, particularly his commitment to pacifism, which he inferred from the command of Jesus to "resist not evil." He was not a political activist and in fact did not call himself an anarchist. As a result, he led no movement, but he had an enormous effect on world literature and was a major influence upon Mohandas Gandhi in his campaign for Indian independence.

INDIVIDUALIST ANARCHISM

Individualist anarchism is considerably different from communist anarchism or anarchosyndicalism, which are collectivist, or from Christian anarchism, which is based on ethical thought. Most forms of anarchism, because of their goal of eliminating injustice and economic exploitation, fit into the extreme left of the political spectrum. Individualist anarchism may be at the opposite extreme. Although it certainly is possible for individualist anarchists to share the goals of collectivist anarchists, in most cases they do not. In fact, in many instances individual anarchism fits into the extreme right, with the primary concerns involving power and ego. It is this kind of right-wing individualism that is the most prevalent form of anarchism apparent today.

Because liberalism introduced individualism to the Western world, it is no doubt true that it influenced individualist anarchism. One could easily interpret the individualist and anti-statist arguments in John Locke's writings as but one step removed. William Godwin quoted Locke approvingly while setting forth his anarchist views but departed from Locke in not accepting the Lockean emphasis upon individual rights and the social contract. He found the utilitarian approach to be more congenial and incorporated the principle of utility into his anarchist ideology.

Godwin assumed that the state would vanish when human beings became enlightened; that is, when each person proceeded honestly and forthrightly to pursue virtue and fulfill duty. What was best for each, interpreted from an enlightened viewpoint, would be best for all. Each person had a right to possess what was necessary and would agree to take no more. Godwin believed in an absolute standard of right that each person of good will would accept. All that would be required would be to develop the correct understanding. It was important that the enlightened person be completely free to act in pursuing the useful, limited only by justice. To this end, no person should be bound, even by a promise. A promise could result in an unacceptable restriction upon one's ability to act to achieve what is right.

Godwin's son-in-law was the noted poet Percy Bysshe Shelley (1792–1822). Shelley's poetic themes often reflect Godwin's influence. In dealing with political subjects, he frequently praised the lone person who triumphs despite overwhelming odds, and he wrote of the weakness of government when faced by determined and enlightened individuals.

Individualist anarchy, which thus began with a concern for achieving the common good through individual action that would benefit each person separately, took a turn to the right following Godwin and Shelley. The work of Max Stirner (1806–1856) began the shift. Stirner (real name Johann Kaspar Schmidt) published little and accomplished little that attracted attention until after his death. His 1843 book *The Ego and His Own* became well known only near the end of the century when anarchism had become associated with violent acts.

Stirner carried individualism to its most extreme, arguing that the only obligation that existed was to oneself. The ego recognized nothing above itself, and morality existed only in doing what one chose to do. The only authority was one's own will. If one chose to be sociable or to give love, it was only because it was pleasing to do so; nothing else could be a justification for anything. The contrast between Stirner's work and his life is remarkable. He was a teacher in a Berlin girls' school and evidently was quite meek and retiring.

The individualist anarchist position in the United States is well represented by Benjamin R. Tucker (1854–1939). Tucker also wrote that the only consideration was one's own pleasure, but he allowed for contracts to be the basis of some sort of society. Stirner had rejected all forms of society, and his work was considerably more violent in its implications than was Tucker's. In permitting contracts, Tucker did not accept Godwin's rejection of promises, nor did he agree with Godwin regarding property ownership. One could own as much property as his power enabled him to seize and keep. In repudiating the state, he of course did not turn to the state to protect property.

It was the attitude toward the state as much as anything else that distinguished individualist anarchists from the early liberals to whom they owed their individualism. The liberals, whatever their anti-statist inclinations may have been, accepted the state as the protector of contracts and property. Anarchists all rejected the state completely, and some, such as Godwin and Stirner, even rejected the idea of contract.

It is interesting to note that, despite their differences, liberalism and individualist anarchism developed in the same direction in the nineteenth century. Each evolved to accept at least a kind of social Darwinism. In both cases, the result was to convert an essentially humanitarian ideology into one of selfishness. In the case of liberalism, the conversion of an ideology of individual rights into one sanctioning exploitation persists, but it is no longer under the name of liberalism. It has become the right wing of what now is called American conservatism. For many of the individualist anarchists, the change has also persisted.

The Libertarian Party in the United States since the 1960s has seen considerable growth, although it remains quite small. The Libertarians reject government regulation in social matters and view today's conservatives as repressive. They also reject governmental regulation of things economic and on that account view today's liberals as repressive. In other words, the Libertarians tend to agree more nearly with today's liberals on matters of social freedom and with today's conservatives regarding freedom from economic regulation. Although they rarely accept the name "anarchist," the Libertarians clearly are in the tradition of individualist anarchism, even though they do not totally reject the state.

Robert Nozick as much as any current writer represents a capitalist form of individualist anarchism.[1] His *Anarchy, State and*

---

[1] Robert Nozick, *Anarchy, State and Utopia* (New York: Basic Books, 1974).

Utopia purported to support individual rights and to view the state as the greatest threat to those rights. His definition of rights, however, was limited almost entirely to property rights. Nozick recognized that the elimination of the state would have been fatal to property rights, so he provided for a minimal state, although he gave the impression that he would have preferred it to be absent had that been feasible. He would have confined the function of the state to very little more than the protection of property. Among the many who criticized Nozick's work as being destructive of the very liberty that he claimed to uphold, George Kateb's points are telling.[2] Kateb said that Nozick's "night watchman state," or minimal state, could become hugely repressive if the protection of property appeared to warrant the creation of an enormous mechanism that would oppress those whom it deemed a threat.

The most extreme of the individualist anarchist capitalists display social Darwinism in an intense form hardly seen since the period around the turn of the century. Some of these are in the Libertarian Party, some not. One such group has chosen Colorado Springs as a base of operation. Their opposition to socialism—echoing Spencer and Sumner—is that it assists the "unfit" to survive. They prefer a state so limited as to perform no function other than to preserve capitalism. Of course they reject public schooling. Even outside of anarchist circles, opposition to public education is becoming increasingly prevalent as a result of the growth of private and church-related schools, and the aggressive actions of certain religious groups. When the anarchist groups reject public schools, it therefore is less startling than it would have been throughout nearly the entire history of the United States until rather recently. What remains startling is their rejection even of public police and military forces. "If you want to protect your property, hire a guard force, the public has no responsibility to do so" is their attitude. If people can afford protection, they can have it; if not they do not deserve it. This version of individualist anarchism fits well into the category of right-wing elitist ideologies, but I include it here because of its relation to anarchism.

---

[2] George Kateb, "The Night Watchman State," *The American Scholar*, 45, no. 1 (Winter 1975–1976), pp. 816–26. See also Douglas Rae's critical review in *The American Political Science Review*, 70 (December 1976), pp. 1289–91.

CRITICISMS OF ANARCHISM

There have been numerous criticisms of anarchism, among which those by two Britishers, the noted playwright George Bernard Shaw (1856–1950) and the equally noted philosopher Bertrand Russell (1872–1970) stand out. Shaw at one time had written in favor of anarchism but changed his opinion as he became more committed to Fabian socialism. In the article "The Impossibilities of Anarchism" published for the Fabian Society as "Fabian Tract 45" in 1893, Shaw dealt first with individualist anarchism, answering Benjamin Tucker on economic grounds. He pointed out that the effort required to perform a task depended upon circumstance; a farmer, for example, could more easily grow a bushel of wheat on good land than on poor, and a bridge owner could accumulate money more easily through tolls if the bridge were in a well travelled spot than elsewhere. Therefore, Tucker's acceptance of the labor theory of value was flawed. He proceeded to dispute the views of communist anarchists by saying that there could be no incentive without compulsion and went on to contrast both forms unfavorably with social democracy.

Bertrand Russell argued with the anarchists that it is not natural for most persons to respect the liberty of others; quite the contrary. Because of this, there would have be some laws, at least, to prevent violence and theft and some enforcement mechanism. He contended that it would be unacceptable to permit private force to develop for such purposes, since it could be used for ill as well as for good. There also would continue to be disagreements under anarchism and a need for dispute settlement. For these and other reasons, he challenged the contention of the anarchists that no state is necessary.[3]

"POLITICAL" ANARCHISM

The common thread among schools of anarchist thought is the rejection of the political process. Many utopian socialists share this characteristic with the anarchists, assuming that while there

---

[3] Bertrand Russell, *Proposed Roads to Freedom: Socialism, Anarchism, and Syndicalism* (London: George Allen and Unwin Ltd., 1919), passim.

will be a state, it will function under the direction of experts or technicians rather than politicians. Politics causes problems, and utopians wish to do away with problems. The anarchists join with them in seeking a problem-free world.

Certainly there are some anti-statist elements inherent in the basis of liberalism, and it is these elements that have encouraged at least a measure of compatibility between liberalism and some types of anarchism. Some thinkers, however, go beyond liberalism and have adopted an approach that is largely that of anarchism, but they do not go so far as to reject the political process or the state. These persons may well deserve the title "anarchist," except that their desire to be practical leads them to reject anarchism's more radical thrust. In order to distinguish them from other anarchists, yet to keep them in the category where they belong, they may be termed "political anarchists."

Assuming the validity of such a category, those who pushed the boundaries of liberalism to their limits might be included. One such figure was among the most radical of the American revolutionaries, Thomas Paine (1737–1809). Paine was not representative of the political thought of the Revolution, nor was he influential in shaping the government that followed. His influence was largely ideological in that he, probably more than any other single person, inspired the revolutionaries to act. His *Common Sense* electrified American opinion, but his radicalism was out of tune with the more moderate spirit of most of his adopted country's citizens, and his influence dwindled sharply. Ultimately, in fact, the American generation to which he had been so committed rejected and largely forgot him.

Paine disputed the prevailing arguments that praised the British system even while they advocated independence. He took the opposite view regarding British government and said that there could be no acceptable justification for hereditary rule. He did not go so far as to accept the anarchist argument that there should be no state and no government, but he removed any mystic trappings surrounding them.

Despite granting that government was necessary, he believed it to be an evil; one that was made necessary only by human nature. As a good Lockean liberal, he accepted the notion of a social contract, but the contract bound only individuals, not citizens and government. Society was natural, but government was

THOMAS PAINE

Some writers have so confounded society with government, as to leave little or no distinction between them; whereas they are not only different, but have different origins. Society is produced by our wants, and government by our wickedness; the former promotes our happiness *positively* by uniting our affections, the latter *negatively* by restraining our vices. The one encourages intercourse, the other creates distinctions. The first is a patron, the last a punisher.

Society in every state is a blessing, but government, even in its best state, is but a necessary evil; in its worst state an intolerable one: for when we suffer, or are exposed to the same miseries *by a government*, which we might expect in a country *without government*, our calamity is heightened by reflecting that we furnish the means by which we suffer. Government, like dress, is the badge of lost innocence.

From *Common Sense* (1776)

artificial. He had no question as to the nature of the best government; it was the one that governed least.

Paine was an uncompromising individualist, and this is the source of much of his radicalism. He had difficulty accepting political authority because of his fervent belief that no person had the right to tell another what to do. One should act on the basis of reason, not authority. If the government issues an order, one should obey not because of the authority of the government, but because reason dictated that it was right to do so. The citizen has no obligation to obey an order that is not reasonable. The one to decide is the citizen, based upon reasoned conscience.

Paine is in keeping with the bulk of liberals, socialists, and anarchists in his belief in the potential of spontaneous direct action by the people. This is a counterpart of his attitude regarding government which should be no more and no less than what the people at any given time decide that it should be. Paine also shared the attitudes of reform liberals and many socialists and anarchists in his desire to alleviate social ills, such as poverty, disease, ignorance, and discrimination.

Almost alone among those in his generation—and in fact among many who came considerably later—he argued for women's rights, pointing out that it was not biology that repressed women, it was laws and public opinion. Equality to Paine meant equality for all. He was far in advance of his time in his social thinking, suggesting what we now call social security nearly a century before any country adopted it and a century and a half before the United States did. He also advocated free public education. Paine even suggested that there be a progressive tax upon income from estates and that inheritances be confiscated in order to provide a grant to all citizens reaching the age of twenty-one so that they all might have a sound economic start in life. Most of Paine's social proposals are to be found in *Agrarian Justice* and his major political ideas in *The Rights of Man* and the interesting series of papers, *The Crisis.*

Clearly, Paine was not an anarchist in the usual sense of the term. Equally clearly, however, he was pushing the boundaries of liberalism in somewhat the same direction as many anarchists. The American transcendentalist writer Henry David Thoreau (1817–1862), who pushed liberalism's boundaries even further presents a better case for being considered a "political" anarchist.

Thoreau's political ideas are essentially the same as those of the most prominent of the transcendentalists Ralph Waldo Emerson (1803–1882). The difference was Thoreau's activism. Emerson was a philosopher, while Thoreau converted transcendentalist philosophy into a true political ideology. In order to put his ideas into practice, he withdrew from society for more than two years to live near Walden Pond, where he provided his own food, shelter, and clothing. His intention, he said, was "to live deliberately." This experience led to his masterpiece *Walden.*

Thoreau, in common with most transcendentalists, believed that institutions corrupted human beings. Beyond that, he rejected the Puritan ethic and argued that work itself was corrupting. Work was necessary, of course, but it was a necessary evil. There was nothing enobling about it. Human beings should live, not work, except insofar as work was essential. The real duty was to be true to one's own conscience, not to surrender to authority, governmental or otherwise, not to work for its own sake, and not to impose one's own ideas upon others.

Thoreau's most important fully political work is his essay "Resistance to Civil Government," usually called "Civil Disobedience." Rather than advocating the immediate elimination of government, he outlined ways in which citizens may resist government when necessary; that is, when its dictates do not conform to conscience. The citizen has not only the right to resist when government is wrong, but the duty to do so, at least passively. Nonviolent noncooperation, he believed, could bring a government down. If citizens refused to carry out immoral orders, no government could enforce its dictates. Because the State of Massachusetts sent troops to fight in the Mexican War and because he believed that the War was an effort to extend the immoral system of slavery, Thoreau refused to pay his tax and went to jail (from which, after one night, Emerson had him released).

Thoreau argued that government was an expedient only. When it serves its purpose, well and good. When it does not, it should not exist. He viewed the individual conscience as the only true government and as possessing the only true authority. In this manner, he pushed the theory of consent to its most extreme. It applied not only to the people collectively, but to each person. Still, he admitted that no person could hope to eradicate every wrong and that there was no obligation to do so. Anyone might properly have other matters to attend to. Each person, though, did have an obligation not to be an agent of injustice to others. This obligation might require one to withdraw support from a policy, actively oppose it, or even oppose the entire government.

Thoreau wrote that all machines had their friction and that it would not be reasonable to expect government to be perfect. There came times though, when the friction grew to be more important than the machine. When government reached that condition, it was time to smash it. He believed that a minority could prevail if it used the proper tactics. During the Vietnam War, many draft resisters adopted Thoreau's approach and refused to register for the draft or to report for induction. There were so many of these on the West Coast that they, as he would have described it, "clogged the system" and rendered it almost ineffective. Ultimately, only in cases where the protesters called attention to themselves or in some way attracted publicity were they prosecuted. There were simply too many for the government to act, too many for the courts to handle, and too many for jails to hold.

HENRY DAVID THOREAU

. . . Can there not be a government in which majorities do not virtually decide right and wrong, but conscience?

It is not a man's duty, as a matter of course, to devote himself to the eradication of any, even the most enormous wrong; he may still properly have other concerns to engage him; but it is his duty, at least, to wash his hands of it, and, if he gives it no thought longer, not to give it practically his support. . . .

If the injustice is part of the necessary friction of the machine of government, let it go, let it go; perchance it will wear smooth,—certainly the machine will wear out. If the injustice has a spring, or a pulley, or a rope, or a crack, exclusively for itself, then perhaps you may consider whether the remedy will not be worse than the evil; but if it is of such a nature that it requires you to be the agent of injustice to another, then, I say, break the law. Let your life be a counter friction to stop the machine. . . .

I do not wish to quarrel with any man or nation. I do not wish to split hairs, to make fine distinctions, or set myself up as better than my neighbors. I seek rather, I may say, even an excuse for conforming to the laws of the land. I am but too ready to conform to them. . . .

However, the government does not concern me much, and I shall bestow the fewest possible thoughts on it.

From "On Resistance to Civil Government" (1848)
(Generally published as "Civil Disobedience")

Had the protest strategy been nationwide, conscription could not have operated.

In general, Thoreau opposed violence, and he certainly did not advocate violent revolution against the state (although he did write in favor of John Brown's violent antislavery raid on the U.S. Arsenal at Harper's Ferry). He did go beyond Paine's principle that the government is best which governs least to say "that government is best which governs not at all." He believed that government was unnecessary if human beings simply followed the dictates of their moral sentiments and their consciences. It was not necessarily wrong, however, for government to exist, nor to cooperate with it. It could be an agent of good. In many ways, his position was that the state and the government were irrelevant. They need not exist; when they did, they had no organic nature of their own and were nothing more than the people who constituted them. They were acceptable so long as they did not interfere with the demands of conscience.

During his lifetime Thoreau was not especially well known, but in an indirect manner he has had enormous influence in world affairs. Mohandas Gandhi, the prime mover in the nonviolent campaign of noncooperation that eventually brought independence to India, Pakistan, and Bangladesh, had read Thoreau and adopted much of his ideology. The prime mover of the American civil rights movement of the 1950s and 1960s was Dr. Martin Luther King, Jr. He had read Gandhi and through his writings was introduced to Thoreau's ideology. King's tactics became those that Thoreau had advocated a century previously. Thus, Thoreau directly affected events in India, and indirectly, by way of Asia, affected the civil rights movement in the United States.

Thoreau did not call directly for the government's elimination. He said that he asked not that there be at once no government but that there be a better government. He also stressed that cooperation is desirable. Because of this, some writers have declared that he was not truly an anarchist. Of course, many anarchists believe in cooperation, so the conclusion is wrong on that account. But inherent in the definition of anarchism is the commitment to eradicating state and government. How can Thoreau's beliefs on this question constitute anarchism? Here, the matter is less clear. Anarchists believe that there should be no government, but nonanarchists believe that state and government are essential. There is a middle ground that this dichotomy does not cover, and Thoreau occupied that middle ground. He did not accept the necessity of government but did not argue as a result that it must not exist. He was an anarchist, but a "political" anarchist.

Robert Paul Wolff has argued similarly for what I call political anarchism. Wolff, as a philosopher, attempted to reconcile the authority of the state with the integrity and autonomy of the individual, and he failed. He said that "it is out of the question to give up the commitment to moral autonomy," and that it appeared as if he must "embrace the doctrine of anarchism and categorically deny *any* claim to legitimate authority by one man over another."[4]

Nevertheless, Wolff was not comfortable with the conclusion that he must abandon the quest for some kind of collective authority, and wrote that he was

> . . . unwilling to accept as final the negative results of our search for a political order which harmonizes authority and autonomy. The state is a social institution, and therefore no more than the totality of the beliefs, expectations, habits, and interacting roles of its members and subjects. When rational men, in full knowledge of the proximate and distant consequences of their actions, determine to set private interest aside and pursue the general good, it *must* be possible for them to create a form of association which accomplishes that end without depriving some of them of their moral autonomy. The state, in contrast to nature, cannot be ineradicably *other*.[5]

Wolff also suggested that, pending the reconciliation of the authority of the state with personal autonomy, human beings may choose to subject themselves to whatever form of government appears at the moment to be best, whether democratic or not. This would appear to be a perfect example of a kind of political anarchism.

It also relates to the ideas of Walt Anderson, who has applied some principles of Abraham H. Maslow's psychological theories to politics in a way that suggests political anarchism. Maslow described persons with the soundest mental health as "self-actualizing" and argued that they may transcend themselves and their cultures to become less oriented to their local groups and more to their species. Anderson pointed out that this idea could undermine traditional notions of authority and political obligation.[6] The attitude of such citizens recalls that of Thoreau regarding the state; it is an attitude of tolerance only. The self-actualizing citizen may well act in a completely conventional manner, but through choice alone.

[4] Robert Paul Wolff, *In Defense of Anarchism* (New York: Harper Torchbooks, 1970), pp. 70–71.
[5] Ibid., p. 78.
[6] Walt Anderson, *Politics and the New Humanism* (Pacific Palisades, California: Goodyear, 1973), p. 39.

The idea that many of a society's strongest and most able members exist within it in a manner different from that of other citizens is profoundly revolutionary. The "self-actualized" choose to accept society's structure and strictures because they have concluded that it is to their benefit, and perhaps that of others, to do so. Should it not be beneficial, they would rebel, reject the government, and, if warranted, reject the state itself. Should they rebel, it would be the result of rational choice, not of pathology, as Freud would assume, or of deprivation as Marxist doctrine would explain it. Depending upon existing conditions, the healthiest citizens might be far from the most likely to become revolutionaries, but they have by far the greatest revolutionary potential.[7]

ANARCHISM IN PERSPECTIVE

Anarchism suffers, at least as much as most political ideologies, from difficulties in definition. Additionally, it is rare for any single ideology to exist at each extreme of the political spectrum, right and left, but varied anarchist beliefs do occupy such divergent positions. Because it has even more versions than most other political ideologies, it is necessary to be especially cautious in attempting to place anarchism in perspective.

Attitude Toward Change

All forms of anarchism reject a conservative emphasis upon tradition and custom. Except possibly for "political anarchism," they are radical in their advocacy of abrupt change, tending to reject as inadequate even calls for moderate change through reform.

Attitude Toward Human Nature

Anarchism, like liberalism, tends to accept human nature as good. This is reflected in its utopian tendency to advocate the elimination of all external limitations or restraints by human institutions upon human conduct. Also like liberalism, however, it has another side. Just as liberalism has its pessimistic strain, dating all the way back to Hobbes, so too are there advocates of

[7] Ibid., pp. 40–45.

anarchism who have a dim view of human nature. Some—though certainly not all—individualist anarchists advocate the removal of institutional restraints to enable the most powerful to dominate others. Their primary concern is not for freedom for its own sake, but for power. They thus substitute social Darwinism for the typical anarchist concern for voluntary cooperation.

Attitude Toward the Potential of Human Reason

In general, systems of anarchist thought incorporate a high regard for human reason. They tend to assume that irrationality causes most human difficulties and to argue that reason, if applied, is adequate to remedy them. Here again, however, individualist anarchists sometimes adopt an irrationalist approach, substituting power or "will" for reason, as do some anarchosyndicalists. The distinction, by and large, is what separates those on the extreme left (Christian anarchists, communist anarchists, "political anarchists," and some individualist anarchists) from those on the extreme right. Anarchosyndicalism in this regard does not fit well into the Left-Right Continuum. It occupies a position on the extreme left in most categorizations, but the acceptance by some anarchosyndicalists such as Sorel of the need for an irrational "great myth" is more characteristic of right-wing ideologies. This is largely a reflection of the inadequacy of the "Left-Right" formulation.

Attitude Toward Human Progress

Most forms of anarchism are highly optimistic regarding the possibility of human progress, assuming that if only corrupting institutions are removed, and reason applied, then progress will follow. The few exceptions to this are some forms of individualist anarchism.

Attitude Toward the Relationship of the Individual to the Community

By definition, anarchism places the individual, rather than the community, at the center of concern. The community has no organic existence and consists of nothing more than the people who compose it. It is rights, rather than duties, that are paramount.

Contrary to common misconception, anarchism does not rule out cooperation or group activity, nor does it inevitably imply rejecting the idea of the good of the whole. Most forms of anarchism, in fact, presuppose highly developed collective activities. They differ from most other political ideologies in their stress on voluntary action and their rejection of coercion, not upon their rejection of the need for collective or public action. Nevertheless, anarchism does emphasize the individual. Most forms of anarchism bear some similarities to liberalism carried to its furthest extreme. There is one point, however, upon which many anarchists differ quite sharply from liberals. There is a strong tendency among anarchists to reject the idea of private property, which liberals consider essential. Some anarchists, of course, do accept it, and those on the right join liberals in emphasizing private property as a fundamental human right.

ANARCHISM TODAY

In the modern world the traditional forms of anarchism have little appeal because they appear to be impractical. "Political" anarchism considers practicality and attempts to combine it with the features of anarchism that have been the most attractive. Because of this it may be that political anarchism is the only anarchist ideology that has the potential to continue to attract adherents. Certainly the Libertarian Party in the United States, which has gained some appeal, however minor, is one in which many members could be considered political anarchists.

Right-Wing Elitism

6

*A*s is true of so many twentieth-century political ideologies, those that reflect the elitism of the far Right grew from the social, economic, political, and intellectual ferment of the nineteenth century. It was not until then that racism became sufficiently well developed as a doctrine to be able to become an integral part of some of the elitist ideologies that were soon to emerge. Among the first systematic racist arguments were those of the French writer Count Joseph Arthur de Gobineau (1816–1882). It was he and his followers who applied the term "Aryan" to a "racial" group whom they believed to be superior to others.

The real Aryans were lighter-skinned invaders who, beginning around 1500 B.C., spread from western Asia into India where they subjugated the native Dravidian population, many of whom they drove into the far south of the subcontinent. The term also refers to the speakers of one of several ancient languages belonging to a related linguistic grouping, which included the invaders of India. These are the only historically accurate uses of the word. The Aryans were not Gobineau's hypothetical "master race" nor, despite Nazi use of a version of the swastika as one of their symbols, were they related to Hitler's subsequent use of the term,

159

which was in the tradition of Gobineau, not that of history or science.

Gobineau sought to explain the decline of civilizations and concluded that it resulted from racial degeneration. His classification of races into a hierarchy of superior and inferior had immediate influence in the United States where Southerners were searching for explanations to justify slavery. One explanation was racial inferiority, and many in the South made efforts to demonstrate it "scientifically." A professor of anatomy, Dr. Josiah C. Nott, for example, had published studies attempting to prove that blacks were biologically inferior. He collaborated with others to edit and distribute an English translation of Gobineau's *The Moral and Intellectual Diversity of Races*. Many other Southerners, such as George Fitzhugh, seized upon Gobineau's ideas and enlarged upon them to argue that the South was composed of "cavalier" stock that was racially superior to the descendents of the Puritans, the "Yankees."

Another influential racist writer of the nineteenth century was Houston Stewart Chamberlain (1855–1927), a German with a British background who was the son-in-law of the composer Richard Wagner (1813–1883). His 1899 book *Foundations of the Nineteenth Century* differed in detail from Gobineau's work, but it also stressed racial distinctions and asserted the superiority of Nordics, or Teutons. He added anti-Semitism to his racism, concluding that Jews were a "race" and that there would be an inevitable struggle between them and the Teutons for control. This emphasis very likely resulted from Chamberlain's association with Wagner, who was noted for his anti-Semitism.

One could argue at length whether such works influenced developments or reflected them. In all probability they did both. The late nineteenth-century embracing of social Darwinism frequently was overtly racist, and many countries began to incorporate racist doctrines into their legislation. Australia barred the immigration of nonwhites, and changed its policy only rather recently. The United States had long had laws, especially in the South, that greatly oppressed blacks, even free blacks. Such Southern laws did not die out until the 1960s. By the late nineteenth century, American legislation came to discriminate against Orientals as well and banned them from becoming residents. Some states also passed legislation denying them the right to own property. In 1924 the Immigration Act specifically made race the basis of immigration policy. Many American jurisdictions forbade marriage between persons of different races until well past the middle of the twentieth century. Similar laws persisted in the Republic of South Africa until 1985. So powerful did the idea of racism become that even today some American writers, such as the educational psychologist Arthur Jensen and the engineer William Shockley, continue to attempt to demonstrate the genetic inferiority in intelligence of blacks.

Probably even more influential than the development of racism was another creation of the nineteenth century: nationalism (see Chapter 9). By the beginning of the century, among the major European powers only Germany and Italy had yet to be consolidated into nation-states, the model for which emerged from the French Revolution. The increase in the power of kings at the expense of feudal lords had been a major step toward the nation-state, and the transfer of sovereignty from king to nation, as symbolized by the Revolution, completed the transition. It was no accident that it was in post-revolutionary France that national conscription developed. It was a reflection of the new conception of the nation as an organic whole, with every citizen under obligation to defend it and work for national goals.

The work of G.W.F. Hegel presents the state as organic, something that transcends the citizens that comprise it, and Hegel made the nation-state the foundation of his philosophy of history. In this way his enormous influence on German thought did contribute to the development of nationalism and to the use of war as an instrument of national policy. But Hegel was a constitutionalist and in no way was he a racist. To interpret his thought as supporting in any direct way the development of fascism or national socialism as ideologies, as many writers have attempted to do, is questionable.[1] The fact remains, however, that Hegel did contribute to the development of some of the practices and institutions that came to serve as fundamental to a variety of regimes, some of which he likely would have opposed strongly.

[1] See, for example, William McGovern, *From Luther to Hitler* (New York: Houghton Mifflin, 1941) and L.T. Hobhouse, *The Metaphysical Theory of the State* (New York: Barnes & Noble, 1960).

It is interesting that nationalism was compatible with virtually any culture or any political system. It seemed to supersede other considerations. However it was applied in a given situation, it always had certain features in common. Above all, it was a rejection not only of the medieval idea of universalism, but of any sort of worldwide brotherhood.

Along with nationalism came its counterpart, the rationalization of violence; at times it became even the idealization of violence (see Chapter 10). This was explicit in many anarchist writings and in much of Marxism, especially as expanded by Lenin, Trotsky, Stalin, and Mao. It was less explicit, but still present, in Western democracies. All nation-states began to build up large military forces and to make the military the foundation of national policy. By the middle of the twentieth century, they had come to accept them as regular parts of national existence and often even of daily life.

No examination of nineteenth-century influences on ideologies of the twentieth century would be complete without consideration of the ideas of the German philosopher Friedrich Nietzsche (1844–1900). Nietzsche wrote of the "will to power" that would develop a "superman" (Übermensch) who had thrown off Judeo-Christian morality and was "beyond good and evil." He rejected the values of democracy, liberalism, and socialism. Their "herd mentality" established the values of slavery, he believed. Nietzsche did take care to point out that he wrote not for ordinary men whom he did not wish to lead away from their moral codes but for a race that did not yet exist.

Nietzsche believed that the Jews had at one time been powerful and self-confident, bold and self-reliant, but that they had degenerated, and that they had contributed their decadent legacy to Christianity, which institutionalized weakness in the West. To this large measure of anti-Semitism, Nietzsche added a belief that Christianity had feminized, or demasculinized, the Western world, destroying values and imposing upon it a slave mentality.

In breaking with centuries of Western thought, Nietzsche rejected the value of reason. It was will and its power alone that could triumph. He asserted that faith in reason and rationality resulted in nihilism.[2] His superman would delight in risk and

---

[2]Friedrich Nietzsche, *The Will to Power* (New York: Random House, 1967), p. 13.

FRIEDRICH NIETZSCHE

. . . [T]he welding of a hitherto unchecked and shapeless populace into a firm form was not only instituted by an act of violence but also carried to its conclusion by nothing but acts of violence . . . the oldest "state" thus appeared as a fearful tyranny, as an oppressive and remorseless machine. . . .

I employed the word "state": it is obvious what is meant—some pack of blond beasts of prey, a conqueror and master race which, organized for war and with the ability to organize, unhesitatingly lays its terrible claws upon a populace perhaps tremendously superior in numbers but still formless and nomad. That is after all how the "state" began on earth: I think that sentimentalism which would have it begin with a "contract" has been disposed of. He who can command, he who is by nature "master," he who is violent in act and bearing—what has he to do with contracts! One does not reckon with such natures; they come like fate, without reason, consideration, or pretext; . . . their work is an instinctive creation and imposition of forms; they are the most involuntary, unconscious artists there are—wherever they appear something new soon arises, a ruling structure that *lives*, in which parts and functions are delimited and coordinated, in which nothing whatever finds a place that has not first been assigned a "meaning" in relation to the whole. They do not know what guilt, responsibility, or consideration are, these organizers. . . .

From *On the Genealogy of Morals* (1877)

danger, and combat would have a redemptive and cleansing effect. Peace and the elimination of violence were reflections of the triumph of weakness and the herd instinct. The new supercaste would be "blond beasts of prey" who would devour the weak and strengthen humanity.[3] Nietzsche wrote that human beings created themselves and had to develop myths and "horizons" to infuse their lives.[4] His stress on struggle, heroism, violent combat against great odds, and irrationalism came to characterize much twentieth-century ideology of the extreme Right.

[3] Ibid., passim.
[4] Nietzsche, *The Use and Abuse of History*, 2nd (revised) ed. (New York: The Liberal Arts Press, Inc., 1957).

Also in sharp contrast to centuries of thought was the emergence of pragmatism. Pragmatism was a philosophy, the most noted exponent of which was the American philosopher, physician, and psychologist William James (1842–1910). In 1907 James set forth the basic principles in _Pragmatism_, which included a revolutionary approach to the nature of truth. Because it identified the truth of an idea with its effect, rather than with conformity to an absolute standard, pragmatism made truth relative and even subject to change.[5] Few twentieth-century political ideologies are completely free from pragmatism's influence, if only in regard to breaking with the standards of the past.

FASCISM

As the memories of the Second World War have faded, there are those who have come to use the word "fascist" to mean someone whose policies they dislike, or sometimes simply to mean "authoritarian." Although authoritarianism is certainly a feature of all fascist regimes, fascism is something considerably more than mere authoritarianism. Fascism is an explicit and well-developed political ideology that grew from the thought and practice of Benito Mussolini (1883–1945), the founder in 1919 of Italian fascism. The word came from the Latin _fasces_, which was a bundle of rods bound around an ax that had been a symbol of authority for officials in ancient Rome.

Mussolini grew up as a socialist and became editor of a socialist journal in Italy, _Avanti_. He had spent time in Switzerland where he studied under the Italian mathematician, economist, and sociologist Vilfredo Pareto (1848–1923). Pareto was an elitist theorist who was no Fascist; in fact he tended to be a Manchester, laissez-faire liberal who admitted to a bias toward liberty.[6] Nevertheless, he was anti-democratic, and his thought contributed in this and other ways to fascist ideology.

Pareto saw the Italian elites as degenerate "foxes" who would be eaten by new "lions." Pareto's system would be cemented by force and would be dominated by elites who did not shy away

---

[5] William James, _Pragmatism_ (New York: Meridian Books, 1955).
[6] James H. Meisel, ed., _Pareto and Mosca_ (Englewood Cliffs, N.J.: Prentice–Hall, 1965), pp. 10–11.

BENITO MUSSOLINI

Fascism combats the whole complex system of democratic ideology, and repudiates it, whether in its theoretical premises or in its practical application. Fascism denies that the majority, by the simple fact that it is a majority, can direct human society . . . and it affirms the immutable, beneficial, and fruitful inequality of mankind. . . . Fascism has taken up an attitude of complete opposition to the doctrines of Liberalism, both in the political field and the field of economics. The foundation of Fascism is the conception of the State, its character, its duty, and its aim. Fascism conceives of the State as an absolute, in comparison with which all individuals or groups are relative, only to be conceived of in their relation to the State. The conception of the Liberal State is not that of a directing force, guiding the play and development, both material and spiritual, of a collective body, but merely a force limited to the function of recording results; on the other hand, the Fascist State is itself conscious, and has itself a will and a personality. . . .

From *The Political and Social Doctrine of Fascism* (1932)

from the use of violence, though he did not seem to glorify violence in the manner of Nietzsche. To Pareto, human affairs tended to be under the dominance of irrationality, and human beings were subject to "residues"—that is unchanging or very slowly changing attitudes—and "derivations"—or rationalizations and myths. Mussolini was highly impressed by Pareto's theories.[7]

Mussolini broke with the socialists over the question of Italian entry into World War I, which the socialists opposed. After the war he returned to form an organization in 1919 to oppose the Left, whom he considered traitors, and to protect returning veterans. This was the *Fasci di Combattimento*, which in 1921 became the Fascist party. By that time, groups of Fascists had been violently attacking and destroying republican, communist, and socialist groups throughout Italy. Mussolini had already come to be known as *Il Duce*, or the leader.

In October of 1922, groups of armed Fascists conducted the famous "March on Rome," which led to the government's resignation. The king named Mussolini as the new prime minister,

[7] Ibid., esp. "Introduction."

and the reign of fascism began. By 1924 Fascists had complete control of the government. In 1929 with the Vatican Accords, Mussolini and Pope Pius XI settled the dispute between Italy and the Vatican over Church lands. Mussolini thus secured the support of the Church and cooperation between Church and state in education. In 1935 Italian troops marched into Ethiopia, thus beginning Mussolini's contribution to what was to become the Second World War.

During this time Mussolini, along with other Italian writers, had been actively developing fascist theory and ideology. Its key points became an exaggerated nationalism, emphasis upon the state, opposition to Marxism, irrationality, a violent social Darwinist struggle, subservience to a leader, and during its later stages, corporativism. It may be helpful to deal with each of these points in some detail.

Nationalism

Nationalism always is a fertile source of symbols that are so essential to political ideology. In the case of Italian fascism, the symbolism was especially strong. Mussolini and the Fascist party constantly stressed the glory of ancient Rome and the role of the Italian Fascist state as the twentieth-century embodiment of that legacy: a new empire. Coupled with this emphasis was pride in the role of Rome as central to the Roman Catholic Church. So intense was fascist nationalism that it has led some scholars to classify it as a special type, which they identify as "integral nationalism."[8] This category would include any nationalism that is particularly comprehensive and militant.

As a consequence, although it is impossible for nationalistic sentiments to be completely free from ethnocentrism, that of Fascists tends to make similar feelings in other movements pale into insignificance by contrast. The extraordinary ethnocentrism that motivated fascism did not necessarily lead to racism and anti-Semitism. These tendencies were generally absent from the Italian Fascist party, although the Fascists began to issue racist and anti-Semitic statements in the late 1930s under pressure from Hitler to conform to Nazi ideology.

[8] Carlton J.H. Hayes, *The Historical Evolution of Modern Nationalism* (New York: Macmillan, 1931).

Statism

In Fascist ideology the state was all-important. No system of thought could place less emphasis upon the individual; fascism was the antithesis of liberalism. The source of Mussolini's greatest opposition to liberalism was that liberal ideology provided the individual with a life outside the reach of the state. According to fascism, however, the individual could find identity only as a part of the state and had no independent existence. It was the state, not the individual, that had significance. This led directly to fascist theories of totalitarianism. The nation was to be all-encompassing, and no conception of rights against the nation or the state existed, not even the right to independence of thought.

One should note, however, that the Italian Fascist state was never totalitarian. Whatever the wishes of Mussolini and the Fascists, totalitarianism in Italy was essentially a matter of rhetoric. Fascist ideology was certainly totalitarian, but the practice did not live up to the ideal nor, despite the harshness of the Fascists, were there true attempts to achieve it.

Or course, fascism conceived of the state as organic, that is, as having an existence above and beyond those who comprise it. So important was the state in fascist ideology that it transcended even nationalism. It was the state that organized human experience and created the nation. Nationality was therefore a creation of the state, rather than the reverse. In the absence of the state there would be nothing except isolated individuals. Mussolini's official expression of the ideology, "The Doctrine of Fascism" argues that the state goes beyond legal existence. It has spiritual authority as the highest expression of humanity.[9] The fascist philosopher Giovanni Gentile (1875–1944), in terms reminiscent of Rousseau, maintained that the state and the individual were one, and that there could be no question of conflict of interest between them;[10] their interests were identical.

All groups and associations existed because the state created them, including the Fascist party, which existed to serve the state. What the state created, it could destroy. Even the family, according to fascist ideology, owed its existence to the state. Families as

---

[9]Benito Mussolini, *Fascism: Doctrine and Institutions* (New York: Howard Fertig, 1968), pp. 11–14.
[10]Giovanni Gentile, *The Genesis and Structure of Society* (Urbana: University of Illinois Press, 1960), pp. 121–29.

well as individuals could not exist independently. In keeping with the obligation of all to serve the state, the highest duty of the family was to produce workers and soldiers for its use.

Opposition to Marxism

An attitude of extreme anticommunism characterized fascism and all similar movements. This was much more than an attempt to gain support, although it succeeded in doing that as well; the fascists saw communism as reflecting and exaggerating the weaknesses that they believed were fundamental to democracy. In what many would perceive as one of the great ironies of history, the fascists saw themselves as advocates of a "spiritual" doctrine in contrast to Marxist materialism. Fascists also rejected the Marxist "scientific" approach and had no faith in the ability of human reason.

However Marxism functioned in practice, it had originated as an attempt to alleviate exploitation. Moreover, in theory it was anti-statist and even foresaw a world in which states had withered away. Marxism's fundamental premise was the class struggle. It was intensely internationalist and provided for cooperation along class lines regardless of state or national boundaries. Nothing could be further from the fascist approach, which was devoid of humanitarian sentiment and was completely grounded in the state. Class struggle was anathema to the Fascists, who stressed instead class allegiance in service to the state.

Irrationality

Many ideologies are predominantly irrational and most—perhaps all—are somewhat so. But only fascism and related ideologies raise irrationalism to a virtue and incorporate it as explicitly fundamental. The Fascist trusts only the will, not reason. This does not mean that Fascists reject thought, but that they conceive of thought and action as intimately related and to a large extent view thought as arising from practice, will, and emotion. Those with the will should seize power and formulate ideas later. In fact, fascist ideology evolved in precisely this manner and grew along with developments. Power determines what should be. To the Fascist, might literally makes right. This can be related to pragmatism, in which there are no absolute standards of truth.

In dealing with society, fascism refuses to accept the science and reason that democracy and Marxism attempt to apply. Instead, it adopts the symbols, emotion, myth, and hatred that can energize the will to power. In this, and other ways as well, fascism explicitly rejects the values of Christianity, which suppresses the individual will to power. More broadly, it rejects the essential values of Western civilization. Nietzsche's irrationalism clearly paved the way for many of the fascist views, as did Sorel's insistence upon the necessity for myths to inspire revolution. However direct or indirect their influence may have been, it is relevant.

In many ways, fascism not only rejects but is a perversion of Western values. It is possible to argue that it adopts certain features of liberalism and conservatism in ways destructive to both and in combinations found in no other ideology. Despite rejecting liberal individualism, for example, the fascist emphasis is on an individual will to power; despite rejecting conservative reverence for tradition and moderation, the Fascist accepts the organic view of the state and the emphasis upon the whole. The result is anything but liberal or conservative.

Violent Social Darwinism

Neither social Darwinism nor violence is unique to fascism. Fascism, however, incorporates a violent struggle for existence, and dominance is also a key component of the ideology. No ideology could do more, not only to justify but actually to glorify both the struggle and the violence. Just as the individual, according to fascism, can find existence only within the state, so can the state and its people achieve the highest form of humanity only through combat. Fascists apply their theories to nationalism and glorify war. They apply them to the defeat of their enemies in coming to power within the state. If they are racist, as with the Nazis, they apply them as well to violence against other races. Fascist ideology attributes to violence a cleansing effect that supposedly eliminates weakness and permits humanity to achieve its highest goals.

The Leadership Principle

Fascists believe not only in a strong leader, but one who has total power. They feel democracy encourages the weak, inhibits all that is capable of attaining glory, and also encourages fragmentation; only the power of the leader can enforce the unity that the strength of the state demands. In a circular fashion, it is this unity that is the source of the leader's power. The leader in theory rules not as a person, but as the embodiment of the state. Because the interests of the people and the state are identical, there can be no conflict.

Corporativism

In developing his "corporate state," Mussolini sought to achieve a middle ground between laissez-faire and its economic cycles on the one hand and bureaucratic nationalized economies on the other. In keeping with fascism's emphasis upon the unity of the state, it sought to achieve harmony between capital and labor through a new form of economic organization: corporativism. This would involve forming organizations composed of both workers and employers in similar industries who would act together through governing councils that in theory represented labor and management equally. Each such organization, or "corporation," would assume control of the relevant section of the economy. The councils jointly would constitute the National Council of Corporations with overall economic control. There are echoes here of the syndicalist theories of George Sorel, although in a vastly different and state-oriented form.

Although corporativism was never fully implemented, there were movements in that direction. In 1939 the state incorporated the National Council of Corporations into a new body, the Council of Fasci and Corporations, which also included two party components. This replaced the remnants of democratically and geographically chosen legislators. In practice, despite the emphasis upon corporativism, all organs, both political and economic, were under the complete domination of Mussolini.

NATIONAL SOCIALISM

As fascism was developing in Italy, similar movements emerged throughout Europe. All of them were related to the general conditions in Europe and elsewhere following the First World War and all reflected specific national situations as well. The most virulent was Germany's national socialism, which in many respects strongly resembled Italian fascism but was not identical. The distinguishing characteristics of national socialism were peculiarly German and unique.

National socialism takes its name from a movement that Adolf Hitler (1889–1945) joined in 1919, the *Nationalsozialistische Deutsche Arbeiterpartei* (NSDAP), or Nazi Party, which means "National Socialist German Workers' Party." Despite the name, and despite Hitler's vague anticapitalist rhetoric, it was by no means a socialist or left-wing party.

In Germany there had been a succession of writers who stressed the superiority of the German people, a strong tradition of discipline and militarism, and a pervasive tradition of romantic myths that exalted feeling, emotion, and Germanic heroism. There also was persistent anti-Semitism. The degree to which such elements of the culture conditioned many Germans to accept national socialism may be debated, but it is clear that they are at least to some extent related to the tendency then in German society to worship untempered power and the society's willingness to accept Hitler's demand for totalitarian discipline and his extremes of irrationalism.

Regardless of these cultural factors, Nazism could not have emerged as such a powerful movement without the great political and economic instability that occurred in Germany in the post-World War I years. Shortly after the formation of the Weimar Republic following the removal of the Kaiser came a ruinous hyperinflation, which wiped out businesses and life savings sometimes literally overnight. Prices went up so rapidly that they actually changed by the hour. Much of the middle class was thoroughly demoralized. After 1924 conditions improved for a few years, but the world-wide depression that followed the 1929 stock market crash in America hit Germany especially hard and shattered much of the confidence that had begun to be reestablished.

This was the situation in which Adolf Hitler began to develop his following and in which his skillful use of German cultural themes began to find a mass audience. Under such conditions, the Nazi party grew rapidly, especially after 1931. One should note that at no time did the Nazis ever receive a majority of the vote in a free election. But Germany, one of the most developed, cultured, and highly educated nations in history, soon came to be Nazi Germany.

Adolf Hitler grew up in Austria on the German border. He was a moody child with a domineering father who scorned his desire to become an artist. He was steeped in German mythology and worshipped the heroes of German history and legend. By the age of fifteen Hitler was orphaned and alone. He struggled to achieve his artistic goals and, while still only in his teens, spent some years in Vienna under conditions of extreme poverty. He did not pass the entrance examinations for the Academy of Art and could not study elsewhere because he had never completed his secondary schooling. What little support he had came from painting postcards and the like and ultimately from charity.

It was during this time of great solitude, despair, and humiliation that he developed the intense hatred that came to be the driving force of his life. He came to despise Marxism and trade unions, and his loathing of Jews, whom he blamed for all of his, and the world's, troubles, was, in his own words, fanatic.[11] Failing in his goal of achieving success in art, he moved to Munich. In 1914 he joined the German army as a fervent German patriot. He rose to the rank of corporal and was wounded in battle. At the war's end, he was in a hospital close to Berlin.

The destruction of the Kaiser's regime brought utter dejection to Hitler, who had viewed imperial Germany as the "Second Reich," the first being the Holy Roman Empire. His deep disillusionment caused him to turn his attention to politics and he channelled his frenzied hatred against all those whom he believed responsible, including Bolsheviks, democrats, socialists, and, above all, Jews. He considered it to be his mission to regenerate the German people in order that they could overthrow the Weimar Republic and create a "Third Reich."

At the time there were numerous radical groups as well as groups of reactionary and embittered former soldiers who perpetuated the "stab in the back" explanation for Germany's defeat. They would gather in various beer halls to complain and to plot. Hitler, still in the army until 1920, served as an undercover informer, infiltrating radical groups and reporting to the army. In 1919 he attended, on assignment, meetings of a radical-sounding

[11] Adolph Hitler, *Mein Kampf* (Boston: Houghton Mifflin, 1962).

group, the German Workers' Party. It was quite different from what he expected. Rather than being leftist, it was bitterly anti-foreign and militantly nationalistic. He found its ideas to be consistent with his and joined the group when invited. According to his membership cards, Hitler was the party's fifty-fifth member and the seventh new member of its executive council.[12] Soon, he was in control.

As a consequence of his party activities, Hitler discovered that he had an electrifying personality. He could bring both men and women under his spell in virtually a hypnotic manner. Individually, or in small groups, many found his charm to be irresistible. But it was before mass audiences that he found his greatest ability: his previously unrecognized oratorical talent. He played upon the people's fears and resentments, appealed to their emotions, promised them greatness, and inspired many to follow without question. Despite his lack of education, his hoarse voice, and his crude manners, he was soon on the way to becoming one of the few truly charismatic political leaders of history.

In devising Nazi ideology, Hitler demonstrated himself to be the equal in skill of any political manipulator who ever lived. Instinctively, he recognized the force of symbols. He adopted the swastika and the straight-armed salute as the signs of the party, which he had re-named the NSDAP. He designed the striking swastika flag—the black crooked cross in a white circle on red—and incorporated the swastika into posters, banners, sashes, and armbands. He made certain that the symbol was widely displayed. He surrounded himself with a group of thugs in brown-shirted uniforms of his own design. These became the "brown shirts," the *Sturmabteilung*, or S.A. These "stormtroopers" became a private army of head breakers who attacked persons and groups deemed to be the enemy. The most violent and cruel of these Nazi enforcers were the elite S.S., the *Schutzstaffel*, Hitler's personal guard, all of whom wore the distinctive black uniform.

In 1923 in the midst of the devastating hyperinflation, Hitler overreached himself. That November, inspired by Mussolini's successful "March on Rome," he led the disastrous "Beer-Hall Putsch." His plan was to seize the government of the German State of Bavaria and thereafter march to Berlin and bring an end

[12]Robert Payne, *The Life and Death of Adolph Hitler* (New York: Praeger, 1973), p. 138.

to the Republic. The Bavarian leaders were meeting in Munich when Hitler marched in, with his troops surrounding the building. He fired a shot into the ceiling and announced that the revolution had begun and that the Republic had fallen. He failed to maintain control, however, and was taken captive.

In 1924 he was tried for treason, found guilty, and sentenced to a light penalty of five years in prison. The court permitted him to expound at length upon his ideology, and he received tremendous publicity. He went to Landsberg Fortress Prison, where he served less than one year before receiving a pardon. While in prison, Hitler set forth in great detail the Nazi ideology; the result was his vitriolic and inflammatory *Mein Kampf* ("my battle," or "my struggle").

The improving economic conditions halted the rapid growth of the Nazi party, and for the few years following Hitler's release from jail, he worked diligently for electoral success, having failed in his attempted coup. The beginning of the depression saved the Nazis and rekindled their appeal. In the elections of 1928 they had won only a few seats in the national legislature, but by 1932 the Nazis had become the largest single party. The elderly President Paul von Hindenburg attempted to secure Nazi participation in a coalition government without giving in to their demands, but eventually he capitulated. On the 30th of January, 1933, he officially named Hitler Chancellor.

Hitler moved quickly to call for new elections to increase his power in the legislature, the Reichstag. His stormtroopers sought to terrorize and destroy opposition groups, and shortly before the elections a fire, which the Nazis blamed on the Communists, consumed the Reichstag Building. Despite the national hysteria, in the March elections the Nazis still did not gain a majority of seats. This did not halt Hitler's quest for absolute power. He made bargains with various Catholic and nationalist groups and intimidated those on the left who refused to support him. On March 23, 1933, under threat of violence from the stormtroopers, the Reichstag surrendered and gave Hitler the two-thirds vote required to endow him with the extraordinary authority that he sought.

Hitler moved quickly to eliminate German federalism and establish a unitary state. He also outlawed all political parties except

ADOLF HITLER

Like the woman . . . who . . . would rather bow to a strong man than dominate a weakling, likewise the masses love a commander . . . and feel inwardly more satisfied by a doctrine, tolerating no other beside itself, than by the granting of liberalistic freedom. . . .

The receptivity of the great masses is very limited, their intelligence is small, but their power of forgetting is enormous. In consequence of these facts, all effective propaganda must be limited to a very few points and must harp on these in slogans until the last member of the public understands what you want him to understand by your slogan. As soon as you sacrifice this slogan and try to be many-sided, the effect will piddle away, for the crowd can neither digest nor retain the material offered. . . .

The magnitude of a lie always contains a certain factor of credibility, since the great masses of people in the very bottom of their hearts tend to be corrupted rather than consciously and purposely evil, and that, therefore, in view of the primitive simplicity of their minds, they more easily fall a victim to a big lie than to a little one, since they themselves lie in little things, but would be ashamed of lies that were too big. Such a falsehood will never enter their heads, and they will not be able to believe in the possibility of such monstrous effrontery and infamous misrepresentation in others; yes, even when enlightened on the subject, they will long doubt and waver, and continue to accept at least one of the causes as true. Therefore, something of even the most insolent lie will always remain and stick—a fact which all the great lie-virtuosi and lying-clubs in this world know only too well and also make the most treacherous use of.

From *Mein Kampf* (1925)

the NSDAP. He purged that party as well and ordered the murder of any official whose loyalty he questioned. When Hindenburg died in August of 1934, Hitler dissolved the office of president. He had achieved total power and imposed upon the people of Germany a rigid totalitarian state. In keeping with his view of the need for *Lebensraum,* or room for living for the German Volk, he directed the nation into rapid militarization and began his march across Europe, beginning the Second World War. Ultimately, he moved into Asia also, attacking the Soviet Union. At home, and in German-occupied areas, Hitler proceeded toward what the Nazis called the "Final Solution," the extermination of all Jews. The Nazis seized Jewish property, herded Jews into concentration camps and systematically murdered them in gas chambers. The sadism of the death camps has become legendary, and Hitler wished for the death of Jews to be as painful and as prolonged as possible.[13] Death camps also awaited other peoples whom the Nazis believed to be inferior, such as Slavs and Gypsies, when they came under German control. Ultimately, the Nazis planned, under the guise of a public-health measure, to even exterminate all so-called "Aryans" who were physically imperfect.[14]

The result of national socialism and the Nazi ideology of Adolf Hitler was the Second World War, the greatest war in history, which caused incalculable suffering and bloodshed. Another result was genocide: a systematic attempt to eliminate a human group. The Nazis murdered an estimated six million Jews and others—not on the battlefield, but in concentration camps.

New York Times writer A. M. Rosenthal has written of Hitler and a few others as "truly dangerous men" who are connected by a "link of hatred so strong as to transcend all bonds of humanity." This is "a hatred built on a vision of existence that excludes the very concept of a common humanity and divides those who live on this Earth into the good and the damned, those worthy of life and those not. It is a vision that starts with words and slogans of a very particular kind, leads to a very particular ideological goal, and thence to the gas chamber or to the holy murdering ground."

He says that "the words the Germans used under Hitler—vermin, parasites, *Untermenschen* ("subhumans")—did lead to the goal of allowing the murderers and the watchers and the knowers in the German nation to think of the victims, especially Jews, as not really human. From that goal to the gas chamber was not so much another step but simply part of the flow of the river of

[13] Ibid., p. 470.
[14] For the details of Hitler's life, see Payne; for the best treatment of the Nazi phenomenon, see William L. Shirer, *The Rise and Fall of the Third Reich* (New York: Simon & Schuster, 1960).

hate."[15] Rosenthal is absolutely correct in identifying ideology as the key, and nothing could display more forcefully its importance. We must therefore examine the important components of the ideology of national socialism.

Nationalism

Nazi ideology, along with fascism, is fervently nationalistic. Fascism is aggressive, but Nazi nationalism is considerably more so, and it takes a somewhat different form from that of the Fascists. It emphasizes the notion of *Lebensraum*, or adequate room to live, for Aryans. In a sense it is territorial. It does, for example, incorporate a fierce romantic attachment to the hills and forests of Germany, which it sees as "natural" dwelling places for Aryans and contrasts them scornfully to urban decadence that it believes to result from Jewish influence. Nazism fully accepts the German myths of *Blut und Boden*, or "blood and soil." In Nazi ideology, blood (race) and ties to the land create the nation.

On the other hand, in a strange way there is a sense in which nazism is international in its outlook. The "Aryan race" is the nation. The Nazis assumed that Aryans should, and would, dominate all other races, wherever located. Some, it would exterminate; others it would enslave. Ultimately, it would cover the earth, no longer to be limited to the lands of the Germans.

View of the State

One of the key differences between nazism and fascism is the Nazi view of the state. Mussolini argued that the state created human beings; it was central to his ideology. The Nazis, by contrast, thought of the state as an instrument, as a means to an end, not as important in itself. The state existed for the Volk, or the people. As a rule Nazis avoided the term in favor of *Reich*, or empire. Hitler thought of the Holy Roman Empire as the "First Reich," Bismarck's creation—the Kaiser's Imperial Germany—as the "Second Reich," and his own "New Order"—Nazi Germany and its conquests—as the "Third Reich," which the Nazis taught would last one thousand years.

[15] A. M. Rosenthal, "Direct Link Between Khomeini and Hitler," *Kansas City Times* (January 13, 1987), p. A7.

Fascist ideology placed the Party at the service of the state. Nazi ideology on the contrary placed the state at the service of the Party. The Party's significance was that it represented the Volk, as a "vanguard," although the Nazis did not use that Leninist term. The parallel with Lenin's view of the Party as the "vanguard of the proletariat" is striking. The nation, or the Volk, created the state as an instrument of its collective will. The highly centralized Nazi state was the means by which Hitler imposed a totalitarian grip upon the society. If humanity has ever seen a truly totalitarian state, it was that of Hitler. It was at least the equal of anything that Mao or Stalin ever achieved.

Opposition to Marxism

Nazism based its opposition to Marxism on the same principles that fascism did. Marx hailed a class struggle that was anathema to the Nazis who believed that unity characterized the nation, conceived of in terms of race, of course, not economic conflict. Marxism ignored national boundaries in favor of economic classes. This internationalism offended the Nazis, whose emphasis was the nation, not a class. As indicated, the Nazi position actually involved an internationalism of sorts, but it was an internationalism in which representatives of one nation—the Aryan race wherever they resided—would impose their will upon all others. Marx would have discarded nations entirely, while Hitler would have his "nation" dominate all others. This was the Nazi *Weltanschauung*, or world view.

The Nazis also rejected Marxist materialism, in favor of their own version of "spiritualism." Their hostility to Marxism was even stronger than that of the Fascists because of Nazi ideas regarding race. Nazis argued that Marx was a Jew, and that communism, therefore, was part of a Jewish conspiracy to degrade humanity.

Irrationality

Both fascism and national socialism were intensely anti-rational, not merely nonrational. Irrationality was explicitly central to the ideology itself. In this, as in almost every aspect, the Nazis were even more extreme than the Fascists. Despite the glories of the Roman Empire, no Italian possessed such a romantic, mythopoetic, heroic view of the world as was common among the Nazis. Nothing could equal the Germanic myths of the Volk and the attachment to blood and soil, as reflected so well in Wagnerian opera, which enthralled Hitler.

These themes led Nazi ideology to stress a primitive sense of tribal oneness that placed the collective above the individual. The Nazi "superman" would seek the benefits of combat, the more violent the better. Nazis assumed violence to be normal and also desirable. Those who triumphed would be destined by nature to do so because of superior ability and will. It was will and intuition that were of prime importance, rather than thought. Nazism was an explicit attack upon human reason. An indication of the Nazi order of values is seen in the title of their famous propaganda film of the early 1930s, "Triumph of the Will."

Violence

The Nazi glorification of violence and combat led directly to a social Darwinist struggle for existence, with the strong devouring the weak. It was violent combat that would establish the leader of the Volk. Further violent combat would bring the Volk, the Aryans, to power over all others within Germany, and then would establish the German nation as the ruler of all others permitted to remain on earth.

As a result, the Nazis developed violence into insitutionalized terror. They directed it against their own people as well as others. The only morality was Nazi morality, which meant Hitler's will. He ruthlessly exterminated opponents, those whose loyalty he questioned—and in fact anyone whom he chose, regardless of loyalty. In the death camps, torture became sport for the guards. Nazi physicians performed unspeakably brutal and painful medical experiments on inmates, often causing mutilation and lingering death. The purpose frequently was nothing other than the satisfaction of idle curiosity. The indiscriminate use of cruelty and terror served both as a psychological release for the Nazis and as a calculated tool to maintain their power and eliminate the possibility of resistance. It was a clear case of an explicit doctrine that might makes right.

Fuehrerprinzip

The Fuehrerprinzip, or leadership principle, was essentially the same as that of the Fascists. One leader would come, through force of personality and will, to rule over all others. The leader would speak for the Party, which spoke for the Volk. He would represent the collective spirit of the Volk, and his will would be one with their collective will. In this mystic fashion, he would be infallible.

Hitler's title *Der Fuehrer*, the leader, was therefore not a modest one. He demanded personal loyalty of all Nazis, and everyone took an oath of allegiance not to the government, the Volk, or the state, but to Hitler personally. Despite the reverence that nazism expressed for the Volk, the leadership principle reflected a fundamental contempt for the masses, even the Aryan masses. They were seen as requiring leadership and domination, which the Nazis were happy to provide.

Economics

The Nazis considered politics to be considerably more important than economics, about which they were rather vague. Hitler initially spoke in generalized terms that were mildly anticapitalist, and this helped increase his appeal among the masses. Such themes dwindled away completely as he gained support from industry and business. Although some Nazis in the early years wrote of corporativism, Hitler did not pick up the theme and made no attempt to establish a corporate state along the lines that Mussolini had suggested.

The Nazis permitted property to be privately held as before, with some exceptions. Even before they began to murder them, the Nazis made Jews ineligible to own property and seized their assets. In keeping with Nazi ideology, all property had to be used to advance the interests of the Party. The government therefore dictated the use to which property would be put and confiscated it as it chose.

Propaganda

Hitler developed propaganda from a skilled art into a science. Nazi ideology specifically dealt with its use. Every bit of information was to be at the service of the Party, and there thus was rigid censorship. Symbols were everywhere: verbal, visual, musical, and physical. Propaganda reduced ideas to their simplest form, and they became slogans, repeated endlessly. Mass rallies, constant repetition, and the presence everywhere of uniforms became fundamental to Nazi life.

All Nazi expression became propaganda. Nazi propaganda experts carefully coordinated their efforts under the leadership of Joseph Goebbels (1897–1945). Goebbels incorporated Hitler's oratorical practices and principles into the massive publicity machine that effectively dominated the consciousness of a society. Among these was the skillful and cynical crafting of language to achieve maximum emotional effect. When the subject was Nazism, the recurring words were "strength," "youth," "vigor," "honor," "glory," "power," "spirit," and the like. When it was the Jews, the words used were "vermin," "lice," "maggots," "stinking," and "scum." The great German language quickly had degenerated into Nazi jargon at which level it remained during Hitler's reign.

One should never underestimate the power of language over thought, and hence over politics and other human affairs.[16] Because we think in words, our choice of words affects our thought. George Orwell's great novel *1984* portrayed a world under totalitarian cruelty in which the regime adopted a new language, "Newspeak," designed to eliminate the possibility of rebellion, even in the privacy of one's mind. The Nazis' effectiveness in that direction had considerable influence on Orwell's ideas.

George Steiner has written that, under Nazi rule, words came to acquire nightmarish definitions after having lost their original meanings. The German words for Jew, Pole, and Russian "came to mean two-legged lice, putrid vermin which good Aryans must squash, as a party manual said, 'like roaches on a dirty wall.' 'Final solution' . . . came to signify the death of six million human beings in gas ovens." The language was perverted not only by "these great bestialities," as Steiner put it. It also came to be twisted to say that white was black, and that night was day, particularly as the tide of the war turned, and Germany came steadily closer to defeat.[17]

[16]Max J. Skidmore, ed., *Word Politics: Essays on Language and Politics* (Palo Alto: James E. Freel and Associates, 1972).
[17]See George Steiner, "The Hollow Miracle," in his *Language and Silence: Essays on Language, Literature and the Inhuman* (New York: Atheneum, 1967); originally published in *The Reporter Magazine* (February 18, 1960); also reprinted in Skidmore, *Word Politics*.

Hitler wrote openly of the "big lie" technique. Lies, like everything else, would be brought to the service of the regime. They were mere tools, means to an end. Nazi Germany was a society filled with flags, posters, banners, books and book burnings, and theatrical techniques, all devoted to arousing emotions and turning them to the service of nazism. As much as anything else, it was Nazi propaganda that enabled Hitler to establish a totalitarian state.

Race

More than any other single factor, it was the idea of race that characterized national socialism. Racism also distinguished nazism from fascism. Hitler seized upon the racist themes reflected in the writings of Gobineau and Chamberlain. Whether he actually had read them is not important. He took the same ideas and developed them into a fanatic preoccupation. The official Nazi "philosopher" of racism was Alfred Rosenberg (1893–1946), whose *Myth of the Twentieth Century* and other writings became Nazi doctrine.

There had long been considerable anti-Semitism in Europe. Hitler and the Nazis refined and intensified resentment and prejudice toward Jews to the extent that it became the central theme of Nazi ideology and of the government that Hitler instituted. At the opposite end of the spectrum was the conception of "Aryan." Hitler was never precise as to what it was he believed an Aryan actually to be. Not all Germans could be so included. The physical type was large, blond, blue-eyed, fair-skinned. The fact that Hitler himself did not fit that type was immaterial, because physical appearance was only one indication. It was the spirit that was the determining factor.

Hitler and the Nazis believed that Aryans were the sole source of all human achievement. The Aryan race was "culture creating." Other races, such as the Japanese, who along with the Italians were Germany's allies in the Second World War, could be "culture bearing." In other words, they could not create culture, but they could maintain it. The bottom classification was reserved for "culture destroying" races, to which he relegated such groups as blacks and Jews. Clearly, there was no scientific or rational basis even for Hitler's ideas as to what constitutes a "race," let alone his evaluation of a particular group.

Uppermost in Hitler's ideology was race as central to art, politics, and all human affairs. His most urgent goal was race preservation. He believed that race mixing was what had prevented Aryans from dominating the world. Lesser races were better or worse depending upon the degree to which they had Aryan blood. Because race preservation superseded everything else in importance, there was no room for personal freedom. Therefore, the Nazis forbade interracial marriage, including marriage between Jews and non-Jews. Moreover, they reserved to themselves the right to order selective breeding among Aryans to improve the race. Non-Aryan races, even if they were German, had no right to live except as Aryans decided to permit them to exist as slaves.

Hitler's crude biological (or genetic) determinism to some extent contradicted his emphasis upon the role of culture and will. Consistency, however, was never of particular concern to Nazis. The sum of their attitudes led directly to the Nazi idea of *Gleichschaltung*, the notion that there is no purpose for any aspect of human existence except to serve the Volk. Such an idea leads directly to the totalitarian state that was the result of Nazi ideology.

SPAIN UNDER FRANCO

General Francisco Franco (1892–1975) came to power in Spain during the Spanish Civil War that lasted from 1936 to 1939. Many consider his rule to have been fascist, but it obscures the nature of fascism to apply the term to every right-wing authoritarian government. Although there certainly were fascists in his government, Franco never called himself a fascist, and his policies generally were not highly ideological as fascist policies are.

Spain had lagged behind most of the rest of Europe in industrializing, there was little constitutional tradition, illiteracy was high, and the middle class was small and weak. Workers were rebellious, and various anarchist and leftist groups were agitating constantly. There were right-wing groups as well, and they were openly hostile to the Republic. To add to the unstable situation, the nation included areas that sought separation, such as the Basque region.

Such conditions brought a military revolt against the Spanish Republic that began the Civil War. Right-wing groups supported the military, while leftists, including communists, came to the aid of the Republic. Among the right-wing groups was a small fascist party, the Falange. After the Republic fell and Franco came to power, he outlawed all other parties. In adopting the Falange as his own, he kept it from obtaining power and bent it to his will. Franco maintained tight control over the Falange and prevented it from developing, or acting upon, a fascist ideology.

Franco's supporters included the Church, the military, and the elite elements of society. During his lengthy rule he carefully crafted coalition support, and compromised as required to maintain his control while reducing unrest to a minimum. His rule was essentially personal and pragmatic, not ideological, and may be classed as a relatively moderate authoritarianism. As the years progressed, Franco permitted numerous reforms, including the introduction of representative institutions, but he kept them under close control.

Succession is difficult for personal governments, but Franco handled it well. As he had provided, a member of Spain's former royal family, the pretender to the throne, Juan Carlos, became king upon Franco's death. The king has instituted constitutional and representative government, and Spain appears to have borne up well following its period of dictatorship. The fact that ideology played hardly any part in the proceedings may be significant.

ARGENTINA UNDER JUAN PERÓN

Like Franco, Juan Perón (1895–1974) came to power following a military coup that established a ruling junta of officers, including Perón, who ultimately won the presidency through popular election in 1946. He was a charismatic speaker whose support came from the nation's unions and the poor, the *descamisados* (shirtless ones) whom he had promised social reforms. Perón followed through with increased benefits and reforms that included women's rights, but he also stifled civil liberties and imposed an authoritarian rule.

His rule was not as harsh as that of Rafael Trujillo in the Dominican Republic, Anastasio Somoza in Nicaragua, or many others in Latin America, but he did use ruthless methods to retain power, including arbitrary arrest and torture of his opponents. Perón attempted to establish an official ideology, very likely totalitarian in character, but it was never sufficiently elaborated to become effective, or even to be subject to clear definition. He and his propaganda officials called it *justicialismo,* and it apparently was an attempt to convince the people that it would be a middle road between capitalism and Marxism, retaining the desirable features of each.

Perón was a leader who made populist appeals and received strong mass support but who did not interfere with the large landholdings or the basic economic structure of the society. He spoke as a nationalist and attempted to move toward economic self-sufficiency for Argentina. He did institute some social reforms but accompanied them with harsh violations of human rights directed at his opposition. While retaining the form of constitutional protections, he ignored their substance and thus subverted the constitutional system. His economic policies, moreover, were inadequate to pay for his rapid industrialization and his social reforms, and he drove Argentina quickly toward bankruptcy.

Initially the Church firmly supported Perón and he even received a decoration from Pope Pius XII. Subsequently, however, his government began to pass laws to which the Church objected, such as establishing procedures for divorce and providing legal protection to illegitimate children equal to that granted legitimate ones. By the mid-1950s, both the Church and the military turned against him, and he fled to exile in 1955 during another military coup.

Perón's rule is difficult to classify. Although many have called him a Fascist or semi-Fascist, he clearly was not in that category. Nor was he a socialist. The descriptive limitations of the left-right continuum here are quite apparent, with Perón demonstrating some characteristics of both.

It is helpful to view Perón in light of the traditions of the region. In many respects he certainly was not the typical Latin American dictator. As an ideologue, however, he does fit the pattern. However much he may have attempted to promulgate an ideology, he did not succeed. His rule remained almost entirely personal. In this regard, he fits well into the category of the Latin *caudillo*, or "man on horseback," who achieves power, and establishes a rule based upon his personality, rather than upon ideology.

THE IDEOLOGY OF IMPERIAL JAPAN

The Japan that entered World War II was a modern nation, but one driven by an ideology that to an unusual degree reflected continuity with ancient traditions. Those traditions contained strong elements of authoritarianism and elitism and had developed through centuries of feudalism. Prominent among them were an emphasis upon hereditary rulers and a glorification of the way of the warrior. The effect of twentieth-century influences was to produce a uniquely Japanese ideology that developed something very close to totalitarianism and led the nation into a disastrous war that caused it in many ways finally, after many centuries, to break with its past. It would not overstate the case to label Japanese ideology as it evolved in the 1930s as fascist.

Beginning early in its existence, Japanese ideology held the emperor to be divine. The emperor spoke for the people, and his will was theirs. There thus could be no question of a representative assembly or of individual rights against the emperor. The emperor obtained his position by inheritance and in theory was supreme. Every subject owed him absolute obedience.

The practice was different from what one might expect under the circumstances. Beginning as early as 1185, the shogun, or supreme military official, came to exercise the real power in the name of the emperor. From that time on, the powerful military dominated society and functioned with relative independence from the government.

As Japan progressed from its earliest beginnings, it looked to China for cultural examples. It adopted Chinese traditions, modified them in keeping with its own character, and produced a thriving culture of its own. Japan was to do the same thing with regard to industrial nations when it confronted them in the late nineteenth and twentieth centuries. The ability to assimilate and modify ingeniously has always been a Japanese strength, but the Japanese have never been content merely to copy; they innovate based upon foreign examples, all the while remaining Japanese.

Although the Japanese drew heavily from Chinese institutions, those institutions took a different form in Japan. The Chinese traditionally held that the emperor ruled with a "mandate from heaven." If a ruler were to violate that mandate, he no longer had the right to rule. The Japanese emphasis was upon rule by inheritance, with no conception of any way in which a ruler might lose the right to rule. In addition, the administrative bureaucracy in Japan also held its position by inheritance, not by examination, as in China. Japan had no educated elite equivalent to China's. As a result, persons in positions of power frequently were incompetent to carry out their responsibilities and had to rely upon others to do so.

In theory, the emperor was supreme, but in reality he relied upon the shogun who was the center of power. The shogun ruled through a privy council, whose Samurai administrators were well educated and capable, as well as formidable warriors. The regional rulers were the Daimyos, who ruled with the assistance of Samurai. In many cases, the Samurai—who were somewhat like knights—wielded the true power. Through the years, the central power weakened progressively and that of the regions grew accordingly.

In the late nineteenth century, the Japanese noted the industrial power of European nations and recognized that they could not survive as a nation without developing power on the European model. Internal struggle brought temporary strength to the emperor and succeeded after centuries in abolishing the shogunate. The Emperor Meiji took the throne in 1866, and reorganized the government in 1867. In the early 1880s, political parties began to develop. The emperor sent Ito Hirobumi to Europe to study constitutions and government, and he came back to recommend a highly authoritarian system that he patterned upon the Prussian institutions that Bismarck had set forth as the basis for the new German Empire.

The constitution provided for civil liberties but also granted the government authority to suppress them legally. It followed Japanese tradition in placing the emperor at the center of power, and required his approval for any amendment. During the ensuing years, the nation established a system of courts and a representative assembly, the Diet. Although the constitution remained authoritarian, political practices were moving in the direction of those in the West.

Such rapid change almost inevitably produces internal tensions, and Japan was no exception. International developments, including war and depression, heightened the tensions. The 1920s and 1930s were a time of instability and turmoil, with numerous groups competing for power. Political assassinations became common, and there were numerous attempted coups. Many antidemocratic, nationalistic societies emerged. They were hostile to the West, to liberalism, to individualism, and to capitalism, and stressed *Kodo*, the "imperial way." The groups were not merely ethnocentric, they were composed of racial and cultural elitists, with little variation from one society to the next. In this setting, party rule became more precarious, and the military once again emerged in the ascendancy.

In keeping with the Japanese past, the military and civilian segments of the cabinet functioned relatively independently. In case of disagreement, the prime minister was supposed to decide. In practice, the solution was to appoint a military officer as prime minister. It was the military as a whole that had come to power, and it was not through a coup, or with any intention of exalting a single officer or group of officers. From 1937 on, the thrust was toward totalitarian thought control. Civil liberties had never been highly advanced in Japan, and those that had existed deteriorated rapidly and vanished under the new rulers.

The Munitions Mobilization Law of 1937 gave the government—the military—complete control over the economy. The General Mobilization Law of 1938 gave the government complete control over workers, and in that same year a new law imposed military control upon the schools, requiring military training, emperor worship, and the development of intense nationalist fervor among pupils. There was total censorship. In 1940, the military government eliminated unions and ordered all workers into one huge government labor association. The government did provide for increased social benefits, such as medical care and other social security programs, but the society became increasingly regimented. In 1941, General Tojo Hideki (1885–1948) became premier, and shortly thereafter Japan attacked Pearl Harbor.

The Japanese political ideology of this period is especially interesting because of its mixture of the traditional and the modern. Japan adopted, and retained, customary Chinese attitudes of racial and cultural superiority but without the moderating influences present in Chinese culture. The Japanese traditionally had emphasized *bushido,* or the way of the warrior. Such a stress on the military was generally absent from Chinese traditions.

Although Chinese religious influence, especially Buddhism, had moderated the Japanese martial zeal somewhat, the military rulers of the 1930s and early 1940s resurrected it with a vengeance. As early as the 1920s, Japanese foreign policy experts had drawn up plans to expand throughout most of Asia with full recognition that this would involve a confrontation with the United States. Although for centuries the emperor had exercised no real power, except briefly, the reverence with which the ideology dealt with him stood the militarists in good stead. They were able to convince young men that battle would be glorious, and that dying for the emperor would be a privilege. An ideology that combines nationalism, racism, cultural elitism, doctrines of total obedience, and a religious duty to die for a political cause, if accepted, cannot help but be extraordinarily powerful.

THE IDEOLOGY OF APARTHEID

As of the late 1980s, apartheid has become a news topic of major concern. Apartheid, or the Republic of South Africa's policies of strict racial separation, has been the target of protests from within that nation, and from around the world. Both the protests and the South African responses are common knowledge, but few persons outside South Africa, other than specialists on the region, are likely to appreciate the degree to which apartheid is a fully formed political, and even religious, ideology.

The predominant Calvinist theology has led many white South Africans to consider themselves a chosen people with God-given entitlements, including a right to the land, and the right to dominate other races whom they consider to be inferior. Afrikaner theologians frequently refer to God's curse on Ham, Noah's younger son, whom they identify as the ancestor of the black race, to justify their views on black inferiority. The same and similar arguments had been a major rationalization for American slavery. P. J. Cilliers, editor-in-chief of the Afrikans daily, *Die Burger,* spoke in 1976 on behalf of many in South Africa who shared the assumption that the Afrikaners were God's chosen people. "Africa's unique white tribe of Afrikaners," he wrote, "see themselves as a sort of Israel in Africa, with a sense of God-guided destiny that it would be as perilous to discount as in the case of the original model."[18]

"The South African racial situation was created by God" constitutes the Afrikaners' basic belief. Consequently, any discussion with Afrikaners about South Africa's past or present is bound to lead to the conclusion: "we are a chosen people entrusted with a divine mission, so all we have done and all we are doing is right."

As Cornevin noted, "when intended for overseas consumption this statement is of course couched in more subtle terms, and most readers of the copious South African propaganda literature do not realize the crucial important of the religious factor in the current impasse of Pretoria's political thought."[19] The regime in Pretoria considers extensive propaganda to be essential to defend South Africa's racial policies, which make it the only state in which "racialism is written into the constitution."[20] The official organ is the *Official Yearbook of the Republic of South Africa*. One theme that it employs is the assertion that in 1652 the "White African tribe of Afrikaners" established itself in the region at approximately the same time that blacks were migrating there from the north, although historians have demonstrated that black settlements preceded those of whites.[21]

The white community of the Republic of South Africa is split into two groups. Afrikaners, the larger group, are descendants of Dutch, German, French Huguenot, and other European settlers. They speak Afrikaans, a variant of Dutch that has evolved through the years into a separate language that many Afrikaner ministers teach is a specific gift from God to distinguish Afrikaners as a chosen people. Virtually all Afrikaners are active in one of several South African offshoots of the Dutch Reformed Church, and the Afrikaner community is extraordinarily homogeneous. The smaller white group is English speaking and is considerably more diverse. It consists largely of the descendants of English settlers. Although

---

[18] See Marianne Cornevin, *Apartheid: Power and Historical Falsification* (Paris: UNESCO, 1980), pp. 32–33; the quotation from Cilliers, reprinted from South Africa's official history, *South Africa, 1977* (Pretoria, 1978), is on p. 33; see also Leonard Thompson, *The Political Mythology of Apartheid* (New Haven: Yale University Press, 1985) and Andre Du Troit, *Afrikaner Political Thought: Analysis and Documents* (Berkeley: University of California Press, 1983).

[19] Ibid., pp. 46–47.

[20] Ibid., p. 11.

[21] Ibid., pp. 11–13; see also "Background Notes: South Africa" (Washington: U.S. Department of State, Bureau of Public Affairs, May 1985), esp. p. 3.

English-speaking South Africans certainly bear much of the responsibility for the conditions under which South Africa's blacks live and work—they control the majority of the nation's wealth and head more than three-fourths of its companies—"since 1948 they have played a secondary role in politics and are far less involved in the official history taught in the schools, which is essentially the history of the Afrikaners."[22]

The nation's highly complicated categories of race include, in simplified form, whites, Africans (blacks), coloureds (those of mixed race), and Asians. The term "blacks" groups together Africans, coloureds, and Asians. Official policy not only separates the races, but wherever possible has encouraged separation between the two white groups. There generally are separate schools for English and Afrikaners, and each stresses the heritage of that particular linguistic group. The racial consciousness of the society is so great that it not only prohibited racial intermarriage until 1985, but many South Africans even frown upon the uncommon intermarriages between members of the two white groups.

The first white settlement in South Africa was in the seventeenth and eighteenth centuries when the Dutch East India Company founded a colony on the Cape of Good Hope. In the nineteenth century the British seized the colony, and many of the Afrikaners fled the settlements to adopt a rural life, where they came to be called "Boers," or farmers. There was continued friction between the Boers and the British and between the whites and the native peoples.

By the end of the nineteenth century there were several Afrikaner states in South Africa, and the white settlers had subjugated the black populations. Control in some areas had gone back and forth between Afrikaners and British, and in the Boer War of 1899–1902, Britain finally conquered the entire region. In 1910 The Union of South Africa came into being as an independent member of the British Commonwealth. It consisted of the Cape Colony, Natal, the Orange Free State, and the Transvaal. In 1948 the Nationalist party took charge and established the official program of apartheid. Criticism of South Africa's racial policies from Britain and elsewhere stung the South Africans, and in 1961 the country withdrew from the British Commonwealth and became the Republic of South Africa.

[22] Ibid., p. 14.

Long before South Africa withdrew from the Commonwealth, it had become a powerful, industrialized nation. The discovery of vast wealth in gold and diamonds drew immigrants from Europe and Asia in the late nineteenth century and shifted the economy away from the pastoral Boer existence. The new wealth served as the basis for the emergence in the twentieth century of a modern, highly developed nation, at least for the white citizens. At the same time, the Afrikaner population increased through high birth rate, while the English were less prolific and more likely to leave for other lands. It was thus that the Afrikaners and their Nationalist party came to dominance.

By the late 1970s, black South Africans increasingly came to protest the conditions placed upon them by the white minority government, which included prohibitions against being in white areas without passes and other restrictions. The government announced that it had created "independent homelands" for certain black groups, but they remained under South African control, and foreign governments refused to recognize them. By the late 1980s, black protests had turned to violence, and the mild reforms that the government adopted had no effect. The United Nations had placed an embargo of arms to the country, and most industrialized nations placed various sanctions upon the regime. The Reagan administration in the United States opposed sanctions, but pressure from allies and strong public sentiment led Congress to force the administration to levy them—although it required overriding a presidential veto to do so.

The cause of the South African turmoil was the policy of apartheid. During the nineteenth and early twentieth centuries, racist sentiment was predominant not only in South Africa but throughout Europe and North America. South Africa's policies were not sufficiently extraordinary to attract much notice from outside the country. As times brought a more enlightened attitude abroad, however, it actually brought a hardening of opinion within South Africa.

This led to extreme restrictions upon the white population of the nation, as well as upon blacks. Although the Afrikaners have been the most militant racists, probably because of their religious orientation, most white South Africans, English or Afrikaner, appear essentially to have shared the same attitudes. This is not to say that there have been no voices calling for reform within both groups, even from within the Dutch Reformed Churches, but thus far they have been largely suppressed.[23] Much of the white society appears to be willing to accept the existence of a police state that is subversive of their freedoms in order to maintain racial dominance. All television is owned and controlled by the state, and in fact South Africa was the last modern state to permit television because of its possible effect upon tradition. The press is owned privately, but censorship laws are strict and the penalties for violation severe, thus reducing criticism to a minimum, however much courageous editors may wish to speak out.[24] The criticisms from within continue to increase, however, and could lead ultimately to significant changes in policy.

Afrikaner solidarity has been maintained by the Church, the Nationalist party, and various Afrikaner associations. The Afrikaner Broederbond, a secret society, was founded in 1918 and appears to include the Afrikaner elite. As Leonard Thompson, one of the keenest observers of South Africa, has written, the society's purpose apparently has been to place militant Afrikaner Nationalist party members into positions of power. In 1949 an investigating committee of one of the branches of the Dutch Reformed Church looked into charges that the society was "dangerous" and "fascist." The conclusion, released in 1951, was that it was "wholesome and healthy, seeking only the progress and best interests of the Afrikaner nation."[25]

In 1944, the Broederbond's chairman, J. C. Van Rooy, expressed the Afrikaner ideology very clearly:

> In every People in the world is embodied a Divine idea and the task of each People is to build upon that Idea and to perfect it. So God created the Afrikaner People with a unique language, a unique philosophy of life, and their own history and tradition in order that they might fulfill a particular calling and destiny here in the southern corner of Africa. We must stand guard on

---

[23] Ibid., pp. 37–46.

[24] For insights into the state of the press in South Africa, see Michael Massing, "Letter from South Africa," *Columbia Journalism Review* (January/February 1987), pp. 35–39.

[25] Leonard Thompson, *The Republic of South Africa* (Boston: Little, Brown, 1966), pp. 134–35.

all that is peculiar to us and build upon it. We must believe that God has called us to be servants of his righteousness in this place. We must walk the way of obedience to faith.

Thompson described how this "neo-Calvinist element" pervaded the ideology as it developed and said that although it has declined, it has "by no means disappeared" during the latter half of this century as Afrikaners have become more urban and secular.[26]

The combination of fierce independence, nationalism, and racism would have been a potent mix in any case—few things can be more powerful in arousing emotions than racial hostility[27]—but buttressed as it was by religion, it became an especially formidable political ideology. The Afrikaners, therefore, translated the ideology into an action group, the Nationalist party, and many came to believe that all true Afrikaners had to affiliate with the Party or else be traitors. Former Prime Minister D. F. Malan (1874–1959) impressed upon the Afrikaners the value of political solidarity. Disunited, they had been defeated constantly; united, they rule. The "lesson has sunk deep into the Afrikaner mores and is transmitted not only by the party itself but also by many organs of the state, notably the public schools, and by the whole gamut of Afrikaner organizations, from the Dutch Reformed Churches to the voluntary associations."[28]

An ideology of superiority thus has resulted from defeat and fear: fear of blacks, fear of the British, and even to some extent fear of British South Africans. This led a number of Afrikaners to support the Nazi cause in the Second World War—although the Union of South Africa entered the war on the side of the Allies—and it has caused many South African schoolbooks to be somewhat ambivalent in their treatment of the Nazis.

Such a background of insecurity has caused South Africa to attempt to build security, as one dissident South African put it, "upon a barrage of laws."[29] The extraordinary powers that the government may exercise legally exceed those in any Western

---

[26] Thompson, *The Political Mythology of Apartheid*, p. 29.
[27] M. Crawford Young, "Patterns of Social Conflict: State, Class, and Ethnicity," *Daedalus*, 111 (Spring 1982).
[28] Thompson, *Republic of South Africa*, p. 152; on South African politics, see also his *South African Politics* (New Haven: Yale University Press, 1982).
[29] Bernard Makhosezwe Magubane, *The Political Economy of Race and Class in South Africa* (New York: Monthly Review Press, 1979).

nation and truly create a police state—for all South Africans. The situation is not, however, monolithic. Although most white South Africans appear to support apartheid, some observers believe that support is lessening, despite the grim developments. In addition, there have always been whites who have spoken out against racism, Afrikaners as well as English. A healthy example of multi-racial cooperation to end apartheid is the "Declaration of Policy" that the Faculty of Education of the University of the Western Cape, an integrated institution, issued in March of 1987. Among other things, it acknowledges that academic freedom cannot be separated from basic civil liberties, that academic freedom is "seriously compromised in South African academic institutions," and that "some form of academic boycott . . . might be an effective strategy" in combatting apartheid. The faculty then committed itself to working for "the establishment of a democratic order in South Africa in the belief that such a dispensation provides the best avenue towards the achievement of a just, humane, and equitable society.[30] As noted earlier, criticisms and calls for reform have even emanated from the Dutch Reformed Churches themselves.

The pressure for change now is considerable. It comes from other countries, from white reformers within the society, from other whites who see "the handwriting on the wall." Most of all, it comes from the black population which has developed a cohesive sense of injustice and determination to change the system. Despite this pressure, the elections on May 6, 1987, gave overwhelming endorsement to the Nationalist party, actually strengthening its position and giving less support to reformers than anticipated. Even groups to the right of the Nationalists gained. The elections were limited to whites only.

There has been considerable violence. Whether the change will come without increasing amounts of bloodshed is doubtful. We are focusing here on ideology as the cause of this country's tragic problem. Ideology, however, because of its rigidities, is unlikely to solve it. If it is ever to be resolved in a humane manner, persons of good will must agree to work together in a spirit of politics—which presupposes compromise—and to turn away from ideology for their solutions.

[30] Faculty of Education, University of the Western Cape, "Declaration of Policy" (photocopy of typescript, March 1987).

RIGHT-WING ELITISM IN PERSPECTIVE

Despite the great variation in right-wing elitist ideologies, they do share certain characteristics. All are antidemocratic in practice and most openly so in theory. Beyond that, all lead to dictatorships and police states. The effect in practice is generally little different, if at all, from the practices that prevail under political systems at the extreme left of the political spectrum, but the professed goals and underlying philosophical justifications for their practices are considerably different. Right-wing ideologies openly acknowledge their elitism, for example, while Marxism-Leninism professes to be egalitarian. To be sure, the Leninist idea of the "vanguard of the proletariat" is also thoroughly elitist, but Marxist-Leninists justify it as being temporary and employed only for expedience, not as an ideal.

Attitude Toward Change

Right-wing elitist ideologies either strongly resist change or seek to restore what they presume to have been an existing order. Once in power, they take extraordinary measures to prevent change by crushing opponents and suppressing ideas.

Attitude Toward Human Nature

The general assumption of right-wing ideologies is that human beings by nature are weak and foolish and incapable of true civilization without the imposition of strong leadership and controls, often harsh controls. They attribute slavish characteristics to most human beings and conclude therefore that most human beings should be treated as slaves.

Attitude Toward the Potential of Human Reason

The strong tendency of right-wing elitists is to take a dim view of the potential of human reason, emphasizing instead will, emotion and the virtues of power. They believe that subordination to authority, not reason, should determine human action and guide society. Although the source of the authority may vary—it may, for example, be based upon tradition, upon the perceived demands of "race" or culture, upon raw power, or upon revealed religion—it is reverence for authority, not reason, that thus is the operative principle.

Attitude Toward Human Progress

Although there are exceptions, in general the far right is optimistic regarding the possibility of human progress. What they interpret as "progress," of course, would not be accepted as such by those who fail to share their views. Fascists expected "progress" in the form of a utopia of national glory based upon the state; national socialists thought that it would be based upon the exaltation of the Volk. Others may see it as founded upon the flowering of a theocracy. Whatever the formulation, most right-wing extremists assume that if only their own prescriptions are followed—or imposed—human societies will prosper and attain glory.

Attitude Toward the Relationship of the Individual to the Community

The extremes of rightest ideology totally submerge the individual into the group. They not only stress duties but recognize no rights. Any "right" that exists is extended by the community, or the leaders, and may be withdrawn at any time for no reason. They may permit private property to exist but always subject to the demands of the leaders. Some ideologies are less extreme than others, but the principle is always to deny that people have inherent rights, and the practice is to accept coercion as standard policy. Although some "individualists" on the far right might seem to be exceptions, even they tend to accept rights as something that powerful individuals create for themselves, not as something inherent or as something that all possess. What they would deny the state in the name of individualism, they are likely to favor appropriating for themselves as power holders.

SOME FINAL THOUGHTS ON AUTHORITARIANISM AND TOTALITARIANISM

The themes of violence, nationalism, and racism were legacies from the nineteenth century to the twentieth. They formed the basis for the new century's ideologies of right-wing elitism. At the same time, another development joined with them to provide the foundation for something even harsher: the totalitarian ideologies that sprang into being in the early years of this century. That new development was technology. The totalitarian states that resulted were of both the left and the right, and their ideologies varied sharply. In practice, the effect on the citizen tended to be the same; the totalitarian reality overshadowed the ideological distinction.

Even in nontotalitarian states, in fact in all modern states, the nineteenth-century legacies of racism, violence, and nationalism coupled with technology have had their effects. Technology permits any government to have considerably greater power over each citizen than it could have previously, and all governments now exercise it. The institutionalization of violence has resulted in the greatest wars in history. It has also resulted in the use of force, not only by totalitarian or other elitist states, but even by Western democracies as they sought to impose their wills upon other peoples, including native peoples in their own lands and those in Asia and Africa as well.

Clearly, there is a vast distinction between all authoritarian regimes—whether on the left or the right—and those regimes typical of the West. The differences, however, should not blind those in the West to the aspects of their own ideologies that can lead in the direction of authoritarianism.

Managerialism/ Professionalism

7

*P*olitics involves the deliberate collective ordering of human affairs. It is a procedure within some sort of framework for arriving at compromise and dispute settlement. "The political method of rule is to listen to . . . other groups so as to conciliate them as far as possible, and to give them a legal position, a sense of security, some clear and reasonably safe means of articulation.[1] By definition, politics deals with disagreements, differences of opinion, and conflicts of interest. The substance of politics therefore involves many things that can be disruptive and inefficient. For nearly as long as human beings have thought about such things, there have been many who have sought to achieve a government without politics.

There are numerous reasons for this. Frequently, there is considerable discomfort with the notion of compromise. Compromise, after all, suggests accepting something that is less than the best. Those whose prime concern is order may see politics as the

---

[1] Bernard Crick, *In Defense of Politics* (Baltimore: Penguin Books, 1964), p. 18.

institutionalization of disorder, and therefore as something to be eliminated. The altruist might see politics as reflecting human selfishness, and also seek a nonpolitical world. The totalitarian recognizes politics as the expression of will other than his own, which he cannot permit. Those who have accepted certain religious teachings as truth could interpret the diversity of politics as a violation of the divine will. Those whose faith is purely in science might find the imprecision and uncertainty of politics unacceptable. Many reasons may be more subtle than these and may go unrecognized—even by those who hold them. Bernard Crick has noted that too frequently governments see politics as an obstacle. "Indeed," he has written, "it is unhappily true, *most* known governments try to repress politics as much as they dare."[2]

The latter part of the nineteenth century was a time of social disruption. Society was rapidly industrializing but had not yet adjusted to the changes. It tended also, especially in the United States, to be a time of inefficiency and corruption in government. Many observers, often quite correctly, associated this with politics. In some instances, therefore, the resulting attempts at reform were not simply efforts to reform politics but also to reduce or even to eliminate politics. In these instances, the reformers sought earnestly and sincerely to create, wherever possible, a nonpolitical government.

During the last century or so, all of these tendencies and others have come together and gained greater strength from the emergence of modern science and technology, thus producing an approach to government that I call "managerialism," or "professionalism." Technology is "simply the activity of applying scientific principles to . . . production. . . . But it has also become perverted into a social doctrine. 'Technology' holds that all the important problems facing human civilization are technical, and that therefore they are all soluble on the basis of existing knowledge or readily attainable knowledge."[3] This approach in its most comprehensive form is built upon several beliefs:

- government consists largely of administration or management;
- administration should be left in the hands of experts and removed from politics;

[2] Ibid., p. 11; see also p. 20.
[3] Ibid., p. 93.

- the result of this would be that government would become relatively nonpolitical;
- being nonpolitical would cause government to become less corrupt and more efficient;
- policy formulation is a relatively limited function;
- policy formulation may be separated from administration;
- policy formulation should be reserved for elected leaders and should be their only function.

A key assumption of managerialism is that management, or administration, not only is the core of governing, but that it may be accomplished professionally and, according to scientific principles, may thereby avoid many of the disagreements that require politics to settle. "The implicit assumption is that *administration* can always be clearly separated from politics, and that if this is done, there is really very little, if anything, that politicians can do that administrators cannot do better."[4] Even more serious is the tendency to which this leads. Managerialism incorporates a "scientific" approach to administration. This does not mean the belief that everything can be done in a scientific manner, "as if by a definite and preconceived technique; but that government should only do those things which can be reduced to such a technique."[5]

Managerialism as an approach to government today is widely—if unconsciously—accepted. This does not mean that everyone who accepts it would apply it to every level of government. Similarly, not everyone who accepts it would accept all of its key beliefs. In fact, the contention that policy and administration may be separated dates from the early theorists of public administration, and modern theory recognizes that it is impossible to separate the two completely. Policy inevitably affects administration and administration cannot be completely free from policy implications. For example, administration involves decisions, and such decisions frequently must be based upon interpretations of policy; hence, they are policy decisions. Nevertheless, the assumption of the early theorists that the two can be totally separate, even though now discarded, continues to exercise some influence.

Managerialism is neither new, nor all-inclusive. Utopian writers for centuries have discussed societies that function without

[4]Ibid., p. 107.
[5]Ibid.

disagreement and without politics. Plato's Republic could be interpreted in this fashion, as could the ultimate societies that Marx and his followers envisioned, and that a host of anarchists sought also; societies, that is, without state, government, conflict, or politics. For all of Marx's disdain of the utopian socialists, his ultimate goal was no less utopian than theirs. In the United States, Bellamy's utopia was explicitly antipolitical, as was the more recent fictional society that the psychologist B. F. Skinner portrays in *Walden Two*. This novel is a reflection of Skinner's behavioristic view of the human condition, which he reduces to stimulus and response. In Skinner's society there would be no such distractions and impediments as "freedom," or "dignity," which he believes in any case to be meaningless—and of course there would be no politics. These are only a few of the huge number of utopian writings from many times, nations, and cultures that not only suggest the possibility of a nonpolitical world, but look forward to it.

No doubt there are many scholars who would question treating managerialism as a political ideology. As indicated, it is not all-inclusive. That is, it need not be an exclusive approach to politics. Many who are committed to liberalism, conservatism, communism, fascism, or numerous other orientations could adopt its approach without disrupting their adherence to another political ideology. In this instance, managerialism is like many other political ideologies. That is, one who accepts it may compartmentalize it to apply to certain circumstances, yet not to others. Human beings have an impressive ability to segment sections of their lives and their thought.

I identify managerialism as a political ideology for two reasons. First, it appears easily to come within our working definition of a political ideology as a form of thought that presents a pattern of complex political ideas simply and in a manner that inspires action to achieve certain goals. Second, it seems worthy of study as a political ideology because of its profound effect upon governments around the world, regardless of the form that those governments take. This should demonstrate the value of our approach to political ideology. It serves to make political relationships clear, rather than to obscure them as a more restricted definition might do.

Merit-based bureaucracies that administer government service reflect the ideology, at least to some extent. Such bureaucracies are widespread, especially in industrialized nations. Moreover, in the United States the highly popular council-manager form of city government is an attempt to ensure city administration by expert professionals. Initially at least, the council-manager movement also was an explicit attempt to remove entire governments as far from politics as possible. It is safe to say that probably no other single ideology has had greater effect upon American municipal government. We will now examine in more detail the effects of managerialism as a political ideology. I cite them not to praise or condemn, but to illustrate their importance.

THE MANAGERIAL STATE

Bureaucracies are not new. Ancient and medieval China, for example, had a highly developed bureaucracy based upon recruitment by examination, similar to the merit systems of today. Today's examinations tend to be related to the technical details of the position, while those of ancient China concerned knowledge of the classics, but the principle of some sort of selection by merit remains. What is new is the pervasive character of bureaucracy, caused by the greatly expanded role of government in this century and the development of the technological ability to reach into every corner of society.

Today we tend to take for granted the superiority of a merit-based civil service that is protected from political interference. It was not always so, even in the United States. When Congress created the Civil Service System in the nineteenth century, it was necessary for supporters of reform to argue long and hard to gain backing for their proposals. The system of political patronage, or the "spoils system," which was based upon the principle "to the victors belong the spoils," still had strong support.

Representative Thomas A. Jenckes, a Republican from Rhode Island, became known as the "father of the Civil Service" because of his strong efforts to achieve a merit system. On January 29, 1867, he spoke to the House of Representatives on behalf of his bill for reform, which he assured his listeners would be nonpartisan. He argued that political partisanship had corrupted politics, and that a merit-based system would ensure that civil servants would be capable and would perform their duties. He condemned the president's power to discharge even those officials whose appointments required Senate confirmation and said that the entire administrative apparatus of the government had been corrupted to serve the cause of partisanship.

Jenckes called for a board of commissioners to examine and appoint public servants, saying that such a system worked well in Great Britain, even with its vast colonial expanses, and would work equally well in the U.S. The reform, he believed, would "stimulate education and bring the best attainable talent into the public service," it would place that service "above all considerations of locality, favoritism, patronage, or party," and would establish it as an honorable career. It would serve the nation better, achieve better administration, protect property and personal rights more effectively, and increase respect for government. Moreover, self-government would have "another of its alien elements of discord removed from it."[6]

Another Republican representative, Frederick E. Woodbridge of Vermont, spoke against the bill, alleging that a merit system would be "anti-democratic." It would duplicate the patterns prevailing in Belgium, Prussia, France, and England and would not reflect American traditions of greater democracy, and of egalitarianism. As for the president's power to remove officials, he admitted that it could be abused, but said that it was essential to ensure performance. He even argued that changes in personnel in the public service were a safeguard for liberty and democracy. "The health of the nation requires," he said, "that the stable shall be occasionally cleaned out."

As for the appointing commissioners, he said that they would exercise enormous power. They could prescribe the examinations, determine where they would be administered, employ any number of assistants, and set up an "inquisitorial court." They could assume dictatorial power in making their determinations. "It might work in Belgium, France, or England, where the masses are mere machines," he thundered, "but in free America it will never work." Yet another Republican colleague, Robert Schenck of Ohio, disputed Woodbridge and supported Jenckes. He said that the proposed reform would indeed be democratic in that it would throw

[6]Thomas A. Jenckes, untitled speech to the House of Representatives, *Congressional Globe*, 39th Congress, 2nd Session (January 29, 1867), pp. 839–41.

"open these places in the different Departments of the Government, to be occupied without distinction by all men, rich and poor, and by persons of both sexes, according to their merits as evidenced and ascertained upon an examination. . . ."[7]

The Jenckes bill failed, but proposals for reform continued to surface and receive attention. Those who favored the spoils system reacted strongly each time. One such supporter of the status quo was Republican Senator Benjamin F. Butler from Massachusetts, who argued simply that those who were in office favored keeping the patronage system and that those who were not worked for reform. "Civil service reform," he said, "is always popular with the 'outs' and never with the 'ins,' unless with those who have a strong expectation of soon going out."[8]

It was not until the assassination of President James A. Garfield in 1881 that the momentum for reform became strong. The assassin, Charles Guiteau, had sought a federal position and had failed to obtain one. Whatever his motives may have been, the public immediately assumed that he shot the president because of the spoils system. The history books tell us that "a disappointed office-seeker" killed President Garfield, and the reformers then portrayed the dead president as a crusader for reform. Despite this, Congress still did not act until after the elections of 1882 made public sentiment on the issue clear. Finally, a large bipartisan majority in the early session of 1883 passed the Pendleton Act that established the basis for the current U.S. Civil Service.

The system that had originally allocated positions based on membership in the elite, and then had adopted the principle of party patronage, had given way to one based at least in part on merit. Most states continued to use the patronage system and instituted reforms only under pressure from the federal government, which during the New Deal days of the 1930s came to require merit systems for selection of state personnel who administered federal programs. These constituted a substantial number of a state's employees. A few states changed their systems only

---

[7] Frederick E. Woodbridge and Robert Schenck, colloquy in the House of Representatives, *Congressional Globe*, 39th Congress, 2nd Session (February 6, 1867), pp. 1034–36.

[8] Benjamin F. Butler, untitled speech to the Senate, *Congressional Globe*, 42nd Congress, 2nd Session (April 18, 1872), Appendix, pp. 267–68.

relatively recently to require merit systems throughout their governments, and even today a few patronage departments continue to exist.

In 1978 a Civil Service Reform Act abolished the old Civil Service Commission, and established in its stead an Office of Personnel Management. This did not change the principle of the Civil Service that removes most personnel matters from the jurisdiction of line administrators in federal agencies. The Office of Personnel Management describes each position carefully, and in detail, and administers examinations to select the appointees who must meet both general and technical requirements. Both law and regulation protect workers from partisan attacks, but they also make it most difficult to discharge those who do not perform well. Few would doubt that such a system encourages impartiality, but critics complain that it also encourages inefficiency, which the early reformers were attempting to eliminate.

Regardless of how they are selected, or where they are located, permanent administrative or bureaucratic structures tend to develop enormous systems of information collection and storage. They are likely to share their information freely with other government agencies, and with government officials. The tendency as regards public disclosure, however, is quite different. Bureaucracies tend to be reluctant to divulge information to the public, and their procedures are likely to make it extremely difficult to correct erroneous information, even if the error can be discovered.

Most administrative hierarchies have clear-cut chains of command, but even so their organizational complexity may make it difficult to assess responsibility for specific actions. This can lead to uncoordinated actions, and even to actions that result from drift and inertia rather than definite policy intentions. There is no shortage of ill intent in the world, but it may be even more disturbing to recognize that ill-conceived actions may occur by accident, with no one having recognized what was happening or being willing to intervene. The bureaucratic structure then may close ranks to defend itself and attempt to justify what was done, rather than correct it.

An equally disturbing feature of a permanent bureaucracy involves responsibility of bureaucrats to the officials whose purpose is to make policy. The function of a bureaucracy is to put policy into practice, to act upon political decisions that others make. Nevertheless, when a bureaucracy is permanent it frequently acts rather independently, regardless of the society's designated leaders. Because policy and administration are so intertwined, the nature of the administrative apparatus inevitably affects the way it implements policy. The bureaucracy may shape programs somewhat differently from the intentions of the policymakers. It may delay programs or sabotage them if bureaucrats believe them unwise or are offended by them. It may carry them out, but very slowly. There are countless ways in which permanent bureaucrats may resist policies that they see as detrimental to their own interests, and when they feel threatened, they are likely to use these methods.

The designated leaders of a society in theory control the bureaucracy, but cannot always do so. In a democratic political system, the people ultimately are supposed to control policy by electing the leaders they wish and deposing others. Choosing leaders, however, may have little effect upon a permanent bureaucracy. There is no effective mechanism even in theory that permits the people to control such an administrative structure because the control would be "political," and one of the purposes of a merit-based civil service is to achieve efficiency and insulate it from "politics." If elected leaders attempt to control the operations of bureaucracies directly, they are likely to face criticism for attempting to politicize the civil service.

The voters have little recourse against a bureaucracy that they dislike when it holds its position by merit, rather than through political appointment. The top positions will be considered as "policy" positions and others as purely administrative or technical. The original theory that separated policy from administration thus continues to some extent to deny political control over the bureaucracy, even though advances in theory have led to a recognition that complete separation of administration from policy is impossible.

Another question concerning the administration of policy involves the extent to which the legislature may delegate authority to the bureaucracy. It would be impossible for a bureaucracy to function if it did not have some authority to issue regulations pertaining to policy implementation. But where should such delegation end? If it is too limited, the bureaucracy could not administer complex legislation; if it is too broad, the bureaucracy begins to perform as if it were a legislature. In any case, issuing regulations is an obvious exercise of a policy function, however closely those regulations may be circumscribed.

Whenever a permanent bureaucracy exists, it develops into a profession, as it was designed to do. The bureaucrat has a specialty, and as a professional, is likely to have become an expert in that subject. Political officials are amateurs with regard to the bureaucrat's specialty. This is true whether those officials are

---

CHRISTOPHER LASCH

As an agency of social discipline, the school, together with other elements in the tutelary complex, both reflects and contributes to the shift from authoritative sanctions to psychological manipulation and surveillance—the redefinition of political authority in therapeutic terms—and to the rise of a professional and managerial elite that governs society not by upholding authoritative moral standards but by defining normal behavior and by invoking allegedly nonpunitive, psychiatric sanctions against deviance.

The extension of these techniques into the political realm transforms politics into another article of consumption. Here again, the emergence of new techniques of control and new styles of political leadership marks the growing influence of the managerial elite. . . .

The growth of a professional civil service, the rise of regulatory commissions, the proliferation of governmental agencies, and the dominance of executive over legislative functions provide merely the most obvious examples of the shift from political to administrative control, in which issues allegedly too abstruse and technical for popular understanding fall under the control of professional experts. Governmental regulation . . . has often been advocated with the explicit objective of insulating business and government against popular ignorance. . . . But even reforms intended to increase popular participation, such as the presidential primary, have had the opposite effect. Twentieth-century politics has come to consist more and more of the study and control of public opinion.

From "Democracy and the 'Crisis of Confidence',"
Democracy, 1:1 (January 1981)

presidents, premiers, ministers, cabinet officers, or other executive officers, or whether they are members of national legislatures, state or provincial legislatures, city councils, or other legislative bodies. How does the amateur deal with the professional? It is quite possible for legislatures to equip themselves with the same kinds of computers and technical experts that the bureaucrats have, but cost and political realities make it difficult for them to do so. Therefore, they generally continue to rely on the bureaucracy for that vital lifeblood of politics: information.

THE COUNCIL-MANAGER FORM OF LOCAL GOVERNMENT

In the United States there are essentially three forms of municipal government. The mayor-council form largely duplicates within cities the standard pattern of American government found at the state and national levels. It incorporates separation of powers, with an elected executive (the mayor), and an elected legislature (the city council). The commission form presents a different pattern and grows less and less popular. This form combines the legislative and executive functions. The voters elect commissioners, each of whom performs a specific executive responsibility. Together, the commissioners sit as the municipal legislature.

It is the popular council-manager form that differs from the standard American model in a way meriting our attention. It attempts to reject politics in the governing of cities by applying to them a structure much like that of the administrative arrangement of a modern corporation. Public school districts and state-supported colleges and universities incorporate similar principles in their administration, but their purposes are narrower and more specialized than those of a government. They therefore do not present the same issues. In this form of municipal government, we find the expression of what is very nearly a pure form of the political ideology of managerialism/professionalism.

In council-manager governments, the voters elect a small city council that serves as the city's legislature; its members will usually be the only elected municipal officials. The council then employs a professional city manager who serves at its pleasure. The manager administers the affairs of the city and has the power to select and discharge the city's department heads. The government is usually nonpartisan, and council candidates run without party labels. Generally, they will be elected at large, thus diluting the effects of sectional sentiment within the city.

This form thus does not incorporate separation of powers as typically understood. In a sense it operates—so far as the executive is concerned—more as if it were parliamentary; that is, the legislature selects, and may dismiss, the chief executive. The parallel is misleading, though, because council members generally serve terms that are staggered so that the entire council cannot lose office simultaneously. Thus changes in the makeup of the council occur, as a rule, gradually, not suddenly as they may in a parliament. Similarly, in a sense, there is a rough kind of separation of powers. The council is forbidden by the council-manager charter from interfering with the details of the city's administration, which in theory must be left to the professional administrator.

The cities of Staunton, Virginia and Sumter, South Carolina each can claim to be the first council-manager city. In 1908 Staunton appointed a "general manager" as the city's administrator but retained other elected officials as well. The Secretary of the National Short Ballot Organization, Richard S. Childs, suggested that cities combine the professional manager with a great restriction on the number of elected officials. In 1912 Sumter did just that, adopting a modern council-manager government. In 1914 Dayton, Ohio became the first relatively large city to do so. Childs became active in the National Municipal League, which was then as it is now a strong advocate of the council-manager system.[9]

As the council-manager system developed, there was considerable attention to the "distinction between 'policy' which was the responsibility of the council and 'administration' which was the responsibility of the manager. Each was warned by professors and practitioners of government to be careful not to interfere with the responsibilities of the other. In more recent years, it has come to be recognized that the distinction between these two functions is at best a fuzzy one and that the two will often overlap."[10]

---

[9] Leonard E. Goodall, *The American Metropolis* (Columbus, Ohio: Charles E. Merrill, 1968), pp. 59–60.
[10] Ibid.

There is no question that, as Adrian wrote, "the plan has had special appeal to Americans who have long wanted to remove 'politics' from municipal government and to place it on a 'businesslike' basis." Nothing could illustrate more vividly the thrust toward managerialism. Adrian proceeded to write that "of course 'politics' is essential in a democracy, in the sense that democracy is the process by which popular wants are compromised and converted into public policy by elected officeholders," and he noted that all municipalities contain politics of this sort, regardless of how governed. The appeal of the plan is that it appeared to the citizenry to minimize political conflict and to provide the expertise that seems so necessary to apply to the complex city operations.[11]

If there remains any doubt regarding the attitude of many council-manager advocates toward politics, an October 1942 editorial in the *National Municipal Review* should lay it to rest. This form of government, it said, "came into being as a result of a demand for business rather than political management of public affairs." Goodall noted the "pervasive influence of the assumption that local government and politics should be separated. The council-management plan was advocated as a means for substituting businesslike management practices for political manipulation." He went on to say that politics, if it has to do with management of conflict, is present in local government as surely as at any other level, but that there was an inherent assumption on the part of the reformers that "local government is somehow different from state and national governments."[12] Actually, this was not necessarily the case. There have been attempts at nonpartisan legislatures at the state level, and Anwar Syed has pointed out that Frank Goodnow, an early theorist of municipal government, "would replace local self-government with local *self-administration*," whereas another such reformer, Luther "Gulick and the other like-minded theorists would substitute self-administration for self-government at the state as well as the local level."[13]

All this is not to say that Americans accepted the council-manager system unanimously, or that there was not frequent strong

[11] Charles R. Adrian, *Governing Our Fifty States and their Communities* (New York: McGraw–Hill, 1978), p. 122.
[12] Goodall, p. 73.
[13] Anwar Syed, *The Political Theory of American Local Government* (New York: Random House, 1966), p. 156.

opposition. As might be expected, there were complaints that city managers were "outsiders" who could not understand local conditions and should not be entrusted with city administration, or that the powers of the manager were "dictatorial." There have also been even more substantial reservations, both initially and through the years.

One difficulty of the manager plan is that it rarely provides the strong policy guidance that complex and troublesome urban conditions demand. The council usually chooses one of its members to serve as mayor, and this official presides over council meetings but otherwise has little power beyond that of any other member. Even if the voters choose the mayor directly, mayoral duties as a rule remain the same. In either case, the mayor's responsibility is essentially ceremonial.

The manager is the focal point of administration. As such, he or she may recommend actions to the council but generally must avoid the appearance of policy involvement. A controversial manager is not likely to remain manager very long. If a strong manager does succeed in becoming a substantial initiator of policy, then policy initiation lies outside the hands of elected officials, a situation that troubles advocates of democracy. In any case, critics of council-manager plans see them as unresponsive to popular will, in that they locate the administration of city services further from the direct control of those whom they affect than do other forms of municipal government.

The critics view such a situation at best as inherently less democratic than other forms. John Harrigan has written that "the evaluation of metropolitan and urban governance in the twentieth century has shown a consistent turning away from the basic democratic principle of a government accountable to the people."[14] In attempting to achieve a government without politics, the reformers typically built into their systems not only the post of manager but also numerous independent boards and commissions with appointed members.

Their concern was to escape from "boss" politics. In viewing cities dominated by political machines and comparing them with others functioning under reform governments, some critics of

---

[14]John J. Harrigan, *Political Change in the Metropolis* (Boston: Little, Brown, 1976), p. 70.

council-manager systems have identified each approach as imposing very high costs, but in each case the costs are different. Boss rule brought both high expenses and the corruption of using public office for private gain. The nonpartisan council-manager government tended to be much more efficient and more honest in the traditional sense, but it imposed costs of another sort: middleclass and business domination, impersonality, and more remote and less accountable government. "Democratic control and participation were sacrificed for efficient management."[15]

James Q. Wilson has noted that "nonpartisanship usually tends to favor Republican—or more correctly, business-oriented—political leaders."[16] In this instance, as in every other, managerialism does not achieve its goal of eliminating politics. Rather, it drives politics underground, away from the public eye. It revises the rules of the game, but the game goes on.

The supporters of council-manager government seem to remain considerably more numerous than the opponents, and through the years they have responded directly to all criticisms. Writing in the *Public Administration Review*, C. A. Harrell and D. G. Weiford concluded that "There is no danger to representative government from the council-manager system." They identified fears that the system is anti-democratic with simple nostalgia and with a failure to recognize that changing times bring changing conditions.[17]

They observed that administrative theory has changed from the simpler models prevailing before the Second World War, when it held that politics and administration could be neatly separated. More recent theory, they pointed out, recognizes that public administration is "an integral part of the political process," and that bureaucracies are part of the "total process of government, which includes the determination of policy." They do not attempt to provide a true justification of their conclusion that council-manager government presents no danger to representative democracy, but they do call for a "wholesale re-examination of

---

[15] Douglas Yates, *The Ungovernable City* (Cambridge: M.I.T. Press, 1978), p. 170.
[16] James Q. Wilson, "Politics and Reform in American Cities," in Robert L. Morlan, ed., *Capitol, Courthouse, and City Hall*, 5th ed. (Boston: Houghton Mifflin, 1977), p. 298.
[17] C. A. Harrell and D. G. Weiford, "The City Manager and the Policy Process," *Public Administration Review*, XIX:2 (Spring 1959), pp. 101–107.

political theory and of the relationship which public administration as a political process bears to the fundamental elements of democracy."

Such a reexamination would have been welcome and would have been more satisfying than assertions that "the public today is better educated and more alert to governmental progress or the lack of it than ever before," that "there must now be unquestioned morality in government," or that "modern local government . . . is held in check by public standards which are higher and more exacting than those of any earlier time." Such assumptions—and they were just that—were unrealistic even when the authors wrote of them, nearly a decade before Watergate. Now they sound hopelessly naive. Hardly more acceptable is their analysis of democracy. They indicated that it has changed, but that reliance upon administrators for policy guidance is no less democratic than earlier systems because "there are sound reasons" for it. There undoubtedly are, but the effect upon democracy remains to be demonstrated.

Their evaluation of council-manager government today is widely accepted. "When measured against the problems of the present and the anticipated greater problems of the future," they wrote, "it is difficult to conceive of a better-balanced, more effective system of local government than the one which has found expression in the elected council and the appointed city manager."[18] There is no question that the council-manager system in general has worked well in small and medium-sized cities with homogeneous populations. In order to understand it as fully as possible, one should recognize both its strengths and its weaknesses. Above all, one should recognize it as the implementation of a specific political ideology: managerialism.

Although they agreed upon seeking less corrupt and more efficient local government, the early reformers were far from unanimous in their motives for advocating council-manager plans. They all sought more "businesslike" government, but for many it was merely a short step from businesslike government to government by and in the interests of business.

Writers differ in their assessment of the reformers' personal intentions. Samuel P. Hays has studied municipal reforms in the

[18] Ibid., p. 107.

Progressive Era and has concluded that they were led by business elites who frequently worked to deny representation to the lower classes.[19] Martin Schiesl disputed this conclusion and argued that the reformers' approach to politics was no less democratic than those that preceded them.[20] Undoubtedly there were those whose concern was to reduce participation by immigrant groups and the poor. Eugene Lewis has written that urban Progressive reformers in fact were almost preoccupied with fear of immigrant groups.[21] Richard McCormick took a more tolerant view of the reformers and wrote that although some did seek "to lessen the political influence of immigrants and Catholics through restrictive election-law reforms, the movement as a whole did not find its basis in such sentiment,"[22] and that "certainly most reformers sincerely believed that the changes they proposed would make their cities more democratic, not less."[23]

Whatever their intentions, the Progressive reformers sought to break the power of the bosses. Because the support of the voters was the source of a boss's power, it followed that it was necessary to restrict the role of the voter, at least of the voter who was likely to support the boss. This often meant that restrictions needed to be applied to the ability of immigrant voters to affect policy. Such concern regarding immigrant power resulted in a broader concern about the role of the general public, bringing about the argument that it was essential to eliminate "politics" from city government. This was simply a subtle form of saying that government should be freed from popular control.[24]

Local government is no less important to the citizen than government at any other level. As a matter of fact, the average citizen is likely to feel the effects of local government more consistently

[19] Samuel P. Hays, "The Politics of Reform in Municipal Government in the Progressive Era," *Pacific Northwest Quarterly*, 55 (October 1964), pp. 157–69.
[20] Martin J. Schiesl, *The Politics of Efficiency: Municipal Administration and Reform in America, 1880–1920* (Berkeley: University of California Press, 1977).
[21] Eugene Lewis, *The Urban Political System* (Hinsdale, N.Y.: Holt, Rinehart & Winston, 1973), p. 75.
[22] Richard L. McCormick, *From Realignment to Reform: Political Change in New York State, 1893–1910* (Ithaca: Cornell University Press, 1981), pp. 106–107.
[23] Ibid., p. 261.
[24] Max J. Skidmore, "Urban America," in B. K. Shrivastava and Thomas W. Casstevens, eds., *American Government and Politics* (Atlantic Highlands, N.J.: Humanities Press, 1980), pp. 257–60.

than the effects of governments at greater distances. The political ideologies that affect local governments are therefore no less important than those that affect government at other levels. Managerialism may be seen more clearly at this level than at any other because of the explicit nature of the council-manager arrangement. Without doubt, there are great strengths that managerialism displays at the same time that it reflects some troublesome elements. No approach to government is perfect, nor is any single approach the best under all conditions. The task is not to achieve perfection but to achieve the best that is possible under the circumstances. To do so requires an understanding of the ideologies at work.

MANAGERIALISM IN PERSPECTIVE

Because managerialism is different from other political ideologies and may exist alongside or as a part of almost any other, it is especially difficult to evaluate it with reference to the typical ideological characteristics. It functions in a chameleon-like manner, adopting the coloration of the system and the overt ideology within which it operates. This explains why it goes generally unrecognized as a political ideology, regardless of its definite political effects.

Attitude Toward Change

Managerialism, "bureaucratism," and professionalism may not be exactly synonymous, but they certainly are closely related. The difficulties of persuading bureaucracies to change are well known and reflect the tendency of managerialism to resist change. An exception to this is technological innovation, which managerialism tends to welcome.

Attitude Toward Human Nature

Managerialism tends to regard human nature as largely irrelevant; the important thing is efficiency and procedure. Human nature should be subject to rules and regulations that reflect the greatest efficiency.

Attitude Toward the Potential of Human Reason

The managerial tendency is to assume that managers should apply reason to the solution of human problems and that the result will be beneficial.

Attitude Toward Human Progress

Managerialism assumes that the application of proper techniques to human affairs will produce the best possible situation. Thus, insofar as inadequate administration exists, progress will result from administrative improvements and is contingent upon such improvements. Managerialism therefore assumes the possibility of progress but not its inevitability. It also does not promise utopian perfection, merely that adopting the best managerial techniques will achieve whatever is possible for humanity.

Attitude Toward the Relationship of the Individual to the Community

Although at first glance it would not seem to take a position on this relationship, managerialism does contain strong anti-individualist implications. Its thrust is to increase the power and efficiency of the state, as opposed to the individual. Beyond that, it would subordinate even the state to the dictates of technology, limiting its actions to those that can be carried out "scientifically." Such a state would be limited to no concern other than the application of the best technique; this would require that human beings be treated as things, as identical units. As Crick put it, the state would become merely a filing cabinet (or a computer, he might now say), "when men can be treated simply as the contents of files."[25]

THE FUTURE OF MANAGERIALISM

The alternative to trained administrators and to professional bureaucracies based on merit is hardly attractive. Would we wish to have less expertise in administering government programs, as temporary and politically appointed bureaucrats would be likely to offer? Would we wish to have administrators who substitute

[25] Crick, p. 107.

personal judgment for the rigid rules and regulations that govern bureaucracy's functioning? Would this be an improvement, or lead to arbitrary and unfair administration? These questions really turn on the issue of managerialism.

What are the alternatives to managerialism in the modern world? Despite the shortcomings of bureaucracies and bureaucratic structures, there are bureaucracies and bureaucrats in every nation that perform with intelligence, dedication, honesty, and efficiency. Moreover, I must point out that it is misleading, even if necessary, to use the term "bureaucracy" as freely as I have used it in this discussion. There are many widely varied institutions and organizations covered by the term. Although for convenience we must use the word, we should also recognize that we must be careful to avoid "the bankruptcy of stereotyped thinking about bureaucracy."[26] Modern society clearly depends upon bureaucracy, and this means permanent bureaucracies. Managerialism therefore is an ideology that is fundamental to the operation of modern society. In discussing its shortcomings, I do not suggest that it can be eliminated, nor necessarily that it should be.

One may recognize the numerous difficulties inherent in merit systems and professional bureaucracies without opposing their existence. This means, of course, that one may recognize the dangers in managerialism without opposing it entirely. The only feasible approach appears to be vigilance, a reasoned analysis to determine where its application is appropriate and consistent with the essential political values and ideologies of the society, and where it is not consistent and therefore not appropriate.

One of the most troublesome issues pertains to control of technological decisions. To a considerable extent, such control is managerial, rather than political. Developments with such profound social effects as the automobile, the telephone, radio and television, and the computer have been placed into widespread service without regard to the political process. Whether deliberate or not, modern society has been revolutionized by forces that to a large extent have been under the direction of managers, in these instances, corporate managers. There appears to be sharp conflict between the goals of rapid technological development and political control of society's direction.

[26]Goodsell, p. 140.

In 1980 the chairman of the commission established to investigate the nuclear accident at Three Mile Island, Dr. John Kemeny, noted that "Jeffersonian democracy cannot work in the year 1980—the world has become too complex." He also remarked that many people say that democracy is not perfect, yet we "muddle through," but that we no longer can do so, and that "the issues we deal with do not lend themselves to that kind of treatment."[27] It may be that the demands of technological change have rendered earlier forms of politics obsolete, but, if so, what are the alternatives?

David Dickson, the Washington news editor for the British magazine *Nature*, has written that "increasingly, the state is taking on the role of an efficient manager . . . eager to maintain discipline and productivity among its work force. There are more than echoes here of the nineteenth-century engineer Frederick Taylor, father of 'scientific management.' " Federal agencies attempt "to promote economic efficiency by limiting political participation in decisions that will determine the shape and direction of technological change."[28] Without deliberate and careful study to determine what can be done, political control in the traditional sense will vanish completely. The managers would seem to be in control, but in reality, even they would be reacting blindly to what they perceive as technology's dictates.

For better or worse, managerialism is here to stay. No nation today, certainly no industrialized nation, could exist without it. It has brought great improvements, not merely dangers. The challenge is to make it compatible with the society's essential values. In liberal democracies, this challenge is reflected in the title of a fine little book by Eugene P. Dvorin and Robert H. Simmons, *From Amoral to Humane Bureaucracy.*[29] Given the characteristics of bureaucracies—their tendencies to be what everyone recognizes by the term "bureaucratic"—the task is not an easy one but also not impossible. With good will and effort, bureaucracy can be made compatible with human values. When and if this occurs, managerialism/professionalism will have proved a boon to humanity. If it fails to occur, it will have contributed greatly to the development of a dehumanized society.

[27] Quoted in David Dickson, "Limiting Democracy: Technocrats and the Liberal State," *Democracy*, 1:1 (January 1981), p. 64.
[28] Ibid., p. 64.
[29] Eugene P. Dvorin and Robert H. Simmons, *From Amoral to Humane Bureaucracy* (New York: Canfield Press of Harper & Row, 1972).

Contemporary Religious Thought and Political Ideologies

8

*I*t would be difficult to overemphasize the effect of religious belief and practice upon politics and political ideology. Anything so central to human experience as religion inevitably affects life in ways far beyond the church, mosque, or temple. In a similar fashion, politics, which deals with collective goals and power relationships within groups, is pervasive wherever there is a human community. Two such important realms of human existence could not fail to influence one another.

Any attempt to understand political ideologies without reference to the effects of religion upon politics would therefore ignore much that is relevant. Our discussion from the very beginning has made clear that political ideologies cannot be studied effectively in a vacuum, and that religious practice and ideas

221

throughout the ages have indelibly influenced political ideology. This means of course that they have influenced political practice as well.

The influence in some cases reflects deliberate efforts to build religion into politics and to establish a political system based upon religion. We see this, for example, in the attempt by Puritans in seventeenth-century New England to establish a "City on a Hill," in the actions by some Sikh and Hindu fundamentalists in India, and in the demands of some proponents of "Liberation Theology," primarily in Latin America. It is evident also in revolutionary Iran, which explicitly has sought since the late 1970s to be a totally fundamentalist Islamic society. It is no less present in the political activity of the "religious right" in the United States, which since the early 1970s has been politically active in an attempt to redirect the nation's entire political system to reflect a particular view of fundamental, evangelical, Christianity. Considerably more moderate Christian examples might be the Christian Democratic parties that are numerous in Western Europe and Latin America, various attempts at Christian socialism, religion-based peace and pacifist groups, and religion-based civil rights movements. These are only a few of the multitude of possible examples of overt attempts to mix religion and politics. Certainly, some aspects of the ideology of apartheid could be included here, as well as among right-wing ideologies, just as some of the belief systems named here could also be included elsewhere.

In any case, as the *Christian Science Monitor* has observed, "to ignore the growing politicization of religion on the world scene is a dangerous mistake. . . . From the key role played in Tibet by Buddhist monks in protests against China to that in Nicaragua by a Roman Catholic prelate, Miguel Cardinal Obando y Bravo, as intermediary in cease-fire talks . . . the blend of politics and religion is becoming a potent Third World force; it deserves both respect and understanding."[1] The effects of religion on political ideology are not limited to the Third World, nor are they limited to overt attempts to combine religion and politics.

It is probably even more frequent that religion influences politics unknowingly. In such cases the influence results from unconscious assumptions that reflect the effects of religion without

---

[1] "Religion in World Politics," *Christian Science Monitor* (November 13, 1987), p. 15.

any intention to combine religion and politics or without even an awareness that religion is involved. Religion is likely to condition outlooks and attitudes to such a degree that it may shape even sincere attempts to establish secular political systems.

Many of humanity's most fundamental beliefs—its ethical system, its views of right and wrong, and so forth—are religious, or related to religion, and certainly a society's basic beliefs will determine its political ideologies. Some such beliefs may well be universal. No society for example would or could permit indiscriminate murder. Many other beliefs will not be universal and will relate specifically to religious and ethical views that may be peculiar to that society, such as matters pertaining to marriage and divorce, culturally prescribed gender roles and the like. However universal or particular certain beliefs might be, objectively viewed, the society is likely to assume that they are universal. Thus in permitting them to shape political institutions, the society can be genuinely unaware that it is building its religious orientation into its politics.

There is yet another manner in which religion may influence political ideology. An ideology may be based upon a reaction against a particular religion. It might even be motivated by hostility against religion in general. Both Lutheranism and Calvinism were reactions against contemporary Roman Catholicism. The political systems that they generated were as much anti-Catholic as they were specifically oriented toward Calvinism or Lutheranism. Many Marxist-Leninist systems are explicitly anti-religious, and to be sure some Marxist-Leninists are motivated as much by hostility toward a religion—or toward religion in general—as by economics or politics.

It is rare for a work on political ideologies to deal with specific religious ideologies, even though hardly anyone would argue that religion has no effect on politics. Some religions take on obvious political characteristics, but a restricted definition of political ideology may obscure this. One advantage of our broad definition is that when circumstances warrant, it can apply to ideologies with primary orientations that are other than political. It can demonstrate when an essentially nonpolitical ideology—economic, religious, or any other—becomes sufficiently political that it should be considered in any comprehensive attempt to understand political ideologies.

Our definition thus achieves its purpose, which is to clarify. In other words, it works and is useful. The ideologies that we will examine in this chapter are not exclusively, or even primarily, political; they are religious. Nevertheless, their political effects justify our treating them under our definition of political ideology.

CHRISTIAN DEMOCRATIC PARTIES

Throughout most of Western Europe and Latin America there are political parties that are specifically religious in their orientation. Their names and character vary somewhat, but generally they are called Christian Democratic parties. They tend to be parties of the center, ranging from conservatives on the moderate right to the more numerous reform groups with mildly leftist agenda. Almost always they are Roman Catholic, although there are two major exceptions to this. The Christian Democratic party of the Netherlands resulted in 1970 from the merger of the Catholic Peoples' party with two small Protestant groups, and the Christian Democratic party of the Federal Republic of Germany also includes Protestants.

Christian democracy has been highly influential since World War II. In recent years it has brought heads of government to power in many nations, including the Federal Republic of Germany, Guatemala, El Salvador, Italy, Chile, Venezuela, and Ecuador. A Christian Democratic party exists in nearly all countries in Latin America and in most Western European states, with considerable strength in several.

Christian democracy has its roots in European developments following the French Revolution. The Revolution unleashed currents in direct opposition to the social and political conservatism of the Roman Catholic church. The result was to force the Church further to the right in its politics, which culminated in 1864 in the *Syllabus of Errors* of Pope Pius IX, who was pope from 1846 to 1878. The pope did not content himself with a discussion of purely religious matters but identified among his eighty errors a long list of political principles and practices. He or other popes had already, in previous encyclicals, condemned as an error each practice on the list. Among the errors were:[2]

[2] Ann Fremantle, ed., *The Papal Encyclicals in their Historical Context* (New York: G. P. Putnam's Sons, 1956), pp. 143–52.

- "15. Every man is free to embrace and profess that religion which, guided by the light of reason, he shall consider true. . . .
- 20. The ecclesiastical power ought not to exercise its authority without the permission and assent of the civil government. . . .
- 24. The Church has not the power of using force, nor has she any temporal power, direct or indirect. . . .
- 27. The sacred ministers of the Church and the Roman pontiff are to be absolutely excluded from every charge and dominion over temporal affairs. . . .
- 42. In the case of conflicting laws enacted by the two powers, the civil law prevails. . . .
- 45. The entire government of public schools . . . may and ought to appertain to the civil power, and . . . no other authority . . . shall be recognized as having any right to interfere. . . .
- 47. The best theory of civil society requires that popular schools . . . and, generally, all public institutes . . . should be freed from all ecclesiastical authority, control, and interference. . . .
- 55. The Church ought to be separated from the State, and the State from the Church. . . .
- 63. It is lawful to refuse obedience to legitimate princes, and even to rebel against them. . . .
- 67. . . . in many cases divorce properly so called may be decreed by the civil authority. . . .
- 77. In the present day it is no longer expedient that the Catholic religion should be held as the only religion of the State, to the exclusion of all other forms of worship. . . .
- 80. The Roman Pontiff can, and ought to, reconcile himself, and come to terms with progress, liberalism and modern civilization."

When Pius died in 1878, however, he was succeeded by Leo XIII, who was pope until 1903. Despite error number 80, Leo's policies in many cases did much to bring the Church to terms with modern civilization. Anne Fremantle calls his eighty-six encyclicals "a collection of statements on various modern problems that is the most important single contribution to Catholic doctrine since the Middle Ages," and she rates Leo as "one of the greatest of all the popes."[3] One of his most famous encyclicals is *Rerum Novarum,* which he issued in May of 1891.[4]

This encyclical, "The Condition of the Working Classes," reversed the tone of Pius IX's pronouncements on social matters. Pope Leo argued that the Church must deal with modern political and social issues and must move to alleviate economic misery. In order to do this, it was necessary to understand the causes of the conditions. Moreover, although he was no less strident than Pius in his denunciation of radical movements, especially those hostile to religion, he recognized that it was important to understand the reasons for their emergence and appeal.

"All agree, and there can be no question whatever," he wrote, "that some remedy must be found, and found quickly for the misery and wretchedness pressing so heavily and unjustly at this moment on the vast majority of the working classes."[5] The pope also reaffirmed his commitment to the institution of private property. He wrote that "to remedy these wrongs the Socialists, working on the poor man's envy of the rich, are striving to do away with private property, and contend that individual possessions should become the common property of all, to be administered by the State or by municipal bodies." To do so, however, would deny the worker the ability to obtain property and thus would "strike at the interests of every wage-earner, since they would deprive him of the liberty of disposing of his wages and thereby of all hope and possibility of increasing his stock and of bettering his condition in life."[6] His conclusion in this regard was that "private ownership is in accordance with the law of nature."[7]

He defended unequal distribution of property and admitted that suffering would always exist, but that "it is shameful and inhuman to treat men like chattels to make money by, or to look upon them merely as so much muscle or physical power."[8] Accordingly, he called upon the rich to use their wealth as if it were common to all and share it with the less fortunate. As for the state, he asserted that "the interests of all, whether high or low,

[3] Ibid., p. 156.
[4] Ibid., pp. 166–95.
[5] Ibid., p. 167.
[6] Ibid., p. 168.
[7] Ibid., p. 170.
[8] Ibid., pp. 173–75.

are equal. The poor are members of the national community equally with the rich." By no means was this an opinion that was universal at the time, nor was his view that it is the state's obligation to alleviate misery. He stated this unequivocally: "The public administration must duly and solicitously provide for the welfare and the comfort of the working classes; otherwise that law of justice will be violated which ordains that each man shall have his due."[9]

Leo further advocated comprehensive arrangements to strengthen the family and to soften economic adversity. These included guilds and trade unions, which the more conservative thinkers at the turn of the century found alarming. What at one time was alarming is now widely accepted. Although at no time did he express a preference for democracy as a political form—following the Church's basic position that political forms are irrelevant if the state is just and gives religion and the Church their due—Leo's social doctrine has become fundamental to much of today's Christian democratic thought and practice, especially as amplified and developed by the French Catholic philosopher and diplomat Jacques Maritain (1882–1973).

Maritain discarded the notion of sovereignty and accepted the separation of church and state, which could be compatible with cooperation between the two. His position traced a moderate path between the excesses of liberal individualistic atomism on the one hand, and that of totalitarianism on the other. Christian Democratic parties strongly reflect his influence.

It was not until after the Second World War that Christian Democratic parties became fully developed. In 1935, just before the War, Eduardo Frei helped to found the National Falange (no relation to the Spanish Falange) in Chile. The Chilean Christian Democratic party grew from this group, and began a movement that spread over nearly all of South and Central America. During this time Christian Democratic parties emerged in Italy and most nations of Western Europe.

In 1966 Frei became President of Chile as a Christian democrat. That same year, Christian Democratic delegates met in Lima, Peru from all Latin American countries, and from ten in Western Europe. By this time, many nations on both continents had elected Christian democrats as leaders. Although there is considerable

[9] Ibid., p. 181.

variation from one party to another, the essential thrust of Christian democracy is toward social reform and steering a middle course between right-wing capitalism and the left. Its essence is Christian teachings and the avoidance of totalitarianism and other extremes at either end of the political spectrum.

In Latin America the strength of Christian democrats has varied according to the ability of each nation to retain democratic processes. In Chile, where Christian democracy began on the continent and had been powerful, it gradually lost power in the late 1960s when the country elected a Marxian socialist, Dr. Salvadore Allende Gossens (1908–1973), as president. Allende was allied with the communists, a small group that dated in that country all the way back to 1912, even before the Russian party. A right-wing military coup in 1973 brought down the Allende government, and also all parties including the Christian democrats, and instituted a harsh military dictatorship under the control of General Augusto Pinochet Ugarte (1915–   ).

In Europe Christian democrats were at the height of their power for more than a decade, beginning in the late 1940s. Their Catholic orientation stressed human brotherhood and international cooperation and influenced the plans in the 1950s for the European Economic Community. After many years of hoping for some sort of European integration, the EEC has emerged as a major step in that direction and as a force in world affairs. Christian democrats certainly assisted in its development.

However their strength waxes and wanes, Christian Democratic parties remain important. Their essentially moderate approach continues to blend religious principle with practical politics and yet avoid Church dominance of the state. They constitute one of the clearest examples of the political effects of religious ideologies, as well as one of the more healthy.

CHRISTIAN SOCIALISM

We have already discussed Christian socialism (especially in the United States) in the chapter on democratic socialism, but because of the close tie between religious and political ideologies, it bears examination here also.

Christian socialists began with Christianity as their starting point, not politics. The social message of Christianity quickly led them to political considerations. In the latter half of the nineteenth century, the harshness of the emerging system of capitalist industrialism—a system that had yet to be modified by any reform or regulation—inspired an enormous number of reformers and new ideologies that sought to alleviate the damage done to society. Some of the reformers were secular in their approach, others were religious.

Among the religious reformers were Christian socialists—critics who charged that capitalism was incompatible with Christianity. Christianity, they argued, was a religion of love and self-denial, whereas capitalism institutionalized selfishness. Christianity demanded cooperation, while capitalism was built upon competition. Christianity was spiritual, and capitalism was materialistic. Capitalism, in fact, elevated to a virtue what Christianity regarded as sin: avarice and greed. Among the commandments that capitalism violated, they believed, was the injunction against covetousness.

Many Christians would have argued that Christians should concern themselves with individual salvation and retreat from the affairs of the world. The degree to which Christians should participate in the political order had been a topic of debate since the days of the early Church. The Christian socialists, of course, rejected this argument. They considered Christianity to require social and political action to assist the downtrodden and to alleviate misery and its causes. Christian socialists interpreted the teachings of Jesus to be more concerned with the conditions of the world and the needs of human beings than with ritual and the minutia of theological considerations.

Outside of the United States, the strongest movement toward Christian socialism was in great Britain. Two clergymen, Charles Kingsley and Frederick Maurice were its most eloquent spokesmen. They argued with grace and style that doing the will of God required the clergy to preach liberty, justice, and brotherhood. The minister who spoke on behalf of equality was speaking God's word. No system that permitted the wealth of a society to be concentrated into a few hands, no system that oppressed the workers, and no system that denied all the people a true place in the political process was compatible with the Kingdom of God and the teachings of Jesus.[10]

Christian socialists, like many others, extended their view of the New Testament to their view of the good society. The religious ideology was paramount, but a specific political ideology was the result. Though now generally overlooked, it continues to find expression—sometimes eloquent expression—as a direct connection between religion and politics.

LIBERATION THEOLOGY

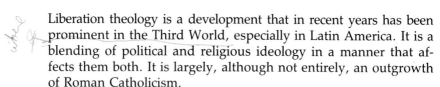

Liberation theology is a development that in recent years has been prominent in the Third World, especially in Latin America. It is a blending of political and religious ideology in a manner that affects them both. It is largely, although not entirely, an outgrowth of Roman Catholicism.

In the years following the Second World War, the Church was alarmed by the increasing secularization among European workers. As other ideologies grew, their commitment to Christianity dwindled. Marxism, especially, was a powerful competitor to Christianity. With its utopian promises and messages of salvation, it often took on much the coloration of a religion in its own right.

In order to persuade workers to return to their religion, the Catholic church encouraged in many European countries, especially France, what came to be called the "Worker Priest Movement."[11] Priests would accept employment as laborers, adopt ordinary dress, and live as the workers lived. The goal was to secure the workers' sympathy and to evangelize.

The movement quickly failed, and the Church suppressed it by the middle 1950s. The difficulty was twofold: it converted few workers and resulted instead in the defection of many priests who adopted the workers' viewpoint and engaged in political action

---

[10]See Stanley E. Baldwin, *Charles Kingsley* (Ithaca: Cornell University Press, 1934) and Robert B. Martin, *The Dust of Combat: The Life of Charles Kingsley* (New York: W. W. Norton, 1960).

[11]John Petrie, ed., *The Worker Priests: A Collective Documentation* (London: Routledge and Kegan Paul, 1956).

along with laboring groups. Most of the priests involved accepted the Church's orders and returned to clerical life, but some were defiant, and there were even those who left the Church to join radical groups, including the Communist party.

The worker priest movement was an indication of alarm within the Church because of the weakening of religion, but to some extent it also reflected concern for the social and economic conditions of the workers. Such concern emerged more strongly in the Second Vatican Council, or Vatican II, in the early 1960s, and the messages of Pope John XXIII. The 1965 encyclical *Gaudium et Spes* (or *Pastoral Constitution on the Church in the World of Today*), for example, directed the Church to attend more to the affairs of the world while maintaining emphasis upon the spiritual.

The Church had always at best been ambivalent regarding the role of social or political action for Christians and frequently had asserted that the Christian as a rule should withdraw from things of the world. After Vatican II, however, there could be no doubt that the Church's position had changed. It not only had come to sanction political and social action but set them forth as obligations of the Catholic community. The 1967 encyclical *Populorum Progressio*, for example, stressed the duty for all Christians to seek peace and justice and to act politically as necessary to attain them.

It was in Latin America that liberation theology burst into full bloom. In 1968 the Second General Council of the Latin American Episcopate convened in Medellin, Colombia to discuss the effects of Vatican II. The outcome was a number of statements that identified capitalism with exploitation, condemned "imperialism" and United States policy toward the Third World, and castigated the ruling elites of Third World nations.

The Council's *Medellin Document on Peace* maintained that the causes of discord in Latin America were the result of international tensions and colonialism, that internal tensions in the various nations were caused by such things as inequality and injustice, and that regional tensions among Latin American nations were caused by militarism among other things. The *Medellin Document on Poverty* identified social service as a Christian duty and urged priests to live among the workers as laborers themselves, much as the worker priests had done in Europe.

In 1976 a number of Catholic bishops from poor countries published "A Letter to Peoples of the Third World." In it they adopted Marxist rhetoric and spoke of the poor as the "proletariat" while calling for revolution. The letter spoke not only of imperialism in the classical sense but also of cultural and economic imperialism. The need, it asserted, was for socialism. Three years later, a statement called the "Preferential Option for the Poor" came from the Conference of Latin American Bishops, meeting in Mexico. The statement is mainly the work of a Peruvian theologian, Father Gustavo Gutierrez, who called upon the poor to become the agents of their own liberation by taking direct action.

Action, or "praxis," is a theme inherent in liberation theology. Jesus did not confine himself to doctrine but took action to aid the poor and liberate them. He promised a new kingdom on earth. Liberation theology looks to the actions, as well as the teachings, of Jesus for its inspiration and argues that true Christianity must base itself upon the example of its founder and become activist. It must seek aggressively to eliminate the ills of the world, to be present "as Jesus was present when the nets were cast by the fishermen on the Sea of Galilee," and to deal with "the insults of industrialism to God's children, humiliated by poverty and treated as a depersonalized thing."[12] In order to accomplish this in Latin America, which has a great shortage of priests, the movement encouraged programs whereby Christian workers—including priests—could be prepared quickly in extension centers, without the formal education normally required of the clergy. This new version of worker priest evangelizes and also goes forth to engage in social activism.

Although the high officials of the Church favor the efforts to alleviate social and economic misery, they are not comfortable with liberation theology. The movement has tended to adopt explicitly Marxist language, which produces uneasiness. Much of liberation theology is built, as is Marxism, upon the notion of class struggle—in this case the poor, rather than the proletariat—which the pope rejects.

In 1984 the Vatican conducted an examination of the teachings and beliefs of many of the movement's leaders. Joseph Cardinal Ratzinger, Prefect for the Sacred Congregation for the Doctrine of the Faith (no longer known by its earlier name, the Inquisition) conducted the investigation and called several of the movement's

---

[12]Melvin Maddocks, "Religion and Politics in the '80s, and Earlier," *Christian Science Monitor* (February 27, 1987), p. 21.

leaders to Rome to testify. Friar Leonardo Boff of Brazil was prominent among them, and his works continue to attract Rome's criticism, as does the Brazilian movement in general.[13] The Vatican, in fact, has censured Boff and once "silenced" him for eleven months.[14]

The Congregation did not condemn liberation theology but expressed concerns.[15] It pointed out that no secular doctrine could replace the scriptures. As for the idea of class struggle, the statement portrayed it as holding forth false hope that would result in worsening of conditions.

Many of the priests active in the liberation theology movement would appear to agree with Brazil's Frei David Raimundo Santos. Frei David studied with Boff and, as a seminarian, read a clandestine photocopy of Marx's *Das Kapital* obtained by some radical students. He now works with, and lives among, the poorest of the poor. "He does not like to talk about politics, because priests like him are often accused of being Marxists, and he is hard put to explain the delicate but, to him, essential difference between being a Marxist and being a Christian who finds Marxist categories of class and capital useful, and even accurate categories with which to describe the life in a place like Campos Eliseos."[16]

The question of ties to Marxism contributed to the suppression of the worker priest movement and continues to make liberation theology a prominent target for its critics. Maddocks has noted that "some have found the worker-priests of France and Belgium and their heirs—the clerics of 'liberation theology' in Latin America today—to be political naifs, manipulated by the shrewd secularists with whom they form 'solidarity.' How much Marxism and how much Christianity are in the mix?" he asked, and said that "the answer is no clearer to their friends than to their enemies. The clerics of liberation theology, like the worker-priests and other adherents of the social gospel, are regarded as too secular by their church, and too religious by the politicians."[17]

---

[13]See Jane Kramer, "Letter From the Elysian Fields," *The New Yorker* (March 2, 1987), pp. 40–75, for an especially vivid portrait of liberation theology in this, the world's largest Roman Catholic country.
[14]Ibid., p. 41.
[15]"Instruction on Certain Aspects of the Theology of Liberation," Second Congregation for the Doctrine of the Faith, The Vatican (September 1984).
[16]Kramer, pp. 40–41.
[17]Maddocks, p. 21.

Liberation theology nevertheless remains vigorous. It appears to be as revolutionary with regard to religious ideology as it is to politics. Where it will lead is uncertain. It could fade away. It might develop into a force that is essentially political or into one that is essentially religious. The potential even exists for a new movement—simultaneously religious and political—that could sever itself from any political or religious structure now existing. Liberation theology bears obvious resemblance to Christian socialism in many respects, but has vastly greater force. Further developments should prove especially interesting for those concerned with political ideologies.

MAINSTREAM RELIGION AND POLITICS

Thus far we have discussed attempts to apply religion directly to politics in such a way as to create specifically religious political ideologies. Such attempts are not the only ways in which religion affects political institutions and ideologies. All of the world's great religions so condition the cultures where they are dominant as to exert a powerful influence, sometimes recognized and sometimes not, on the resulting politics.

Two of the most widespread non-Christian religions are Islam and Hinduism. In neither of these systems of belief is there anything corresponding to the Christian notion of a church. Questions of church-state relationships therefore become less relevant than in Christianity, while at the same time the relation between religion and the state becomes if possible even more complicated.

Islam's founder, Muhammad, grew up in Mecca, where he criticized false gods and the selfishness of the wealthy. He left in A.D. 622 to settle in Medina somewhat to the north. There, he established a nation of believers, which by the time of his death in 632, dominated the entire Arabian Peninsula. His successors, the caliphs, who were regarded as both guardians of the faith and political leaders, expanded Islam's domain as far east as China and Southeast Asia, into the South Asian subcontinent of India, and as far west as Spain.

Islam began with an explicitly political character. That character remains today. Muhammad was the political as well as the religious head of the community, and thus Islam and politics are almost impossible to divorce, even theoretically. "Islam is unique among the world's major monotheistic faiths in that it is not just a religion but a religious polity complete with rules of law, the Sharia."[18] The political institutions of the Muslim world vary according to the country. In some cases, such as Iran, Saudi Arabia, and perhaps Pakistan in the last decade, they are a direct outgrowth of the religion. Even in the most secular of Muslim countries there is a direct relationship.

The major doctrinal split among Muslims is among the Shiite faction dominant in Iran and the Sunni. This explains part, though by no means all, of the hostility between Iran and Iraq, which is Sunni. The conservative Sunni leaders in Saudi Arabia and elsewhere have long accused the Iranians of using religion to achieve their political goals at the expense of other Muslims. Mecca is in Saudi Arabia, and the *Hajj*, a pilgrimage to Mecca (to be made at least once, is a spiritual duty of each devout Muslim). The Saudis contend that Iranian agents have sought to undermine the Saudi government under cover of the pilgrimage, and in 1987 there was a battle between Iranians and Saudi forces in Mecca at Islam's most holy shrine.

The Saudis, however, have themselves used religion for explicitly political purposes. As Shireen Hunter (Deputy Director of Mideast Studies at the Center for Strategic and International Studies) has written, the House of Saud justified its assumption of power by the Koran, and used its authority to impose rigid controls over the citizenry. It is skillful at using its custodianship of Mecca to increase its prestige and influence within the Muslim world. Moreover, the Saudis have built mosques and contributed large amounts of funds to encourage Islamic organizations throughout the extensive Muslim world. Their purpose has been to encourage conservatism and stability, but it has had the unintended effect of creating Islamic revolutionary consciousness as well.[19]

The majority of the world's Muslims are not in the Middle East but in South and Southeast Asia. Indonesia is the largest Muslim country and the most advanced. It is there that we find

[18]Robin Wright, "Quiet Revolution: Islamic Movement's New Phase," *Christian Science Monitor* (November 6, 1987), pp. 18–19; quotation from p. 19.

[19]Shireen T. Hunter, "Revolution in the Persian Gulf Will Get Messier," *Kansas City Times* (August 21, 1987), p. 21.

the most activity in "rethinking fundamental Islamic concepts of church and state. In the process, Moslem scholars say, they are modernizing and liberalizing their religion, creating models for the larger Islamic world." Indonesian intellectuals are attempting to introduce modernity into their religious lives and are "debating not only the Islamic tenet that there can be no division between religious and civil authority, but also cultural, social and economic issues, and attitudes toward ecumenism and 'interfaith activities.' "[20]

The difference in Muslim cultures and religious understandings is illustrated by the situation that resulted in the 1970s when the Saudis invited five Indonesian students to Mecca as official guests. "One of them wrote an article saying it was an anti-Islamic place, because of the treatment of women and so on. Never was another Indonesian student invited again."[21]

Indonesian thinkers recognize that secular education is not the full answer and are seeking new ways in which to use traditional Indonesian civic and religious institutions to provide an effective accommodation to modern conditions. Adi Sasono directs the Institute for Development Studies in Indonesia and also administers the library at Djakarta's largest mosque. He believes that the most urgent task now facing Islam is how to deal with developmental issues, and not arguments over orthodoxy. He stresses that the Koran "is a source of values to be interpreted in our time and place. Islam should be a social ethic, a source of social justice."[22]

The difficulties that Islam is facing in adjusting to the modern world result partly from its unique mixture of politics and religion. More important, however, is Islam's prevalence in traditional cultures that until recently have remained rather isolated from the rest of the world. Those non-Muslims who believe it impossible for Islam to advance should take note of the liberalizing tendencies in most other religions. Christianity, for example, has adjusted quite well, both theologically and practically, to the modern world. Yet, it was not long ago that Christianity appeared to be wedded to a rigid and anti-scientific orthodoxy and to be as traditional as Islam may seem today.

---

[20] Barbara Crossette, "Indonesia Moslems Confront Change But Are Seeking to 'Tame' Excesses," *New York Times* (February 5, 1987), p. 6Y.
[21] Ibid.
[22] Ibid.

Islam is one of the newer of the world's great religions, while Hinduism is among the most ancient. Although some other countries, such as Nepal, are predominantly Hindu, it is to India that one turns when considering Hinduism. India considers itself to be the world's most religious nation, and in some ways this is certainly true. Hinduism, like Islam, is as much a system of ritual and practices, a way of life, as it is a system of beliefs.

Modern India is a secular, democratic state. It has incorporated Western ideas of liberal democracy, and its legal system provides for protection of civil liberties. Its governmental institutions would strike the casual observer as quite similar to those in the West and considerably more Western in style than Asian. Despite the secular nature of the state, one does not have to delve very deeply to discover the Hindu influences that remain predominant.

The most notable feature of Hinduism is caste. Modern India has officially outlawed discrimination based upon caste and in fact has elaborate "affirmative action" programs for "scheduled" tribes and castes, those of low status and characteristic poverty. The caste system itself nevertheless remains powerful and conditions much of Indian life and politics.

The thousands of castes fall within four major groupings. These were defined in the ancient *Laws of Manu*, which also prescribed elaborate rules for personal behavior. The groupings were based upon categories of employment and to some extent even today influence the Indian citizen's choice of occupation, especially in rural areas. In cities and among the more highly educated and the more westernized, the caste system has become vague and much weaker. Even there, however, it retains considerable force. The highest grouping is that of the Brahmins, who traditionally were priests and teachers. Those Hindus who have no caste historically have been outcasts—"untouchables." The origins of Hindu caste are lost in history. It was present as early as 500 B.C., and it may date back as far as 3,000 years.

Caste is completely hereditary. Each caste mandates marriage as a duty, and there are complicated rules of marriage prescriptions and prohibitions that vary from caste to caste. There is no moving up; if one rises in the social order the caste remains the same. Other restrictions vary with caste and pertain to food and drink and purity rituals, including touch. Traditionally, one may not eat anything that a person from a lower caste has touched.

Such complicated arrangements have even resulted in the paradox of Brahmin cooks in restaurants, because their caste prevents them from polluting food by their touch.

Another prominent feature of Hinduism and Indian life is the extended family. The traditional Indian household includes married sons and their families living together with their parents. The father controls the family finances, allocating allowances to the sons from their earnings, and the mother dominates the daughters-in-law. This pattern is less and less common in the cities, but even there is frequent outside the middle classes, and it still prevails in the villages. Family concerns thus greatly affect politics, and the family unit can be politically powerful.

The position of women traditionally was strictly subordinate among the Hindus. According to Manu, the wife was supposed to worship her husband as a god, walk behind him in public, refrain from eating even in private until her husband had finished, and practice complete seclusion from the world—or often even commit suicide by throwing herself upon his funeral pyre (*sutee*)—if her husband died. She was, however, to be venerated by her children and loved by her husband, and she controlled the domestic aspects of the household—subject, of course, to the dictates of her mother-in-law.

Indian legislation now has sanctioned divorce, although it remains uncommon, and today women are legally equal. The social patterns still are essentially traditional, however. Because of the enormous complexity of caste rules and regulations, it has been difficult for the Indians to devise a uniform civil code. Would it ever be possible to permit legal adoption, for example? To do so might result in an untouchable being reared in a Brahmin family as a Brahmin. This would pollute any Hindu of caste who came into contact with him or her, and the pollution would go unrecognized, thus making it impossible for the polluted one to know that it was necessary to engage in the essential cleansing rituals.

Because Hinduism stresses reincarnation and a continual cycle of birth and rebirth, it has frequently made reform difficult. If conditions are bad in this world, they are that way as punishment for transgressions in previous lives. To attempt to change them could be interpreted as an attempt to interfere with the divine order. Much political energy in India is directed toward such questions as cow slaughter and protective legislation for the ever-present cows that wander everywhere, consuming scarce vegetation, but are sacred to the Hindus.

Indian social institutions are among the world's most traditional. The Hindu religion is pervasive—despite the huge number of other religions throughout India—and at least in its most traditional forms engenders a political quietism that discourages positive action to improve conditions. As a way of life, Hinduism affects even those Hindus who are not religious and who profess little or nothing in the way of belief. In view of such manifest difficulties, the progress that India has made is remarkable. Hinduism can change and develop, and it has done so throughout millenia. To a great extent the example of that most deeply committed Hindu Mohandas Gandhi, the architect of Indian independence, has inspired Hinduism to accept such foreign notions as being "one's brother's keeper," and Indian legislation largely reflects this obligation.

India is developing, and it is coming to terms with the West and the modern world. At the same time, it clearly remains Hindu, and its actions and institutions—however secular they may be—retain their Hindu flavor. Thus Hinduism continues strongly to affect Indian political ideologies. With Hinduism, the effect is less overtly political than it is simply assumed, because of the way one lives. With Christianity, the situation is different, and varies from nation to nation.

Initially, Christianity separated itself from the world and was totally nonpolitical. The Christian quite naturally came to accept the church as something different from the state. This remained so even when church and state became entwined politically. Hindus had no church to separate, and even Hindu worship remained personal, with no mass services. The complexity of the relationship between Christianity and state in Christian areas must be examined for insights into the political ideologies of those regions.

In Western Europe Christianity has had a historic connection with the state. Although there is religious freedom throughout the Continent and in Great Britain, some countries maintain established churches, that is, the civil authority protects and supports the church and grants it official status. The United Kingdom is an example. The monarch not only is head of state but is also head of the Church of England, which remains the official church of the realm, and Anglican bishops and archbishops sit by right in the House of Lords. The Federal Republic of Germany (West Germany), which has no established church, provides a different kind of example. There the government provides chairs of Catholic theology and Protestant theology in the universities. In the United States, the situation is vastly different.

Although the U.S. Constitution forbade the national government from establishing religion, its Bill of Rights did not apply to the states until the twentieth century. It was not until 1925 that the Supreme Court first decided that any of the protections of the Bill of Rights limited the power of a state government over that state's citizens. For some years after the ratification of the Constitution, several of the states had established churches supported by tax funds. At one time or another, they existed in nine of the thirteen states.

In the South where the official church was Anglican, the Revolution led to anti-English sentiment that facilitated disestablishment; it came before 1800. In New England, however, there was no patriotic issue and establishment persisted well into the nineteenth century. Massachusetts, in fact, did not vote disestablishment until 1833.

Nevertheless, there was strong sentiment that religion and government should be kept separate. In 1786 Virginia adopted a Statute of Religious Freedom that Thomas Jefferson had written. "Almighty God hath created the mind free," it said, and added that all attempts to coerce belief "tend only to beget habits of hypocrisy and meanness. . . ." It asserted that "rulers, civil as well as ecclesiastical" were "themselves but fallible and uninspired men" who set their own opinions over those of others as if they were infallible and imposed them upon the people.

Therefore, the General Assembly declared "that no man shall be compelled to frequent or support any religious worship, place, or ministry whatsoever, nor shall be enforced, restrained, molested, or burthened in his body or goods, nor shall otherwise suffer, on account of his religious opinions or belief; but that all men shall be free to profess, and by argument to maintain, their opinions in matters of religion, and that the same shall in no wise diminish, enlarge, or affect their civil capacities." The Assembly declared that it recognized that its opinions could not bind its successors, and that as a result it would not have the force of law if it were to assert that the act were irrevocable. Nevertheless, it asserted that the rights it discussed were the "natural rights of mankind," and that "if any act shall be hereafter passed to repeal the present or to narrow its operation, such act will be an infringement of natural right."[23]

In 1796 President George Washington's administration negotiated a treaty with a Muslim nation, Tripoli, which the Senate ratified with the required two-thirds vote. The treaty declared that there was no basis for friction between the two countries as a result of religion because "the government of the United States of America is not, in any sense, founded on the Christian religion." Both Thomas Jefferson and James Madison refused to proclaim Thanksgiving Days during their presidencies, believing that it would be unconstitutional to do so,[24] although this was probably contrary to prevailing opinion.

The fundamental constitutional provision concerning the role of government as regards religion is the First Amendment, which declares that "Congress shall make no law respecting an establishment of religion, or prohibiting the free exercise thereof." Despite the language that refers only to the national government, the Supreme Court for decades has determined that the First Amendment restricts states as well. The constitutional basis for such interpretations is the Fourteenth Amendment, which says that "No State shall make or enforce any law which shall abridge the privileges or immunities of citizens of the United States."

It was many years after its ratification before the Court began to rule that this clause in the Fourteenth Amendment had extended some provisions of the Bill of Rights to protect citizens from state, as well as federal, action. Once it began to rule in this manner, however, the Court has consistently sought in major matters to keep government and religion separate. Yet there are those who contend that the prohibition against establishment of religion means only that there can be no established churches as they existed in Europe at the time that the nation ratified the First Amendment. They argue that it is proper for the state to support

---

[23] Included in Merrill D. Peterson, ed., *The Portable Thomas Jefferson* (New York: Viking, 1975), pp. 251–53.
[24] C. Herman Pritchett, *The American Constitution*, 2nd. ed. (New York: McGraw–Hill, 1968), pp. 568–69.

religion so long as it supports all religions equally and does not discriminate.

The generally accepted view is that the Constitution requires a "wall of separation" between religion and the state. There is considerable evidence that this view is the one that the Framers intended.[25] The First Congress rejected proposals that would merely have outlawed discrimination and insisted on language prohibiting "an establishment of religion," not merely an established church. Moreover, the phrase "establishment of religion" had a different meaning in the United States in 1791 from the one that it had at the time in Europe.

> In America there was no establishment of a single church, as in England. Four states had never adopted any establishment practices. Three had abolished their establishments during the Revolution. The remaining six states—Massachusetts, New Hampshire, Connecticut, Maryland, South Carolina, and Georgia—changed to comprehensive or 'multiple' establishments. That is, aid was provided to all churches in each state on a nonpreferential basis, except that the establishment was limited to churches of the Protestant religion in three states, and to those of the Christian religion in the other three states. Since there were almost no Catholics in the first group of states, and very few Jews in any state, this meant that the multiple establishment practices included every religious group with enough members to form a church. It was this nonpreferential assistance to organized churches that constituted "establishment of religion" in 1791, and it was this practice that the amendment forbade Congress to adopt.[26]

Most Americans appear to be comfortable with the separation of church and state and to accept a secular nation as necessary in order to ensure religious freedom. Despite this, it seems clear that religion has so influenced American institutions that it is pervasive in the culture. Although that influential religion is not a specific sect, neither is it a generalized "belief in God."

Robert N. Bellah was one of the first to note this.[27] He indicated that there is "an elaborate and well-institutionalized civil

---

[25] See Pritchett, pp. 567–79, on the establishment of religion.
[26] Pritchett, p. 568.
[27] Robert N. Bellah, "Civil Religion in America," *Daedalus*, 96:1 (Winter 1967), pp. 1–21.

MICHAEL NOVAK

It is difficult to see how political scientists can understand political events in Viet-Nam, or even the different political styles of such American politicians as Goldwater, Johnson, Stevenson, and Kennedy, without a knowledge of the alternative experiences of religion.

The cautious observer, consequently, will not wish to assent too quickly to the proposition that the transformations being undergone by Christianity in our time are all in the direction of capitulation to atheistic or agnostic secularism. Contemporary atheistic secularism, particularly in America, carries so great a weight of Christian conviction that it does not confront a sophisticated Christianity so much with an antithesis as with a sympathetic stimulus. In our society there are real differences between the world view of the agnostic and that of the Christian. These differences must be located with care; conclusions about their practical consequences ought not to be rashly and ideologically assumed.

In the first place, American atheists or agnostics are not often tempted by nihilism. Dostoevski once wrote that if there is no God, everything is permitted. But nontheistic humanists in the United States do not appear to be less moral, less critical, less concerned with values than theistic Americans. On the contrary, nontheists in America appear to retain a profound conviction concerning the possibilities of intelligence in history, a fundamental and hopeful orientation toward a better future for men, a marked capacity to accept responsibility and to act, and a profound respect for the human person and his freedom. These are startling values, on the face of it; but we take them so for granted that we do not wonder about them.

From "Christianity: Renewed or Slowly Abandoned?"
Daedalus, 96:1 (Winter 1967)

---

religion in America"[28] and noted that while the term was Rousseau's, he did not claim a Rousseauean influence. Bellah began his argument by citing the numerous references that American presidents make in their speeches to God, saying that it was more than a mere need to appeal to the voters. "Although matters of

[28] Ibid., p. 1.

personal religious belief, worship, and association are considered to be strictly private affairs," he wrote, "there are, at the same time, certain common elements of religious orientation that the great majority of Americans share. These have played a crucial role in the development of American institutions and still provide a religious dimension for the whole fabric of American life, including the political sphere."[29]

He described this "civil religion" as involving rituals, beliefs, and symbols. He granted that it drew much from Christianity, but that it was separate and distinct, asserting that it "is clearly not itself Christianity."[30] This is open to question, as we shall see. Bellah saw it as a true religion, but one that is broad and encompassing by virtue of its avoidance of the personal features and its concentration on those elements that can pertain to the body politic.

Franklin H. Littell wrote of the extremes of a "myth of a Christian America" on the one hand, and an "ideology of secularism" on the other.[31] He distinguished between the latter and the "historical process of secularization." Littell argued that the United States is neither "Christian America" nor dominated by the "ideology of secularism," and he admitted that religious purposes may be the basis of laws, if those laws incorporate the necessary secular justifications.

"The form of words is important," he said, "Sabbath observance may be enjoined among believers and maintained within the church by the authority of Holy Writ. In the public forum, however, the case for Sabbath observance must be made on the basis of protecting individuals and society from excessive work hours and ensuring them a decent alternation of work and rest."[32] The point is a good one. America is not a "Christian nation," but much in its traditions and institutions results directly from religion—specifically from its Judeo-Christian heritage. Sometimes the religious influence is unrecognized. At other times it must be disguised or reconciled with the secular state by nothing other than rhetoric.

---

[29] Ibid., pp. 3–4.
[30] Ibid., p. 7.
[31] Franklin H. Littell, "The Churches and the Body Politic," *Daedalus*, 96:1 (Winter 1967), pp. 22–42; see p. 30.
[32] Ibid., p. 39.

A non-Christian observer is considerably more likely to detect an explicitly Christian character to American politics and institutions than a Christian supporter of the separation of church and state. Milton Himmelfarb[33] has provided a Jewish perspective that many Christian observers, including Littell,[34] would dispute. He has argued that "in every Western nation, Christianity is too inseparable from the national culture for religious neutrality to be truly possible." He proceeded to say that a political revolution would be inadequate to change the situation, and that "what is needed is a cultural revolution, or more accurately, a linguistic one. If national languages persist, so will national cultures, and so will the Christianity or the Christian influence—or symbolism, or vocabulary—that is so deeply imbedded in Western culture."[35] He put it even more bluntly by saying that Christian propaganda is "ineradicably a part of our secular culture," and he specifically included America as well.[36]

It may be true that Himmelfarb overstated his case. It may also be true that Christians tend to be too close to the situation to be able to evaluate it accurately. In any case, mainstream Christianity has clearly influenced many institutions, including political institutions, in Western culture—even in the secular United States which maintains religious freedom and the separation of church and state as among the cardinal tenets of its political philosophy.

THE RELIGIOUS RIGHT IN THE UNITED STATES

In the late 1950s, the Reverend Henry P. Van Dusen of Union Theological Seminary wrote an article for what was then one of the most popular American periodicals, *Life* magazine, in which he spoke of a "third force in Christendom" that was competing with traditional Catholics and Protestants. "Van Dusen concentrated upon the rapidly expanding pentecostal, holiness, and Adventist groups that have attracted so much attention in recent years—the Churches of Christ, Assemblies of God, Church of God

[33]Milton Himmelfarb, "Secular Society? A Jewish Perspective," *Daedalus*, 96:1 (Winter 1967), pp. 220–36.
[34]Littell, p. 27.
[35]Himmelfarb, p. 224.
[36]Ibid., pp. 225 and 230.

in Christ, Seventh Day Adventists, Church of the Nazarene, and Jehovah's Witnesses," referring to them as "third-force" or "fringe-sect" groups.[37]

From around 1910 until 1930, there were groups calling themselves "conservatives," "evangelicals," or "fundamentalists," who worked within traditional denominations seeking control. "Fundamentalism was a term coined about 1910 in order to define those who opposed the modernist and Social Gospel movements within the established denominations." They fought to impose their own views of orthodoxy to the exclusion of all ideas disagreeing with theirs. They taught that the Bible was without error, was the total truth, and that their scriptural interpretations were the only acceptable ones. "These fights . . . produced serious problems in every major denomination in the North. They were especially bitter among the northern Baptists, Methodists, Presbyterians, and Disciples. Eventually, by the mid-1920s, the fundamentalists had become so narrowly dogmatic, so bitterly intransigent, that they lost the good will of the moderates who had formerly given them some sympathy."[38]

McLoughlin described these groups as joining Southern denominations, where modernism or liberal interpretations of scripture had never been strong or leaving the mainstream to affiliate with those groups that he calls the "fringe sects." Some in the 1930s were so embittered that they joined right-wing extremist political groups, usually anti-Semitic and quasi-fascist. There, they could direct "their diatribes against political as well as theological Liberalism."[39] Most, however, remained within the mainstream politically and kept religion and politics separate. H. Richard Niebuhr has referred to the fundamentalists and their sects as "the disinherited." McLoughlin added that "whether one calls them disinherited or alienated, they are essentially apolitical and withdrawn. They have washed their hands of this world except to proselytize for followers. . . ."[40]

Throughout the 1970s, however, the situation changed sharply. Television as a medium gave daily exposure to fundamentalist ministers. Many developed considerable skill in persuasion, which

[37]William G. McLoughlin, "Is There a Third Force in Christendom?," *Daedalus*, 96:1 (Winter 1967), pp. 43–68; see p. 43.
[38]Ibid., p. 56.
[39]Ibid., pp. 56–57.
[40]Ibid., p. 55.

RICHARD A. VIGUERIE

The potential of . . . a coalition is tremendous. There are an estimated 85 million Americans—50 million born-again Protestants, 30
million morally conservative Catholics, 3 million Mormons and 2
million Orthodox and Conservative Jews—with whom to build a
pro-family, Bible-believing coalition.

Church leaders acknowledge that overcoming age-old suspi-
cions among Catholics, Protestants and Jews won't be easy. But
increasing threats from big government and big business (like mass
media fascination with exploiting sex) make coming together an
absolute necessity.

From *The New Right: We're Ready to Lead* (1980)

enabled them to amass fortunes from contributions. As their fortunes grew, so did their sophistication. They recognized that the
same appeal that brought converts and funds might also bring
them political power, and they recognized the power of organization. Their efforts contributed greatly to the elections of Ronald
Reagan to the presidency in 1980 and 1984. Mr. Reagan opposed
abortion, favored prayer in public schools, and opposed the Equal
Rights Amendment; all key elements of the agenda of the religious right.

One of the results was the Adolescent Family Life Act of 1981
that authorized payment of government funds to teach sexual
morality to teenagers. About twenty percent of the money spent
under this law went to church groups, mainly Roman Catholic.
Several religious groups joined together to challenge the act, asserting that the provision making church groups eligible for use
of federal funds violated the First Amendment. U.S. District Judge
Charles Richey ruled in 1987 that the law was, indeed, unconstitutional, and the Reagan administration appealed the case and
was "placed in the position of defending before the U.S. Supreme
Court the *religious* aspects of" the law. "One of the plaintiffs in
the Supreme Court case, the Rev. W. Emmett Cocke, a Methodist
minister from Virginia, says he opposes the law because it dis-
criminates against his church. 'Those of us who believe in the
legal option of abortion are disqualified from even making an application [for a federal grant],' Mr. Cocke explains." The major

opposition to the act involves only the aid to religious instruction. This appears to have been the first time that any court has invalidated a federal law as "an impermissible establishment of religion,"[41] but in 1988, the Supreme Court upheld the law.

Much of the concern of many fundamentalists as they became active in politics was directed toward an attack upon what they termed "secular humanism," which was a vague formulation that meant essentially whatever disagreed with their interpretations of the Bible. To observers not sharing their point of view, the agenda of these critics appeared to be at least as much political as it was religious. A representative example of their beliefs and strategies may be found in a book by the Reverend Tim LaHaye, *The Battle for the Mind*. LaHaye was a member of the board of directors for the Reverend Jerry Falwell's political pressure group, the Moral Majority, and produced his book specifically to combat "secular humanism," which he believed to be an anti-Christian religion.

LaHaye's confusion regarding humanism became clear when he wrote that Hitler would have imposed a "humanistic totalitarianism" upon the world. He proceeded to add that "humanists are not qualified to hold public office," that public education is "brainwashing," and that what America needed was "pro-moral leaders who will return our country to the biblical base upon which it was founded."[42] He argued that "our unique check-and-balance system of government would never have been conceived by humanism. It is borrowed directly from Scripture."[43] It was federal aid to education that he believed caused the growth of "secular humanism" because, he said, it transferred control of schools to the federal government.[44] LaHaye wrote that the theory of evolution underlay all secular education. In addition to biology, he included political science and sociology, and said that it also adversely affected art, music, and literature.[45]

His prescription was for "Bible-believing pastors" to exhort their congregations to vote, and he encouraged them to select parishioners to run for political office. Their goal would be to cleanse

---

[41] Curtis J. Sitomer, "Morals and Public Money," *Christian Science Monitor* (November 19, 1987), p. 21; quotations are from this article.
[42] Tim LaHaye, *The Battle for the Mind* (Old Tappan, N.J.: Fleming H. Revell Co., 1980), p. 36.
[43] Ibid., p. 39.
[44] Ibid., p. 45.
[45] Ibid., p. 61.

books, radio, movies, and television of "secular humanistic" influences. A hint of his attitude toward religious freedom was his comment that there was a "well-known parallel between the social positions of the Methodist Church and the Communist party."[46] He concluded that only politicians who were not "pro-moral, pro-American, and Christian" could have voted for the Panama Canal treaties, approved social welfare programs, opposed prayer in the schools, or favored limitations on armaments. An appendix to his book includes a questionnaire for submission to political candidates. Among the questions that sought to determine their "Position on Morals" were: "Do you favor passage of the Equal Rights Amendment?" "Except in wartime or dire emergency would you vote for government spending that exceeds revenues?" "Do you favor a reduction in government?" Clearly such items are political rather than religious and cannot qualify as seeking information on "morals."

The whole thrust of the attack by certain fundamentalists upon "secular humanism" has been to define "religion" so broadly that it includes virtually everything, making the term essentially meaningless. This is intentional. The fundamentalists' approach is to define whatever is not explicitly religious as being part of "the religion of secular humanism." This is not so farfetched as it sounds. In March 1987, fundamentalist pressure groups succeeded in convincing a U.S. District Court in Alabama that "secular humanism" was indeed a religion as Judge Brevard Hand so ruled. He proceeded to issue an order banning dozens of textbooks from the classrooms of Alabama schools. As was to have been expected, the Court of Appeals overturned this most extraordinary court decision.

There is a hidden agenda here. If the reasoning of these fundamentalists is accepted, if virtually everything is part of a religion, then it becomes impossible for schools not to engage in religious teaching. If it is impossible to avoid teaching religion in schools, then even public schools must teach religion. If it is accepted that they teach religion, then the public schools may teach fundamentalist Christianity. This is the goal.

Writings such as LaHaye's are characteristic of the political ideology that results from a certain approach to religion. They

[46]Ibid., p. 164.

also reflect the alienation that prevails among those adopting this approach. One can readily understand—and sympathize with—the plight that such people face, whether they are American evangelicals, Islamic traditionalists, or committed fundamentalists of any religion. The world that they see functions so often in a manner that violates their basic beliefs about the way things should be. No one should be astonished that many of those who retain their rigid beliefs against any compromise become alienated. Such alienated groups strike out forcefully at modern science and at conditions that they fail to understand. Their most salient characteristic is fear. The narrow and rigid indoctrination that they define as education does nothing to increase their understanding of the complexities of the world, and can only increase their fright and bitterness, hence their alienation from a form of politics that recognizes diversity, ambiguity, and uncertainty in the world.

There is a great consistency between right-wing religious ideologies and right-wing political ideologies. Just how far right these ideologies are may be inferred from a final quotation from La-Haye: "Democracy leads to anarchy. Americans have always preferred a government of laws, where the good of the many is preferred to the good of the individual. Otherwise chaos will open the door to a totalitarian dictator. 'Democracy' is a fantasy!"[47]

RELIGIOUS STRIFE IN NORTHERN IRELAND

Catholic Ireland was never content within the Protestant British Empire. The British Parliament adopted the Government of Ireland Act in 1920 in response to Irish sentiment favoring independence and after considerable violence and bloodshed. The act provided independent status to Ireland similar to that held by Australia, New Zealand, and Canada. Irish nationalists remained uncomfortable, however, and ultimately Ireland completely severed its ties with the Commonwealth.

The 1920 act separated the six, largely Protestant, counties in the north from the rest of the nation. These counties, often called Ulster, include about one-sixth of the area of the island but are

[47]LaHaye, p. 89.

more heavily populated than the southern counties and contain more than one-third of the Irish population. Whereas the Irish state is overwhelmingly Catholic and provides a special place in its legal system for the Roman Catholic church, Northern Ireland is approximately two-thirds Protestant. In 1921 King George V opened the first session of the Parliament of Northern Ireland. In 1949, after Ireland had left the Commonwealth, the British Parliament adopted the Ireland Act declaring that Northern Ireland is an integral part of the United Kingdom, and that it will remain so unless the people of Ulster choose to leave.

Militant Irish nationalists in Ireland have always been outraged at the separation, but the Protestants of Northern Ireland have feared Catholic domination. For example, for all practical purposes there is no divorce permitted in Ireland. Moreover, economic conditions are better in the more highly industrialized Northern nation, and many there have strong ties to England. The Catholics in Ulster, however, have complained of discrimination by Protestants, and many have favored union with Ireland.

The result has been tragic, with the violent Provisional Wing of the Irish Republican Army conducting guerrilla warfare against the government of Northern Ireland, and an equally violent Ulster Defense League, formed by extremist Protestants, that commits acts of violence against Catholics. British troops for years have been stationed in Northern Ireland in an attempt to achieve order. Their occupation has been harsh, with numerous violations of civil liberties.

Because of an inflammable mix of religious ideologies and nationalist sentiments, Northern Ireland has become one of the world's most troubled areas. It does not appear as if any settlement is near. Some would say that, despite recent compromises, one does not appear even to be possible.

SIKH MILITANCY

The Indian State of Punjab contains a concentration of Sikhs, who are in the majority there. Sikh men may be recognized by their full beards and their distinctive turbans that cover uncut hair. They all have the name Singh, which means "lion." For generations, Sikhs have been prominent in military, police, and other security forces throughout India.

Sikh fundamentalists have for some time sought to impose a theocracy upon the Punjab, or even to establish it as an independent Sikh nation. About one-third of the population, however, is Hindu. Sikh terrorists have murdered Hindus, or burned their property, and then fled to Sikh temples, where historically they have found sanctuary. One especially tragic element of the situation is that moderate Sikhs have tended not to speak out against the extremists for fear of appearing hostile to their own religion— or often even fearing reprisals.

In June of 1984, Prime Minister Indira Gandhi sent troops into the Punjab and raided the Golden Temple in Amritsar, the most holy of all Sikh shrines. Because it previously had been "off limits" to the authorities, the temple sheltered many notorious Sikh extremists who had for all practical purposes turned it into an armed fortress. The raid resulted in extensive damage to temple buildings, and led to the deaths of some thousand Sikhs. It had another consequence as well. Mrs. Gandhi's Sikh bodyguards assassinated her.

The assassination caused riots throughout the country. Many fundamentalist Hindus who hoped for a Hindu theocracy encouraged the turmoil. Sikhs throughout India became the victims of attacks. The new Prime Minister, the late Prime Minister's son Rajiv Gandhi, quickly moved to achieve some sort of accord with Sikh leaders, and he and Harchand Singh Longowal, the president of the Sikh party, arrived at a compromise agreement. Sikh extremists refused to accept the agreement, however, and assassinated Longowal.

The turmoil continued, and once again Sikh militants occupied the Golden Temple. This time, the state government took action. This led to a tremendous outcry even from moderate Sikhs who considered the Sikh-dominated state government to have acted against the interests of the Sikh religion.

As of 1988, the extremists are selling—at giveaway prices— audio cassettes of songs praising martyred Sikh terrorists. They continue to murder Hindus in the Punjab and even fire into crowds of Sikhs and Hindus to create terror. They have assassinated journalists and have even killed other Sikhs who have spoken out against them, not only in the Punjab, but throughout India. Many parts of India now resemble an armed camp. The intention appears to be to create such terror that the government will agree to demands for a separate state.

Fundamentalist Hindus similarly engage in terrorist acts against Sikhs, and the climate is worsening. The Sikh religion originally sought to be a bridge between Hinduism and Islam, but despite Hindu polytheism and Sikh monotheism, Sikhs generally have been closer to Hindus than to Muslims. Now, however, the Sikh militants are stressing their monotheistic similarity with Islam, and they receive arms from Pakistan. Pakistan, of course, not only is Islamic, but since partition has been hostile to India. This creates special opportunities for fundamentalists of all kinds to cause untold mischief.[48] They are not wasting the opportunity.

ISLAMIC FUNDAMENTALISM

Islam, like Christianity, is multi-faceted and far from monolithic. Both religions can adapt to modern conditions and provide for change and development. Both, however, can also be interpreted in rigid ways that prevent not only progress, but also sympathy toward anyone whose belief is different. An extreme adherence to unwavering traditionalism often reflects a defensive reaction that results from insecurity. It also is likely to vest extraordinary power in the hands of a leader, whether a John Calvin, an Oliver Cromwell, or an Ayatollah Ruhollah Khomeini.

Essentially, Islam teaches brotherhood. Its spirit, like that of early Christianity, is internationalist, with a stress upon the kinship of all true believers. In the hands of fundamentalists, these beliefs can be interpreted to require war against nonbelievers and to require the establishment of Muslim regimes wherever nation-states exist, which joins with Arab nationalism to add to the hostility against Israel.

It would require a complete book and more to discuss in detail the tensions of the Middle East or the terrorist activities elsewhere that result from those tensions. Many factors are involved.

[48] Ved Mehta, "Letter From New Delhi," *The New Yorker* (January 19, 1987), p. 52–69.

They include among other things Arab nationalism, disputes between Islamic nations such as Iraq and Iran, disputes with non-Islamic nations, reactions against Zionism, and resentment against the developed world. There are even tensions resulting from the incompatibility between the statist orientation of Arab nationalism and the universalism of Islam.

There is no doubt, however, that a contributing factor in the trouble is Islamic fundamentalism, defined as an uncompromising belief in a rigid interpretation of Islamic law and tradition. Islamic political theory envisages ultimate universal sovereignty based upon Islam and therefore causes unusual resentment against a Jewish state. When Islamic leaders discuss politics and policy, they generally—with the exception of the Iranian leaders—speak in nationalistic and therefore secular terms. The people, on the other hand, tend to respond to nationalistic appeals from a religious, and frequently fundamentalist, foundation.

It is impossible to understand the Middle East without understanding something of Islam, and also Judaism, but, despite appearances, the fundamental conflict between Israel and the Arab states is not religious; it is nationalistic. The history is complicated by colonialism, national differences, and the reality in the Arab world of having once been cultural and technological leaders but now remaining largely "underdeveloped."

There are nevertheless extraordinary tensions in the Middle East and elsewhere that do result primarily from religion. When Iranians fought with the Saudis in Mecca, the "Saudis, who have relied on Islam as a pillar of their security, were now being challenged in the name of Islam for their siding with the godless West in the Persian Gulf War."[49] In Egypt, "everyone is trying to out-Islamicize each other," which only illustrates the political force that religion is generating. Islamic populism is likely to be "the most important ideological force in the world" over the next forty years, one observer remarked. Not only do Iraq and Iran continue their war, but Tunisia has an outlawed organization, the Islamic Tendency Movement, that "has the support of up to 25 percent of the population, according to Western diplomats." In addition, "University campuses in Jordan, Kuwait, and Morocco are now

[49]Hunter, p. A–15.

astir with fundamentalist politicking," and "fundamentalists are no longer limited to the radical fringe." Their campaigns now are much more than violent or aggressive acts and are seeking to provide constructive alternatives.[50] The Middle East is nothing if not complex, and the same is true of Islam. Even Islamic fundamentalism is not monolithic, and Muslim fundamentalists may disagree with one another just as Christian fundamentalists do.

RELIGIOUS THOUGHT AND POLITICAL IDEOLOGIES IN PERSPECTIVE

The effect of religion pervades human life. Although religious thought is not primarily political and includes much more than politics, it inevitably affects politics and political ideology. At times, religious ideologies become so influential on politics that they must be examined in order to gain understanding of political ideology as a phenomenon.

Attitude Toward Change

When religious ideologies become political, they are like most other political ideologies regarding their attitude toward change. They can range all the way from supporting radical revolution, through advocating reform-oriented change, to the extremes of protecting the status quo or calling for reactionary revolution to return to a supposedly superior earlier state of affairs. Although there are major exceptions, the tendency of religious organizations themselves is to resist change.

Attitude Toward Human Nature

Religiously oriented political ideologies are as varied in their attitude toward human nature as are any other political ideologies. Without exception, however, religions by definition look outside the human community for inspiration, and the nature of the inspiration that they seek determines their attitude toward

[50]Wright, p. 18.

human nature. The range is extreme, from the total depravity assumed by the Calvinists to the virtual perfection assumed possible by the American Transcendentalists, and these examples are completely within the confines of Christian tradition.

Attitude Toward the Potential of Human Reason

Here, again, the range is extraordinary, but the strong tendency of religious-based political ideologies is to be skeptical with regard to the ability of human reason.

Attitude Toward Human Progress

Religion-based political ideologies tend to be optimistic regarding the possibility of human progress, if humanity relies adequately upon religious principles for guidance. There are exceptions; in some cases cyclical notions of reality replace assumptions of linear progress, while in others, any progress is doubtful. Here again however there is broad variation.

Attitude Toward the Relationship of the Individual to the Community

Religions vary in this regard as do political ideologies. When religious ideologies become political, they tend to stress group identity, although there are some exceptions.

CONCLUSION

Religion can have a huge impact upon political ideology. The *Christian Science Monitor* has said in an editorial that "Many Westerners may be troubled by what they see as the intrusion of religion into the secular world; yet the rising role of religion in politics should neither be feared nor automatically opposed."[51] This is certainly correct, but all political movements reflect political ideologies, and it is dangerous to fail to understand them. The same holds true for the new combinations of religion and politics.

[51] "Religion in World Politics," *Christian Science Monitor* (November 13, 1987), p. 15.

At certain times, like the present, fundamentalist religion incites such fervor that it assumes proportions rivalling the influence of mainstream religions. Upon occasion it may even exceed that influence. Nevertheless, the force with which to reckon is not fundamentalism. There is no such single entity. Rather the force is the fundamentalists themselves, whose religion teaches them that they—and they alone—represent the truth. To this extent, their concern is religious. Fundamentalists of all kinds, however—Christian, Sikh, Islamic, Hindu, and others—are likely to attempt to impose their particular version of the truth upon others. When this happens, religious ideology becomes political ideology. As so often happens, the political ideology that grows out of fundamentalist religious ideology leads directly to human misery.

One must remember, of course, that religions as such are certainly not political ideologies primarily. Even so, the complex interrelationships between politics and religion are pervasive. They so permeate institutions—again, even in America—that one could not fully understand political ideologies without having some understanding also of the effects, historical and contemporary, of the ideologies of religion.

Nationalism and the Nation-State

9

*F*ar back into the distant past, visionaries have dreamed of a world of peace and cooperation. In Ancient Greece the Stoics taught that all human beings shared a common rationality and were subject to the same natural law, one that transcended human groups. Christianity developed this theme into the brotherhood of man. Numerous reform ideologies emerged in the nineteenth century, incorporating similar ideas. Despite the hopeful dreams, the tradition of spiritual and philosophical thought, and the ideologies of reform, the current reality is something very different. The world has retreated from the universalism of the ancient empires—including that of Rome—and from the idea of a universal church. Today's reality is fragmented by nationalism, and by its outgrowth, the nation-state.

No force now has greater influence upon world affairs than nationalism nor is any other so responsible for political action and reaction. The association with one's own nation and the recognition of states other than one's own are fundamental to modern political organization. The nation-state is so pervasive that it is difficult to conceive of a world without it. Yet both nationalism and nation-states are relatively recent phenomena. They are products of history, but are so basic to modern consciousness that they seem otherwise, and appear instead to be products of nature.

It would be almost impossible to overemphasize nationalism's influence upon other political ideologies. In one way or another it affects them all. Nationalism, in fact, may well be the most important of all political ideologies existing today.

THE CHARACTERISTICS OF NATIONALISM

There is considerable confusion as to the nature of this prominent feature of current politics, and no single definition could satisfy everyone. Nationalism is a political ideology built upon the central theme of identification with the nation. Strictly speaking, there is a distinction between the terms "nation" and "state." A nation is a large group of people—with or without a government, with or without a country—who believe that they belong together because of certain characteristics that separate them from others. A state may embody a particular nation but may incorporate others as well, or it may be based upon something apart from nationhood. In any case, a state is a political arrangement, while a nation is more a social and psychological phenomenon.

Nationalism involves a group's perception of itself as distinct from others, and the awareness of its members as components of the group. It also involves the group's desire to protect and preserve its identity and to enhance its power and status as a nation. It is this that leads nationalism often to become territorial, to develop an attachment to a certain land as home. It is the perception, or the belief, that is important. Many factors may serve as the explanation for "nationhood," including common culture, language, historical experiences, religion, and the like. The important factor is not whether the explanation is correct, but rather that the group believes it to be true.

Nations seek explanation for their character in the past, real or imagined. The glories of Rome, of Ancient Greece, and of mythical Germanic tribes are but a few of the many themes from the past that have provided myths and traditions leading to a

ADAM SMITH

The love of our own nation often disposes us to view with the most malignant jealousy and envy the prosperity and aggrandizement of any other neighbouring nations . . . .

The love of our own country seems not to be derived from the love of mankind. The former sentiment is altogether independent of the latter, and seems sometimes even to dispose us to act inconsistently with it. France may contain, perhaps, near three times the number of inhabitants which Great Britain contains. In the great society of mankind, therefore, the prosperity of France should appear to be an object of much greater importance than that of Great Britain. The British subject, however, who, upon that account, should prefer upon all occasions the prosperity of the former to that of the latter country, would not be thought a good citizen of Great Britain. We do not love our country merely as a part of the great society of mankind; we love it for its own sake, and independently of any such consideration.

From *The Theory of Moral Sentiments* (1774)

sense of national consciousness for one group or another. Frequently, the tie of language is overwhelming, although not always. Germany and Austria are separate countries, regardless of their common language, and Switzerland is a multi-lingual state. Nevertheless, the force of language should not be underestimated. Religion, similarly, often plays a key role. The tendency of Hindu India, for example, has been to incorporate other Hindu states, although some, such as Nepal, remain independent. The Nazis invoked "race" as a characteristic of nationalism. Their emphasis was extreme, but ethnic identity frequently does undergird nationalistic sentiment. However strong other characteristics may be, a perception of a common history or cultural tradition will almost always be an essential element of nationalism. It is worth repeating that the accuracy of this perception is immaterial. A nation will have a common heritage, whether real or imagined.

Nationalism, then, is a group ideology. It is a condition created by tradition and culture that leads to a psychology of loyalty

ERNEST RENAN

Human society assumes the most varied forms. . . .

It is quite true that most modern nations have been made by a family of feudal origin. . . .

Is, however, such a law absolute? Doubtless, it is not.

On what criterion is . . . national right to be based? . . .

Ethnographic considerations have . . . played no part in the formation of modern nations. . . . The truth is that no race is pure. . . . Language invites union, without, however, compelling it. . . . Above French, German or Italian culture, there stands human culture.

Nor can religion provide a satisfactory basis for a modern nationality. . . . [T]he masses no longer have any uniform belief. . . . Religion has become a matter to be decided by the individual according to his conscience. . . .

Community of interest is certainly a powerful bond. . . . But do interests suffice to make a nation? I do not believe it. . . . a Customs Union is not a country.

Geography . . . certainly plays a considerable part. . . . But can one say . . . that a nation's boundaries are to be found written on the map . . . ? I know no doctrine more arbitrary or fatal than this, which can be used to justify all kinds of violence. . . .

A nation is a soul, a spiritual principle. Two things, which are really only one, go to make up this soul or spiritual principle. . . . The one is the possession in common of a rich heritage of memories; and the other is actual agreement, the desire to live together, and the will to continue to make the most of the joint inheritance.

From "What is a Nation?," delivered at the Sorbonne
on March 11, 1882

to the nation as the supreme element in human affairs. It is separatist and sets the nation apart, asserting the innate superiority of the group to those outside. Historically, regardless of technical distinctions, it is associated with the nation-state. Contemporary nationalism is in fact so completely entwined with notions of the state that it makes little sense to consider them in isolation from one another. Even when it transcends the state—as Arab nationalism in theory does—it tends to give way to the interests of various states—as Arab nationalism in practice does.

Yehoshua Arieli has provided one of the most perceptive discussions on this subject. He has written that nationalism is of relatively recent origin and that "it aims at the creation and maintenance of a community of life and destiny with a will and purpose expressed in the state and a unity embodied in the nation. Such unity is conscious and is maintained by a system of symbols, values, and notions. . . . Nationalism rises beyond the loyalties to ancient traditions or the attachment of men to their land, their homes, and the localities to which they belong. It is founded upon generalizations and a conceptual framework of orientation—in short, upon ideology."[1]

In early stages, nationalism generally leads to attempts to embody the nation in a political organization, which, if successful, becomes a nation-state. When already embodied in a nation-state, it frequently becomes expansionist, or imperialistic, seeking to bring other states and nations under control. Alternatively, when several nationalities exist within a state, nationalism may lead to attempts by one group to dominate others, or to separate and establish a separate state. There is no shortage of examples.

THE DEVELOPMENT OF NATIONALISM

Nationalism in the modern sense, in common with so many other political and social phenomena, emerged as the French Revolution shattered older political realities. In feudal Europe the greatest powers were the Church and the emperor, who constantly competed for supremacy. Neither there nor in Asia, Africa, or elsewhere was there a single force sufficiently strong to overcome political and cultural differences and unite peoples on a large scale. The older empires had absorbed groups in a cosmopolitan manner, embracing a huge variety of languages and cultures. They provided stability and order, but they did not provide neat divisions of political responsibilities. There were many overlapping

[1] Yehoshua Arieli, *Individualism and Nationalism in American Ideology* (Baltimore: Penguin Books, 1966), p. 1.

jurisdictions and numerous subordinate officials, and agencies competed with one another for authority. At times, they even competed for power with the central authority, especially in remote regions. Nationalism and the nation-state did not exist, as is evident in the histories of the great empires of Africa, South America, Asia, and the greatest of them all, Rome. China, India, and Russia did manage to survive and complete the transition into modern nation-states, but not until well into the twentieth century.

It was the French Revolution, not any of the great empires, that laid the foundation for modern nationalism and for the development of the nation-state. As noted in Chapter 6, a major development in this direction had been the weakening of feudal lords and the emergence of the king as sovereign. When the Revolution completed the transfer of sovereignty from king to nation, with the emphasis upon the state as an organic whole, it was the final step. Of course, no social or political development occurs in a vacuum, and any new ideology builds to an extent upon previous themes. For example, many if not most tribal societies had mechanisms for political consultation and participation. The ancient Jews contributed the notion of progress and a moral purpose in politics. The idea of the rule of law came from the Greeks. Such political ideas and practices laid the groundwork for modern political structures and ideologies, but a major element was missing until the Revolution in France.

It was then that truly mass politics emerged, and it was mass politics that created the conditions required for the development of nationalism and for the nation-state. Following the Revolution, France became a nation in the modern sense. It demanded total loyalty, even devotion, from its citizens. It became the duty of the entire population to protect the state, and the state became the protector of the people and came to dominate them. It is significant that national military conscription grew out of the conditions in the new nation.

Just as Jean Jacques Rousseau was the philosopher of the French Revolution, so also is he the philosopher of nationalism. However one interprets Rousseau's theory of the general will, it provided a basis for community life and for national sentiment. After Rousseau, the relationship between the state and the people was irrevocably altered. National consciousness demanded a national state, and the nation-state demanded sacrifice along the lines of John Kennedy's famous exhortation, "Ask not what your country can do for you, ask what you can do for your country!" Those who see Rousseau as providing the basis for totalitarianism may well be equally uncomfortable with such expressions that have their ideological roots in Rousseau's philosophy.

Nationalism burgeoned throughout Europe following the Revolution. As the militant French nation sought to expand throughout the Continent, other peoples reacted by producing their own versions. For many years, friction between France and England had worked to develop national consciousness among both the English and French. The impact of revolutionary France was such that it came to threaten the entire Continent, not merely Britain, and spread nationalistic ideology far from its beginnings. In many instances, it took considerable time for the new ideologies to produce nation-states—Italy and Germany, for example, did not emerge as states until 1870 and 1871 respectively—but nationalistic ideologies were powerful long before. Italian nationalism was fully developed by the 1820s, and German nationalism under the militant leadership of Prussia had been an influential force for many years prior to German consolidation.

Wherever one looks in nineteenth-century Europe—France, Great Britain, Spain, Italy, Germany, Russia, Belgium, the Netherlands, or elsewhere—the most distinctive feature is the struggle for or against conquest, with France at the center. French nationalism and the ensuing turmoil actually created rival nationalist ideologies. Nationalism therefore began directly as a result of war and violence and continues to be the major force encouraging violence in the modern world.

It would hardly be possible to overstate its importance. By the end of World War I, the nation-state was predominant in Europe. Before the middle of the twentieth century, it was virtually universal, not only there, but throughout the world. Nationalism had succeeded in destroying the older empires that had included various nations together under rather loose political arrangements. Where nation-states included different nations, the emphasis came to be upon the state as the creator of a nation of its own, superseding previous national differences. This was a much more assertive political force than that of the cosmopolitan empires, which had tended to exist simultaneously with distinctive national cultures.

The ideological principle of self-determination for nations was the basis for nationalism, and for the creation of nation-states. Ironically, the nation state as an institution became so powerful that it came in many instances to represent a new form of nationalism. This new nationalism retained the language of the old but came to define the state, itself, as the nation. This is the situation that tends to exist today, and that is the reason we generally think now of any state as a "nation-state" and use the terms "nation," "state," and "nation-state" interchangeably. The usage is not precise, and historically is inaccurate, but it does reflect modern realities rather accurately.

Italians and Germans in the early nineteenth century are examples of nations that were divided into many states. In asserting the right of nations to become states, the emphasis upon the state became so strong in many instances as to overshadow concern for nations. "Nationalism" now often refers to identification with the state. The tendency is so powerful that identification with a group within the state—as opposed to identification with the state itself—will often be interpreted as being "unpatriotic." Thus, nationalism, which originally was an ideology of self-determination for national groupings, has come to be a statist ideology that subordinates all else to the demands of the state, generally called the nation-state.

MODERN MANIFESTATIONS OF NATIONALISM: THE MIDDLE EAST

The term "Zionism" refers to the movement to establish a Jewish national state, which led to the creation of Israel following the Second World War. Although he was not the first Zionist, the Austrian journalist Theodor Herzl (1860–1904) provided the energy and organization that helped Zionism become a major force. In late August of 1897, largely at his urging, Jewish representatives from many nations met in Basle, Switzerland to form the First World Zionist Congress. Over two hundred delegates attended. They created the World Zionist Organization, elected Herzl president, and called for the establishment of a Jewish state in Palestine. Zionists then became active in many nations, comprising a nationalist movement that was unique. It was not a reaction to colonialism and had no territorial base to defend. Rather, it sought to secure a land in which to collect a widely dispersed population.

As political activists, Zionists did not demand political orthodoxy. In working toward their goal, they functioned within a variety of political parties. Among their ranks were conservatives and liberals, capitalists and socialists (both Marxists and non-Marxists). Some sought a theocracy, but most favored a state that would provide a homeland for Jews but which would be secular. Although the movement received widespread support among Jewish groups, not all Jews agreed, then or now, that Zionism was appropriate.

Herzl had concluded that Jews throughout the world had sufficient similarities in culture to be able to form a cohesive nation. His experience in Austria, where anti-Semitism was probably greater at the time than anywhere except for Eastern Europe, convinced him that a state of their own was essential if Jews were to escape persecution. Regardless of the fact that Jews were living comfortably in the United States, he rejected emigration to existing nations in the Western Hemisphere as a solution, insisting that self-government was essential, preferably through settlement in Palestine (though earlier he had entertained Argentina as a possibility). He outlined his goals in various writings, such as his 1896 *Der Judenstadt,* arguing for the necessity of a Jewish state, and his 1902 novel, *Altneuland,* in which he advocated peace and cooperation with non-Jewish Palestinians.

The Zionist movement soon received a major endorsement from the British government. The Balfour Declaration of November 2, 1917 declared that Great Britain favored "the establishment in Palestine of a national home for the Jewish people" and indicated that it should be "clearly understood that nothing shall be done which may prejudice the civil and religious rights of existing non-Jewish communities in Palestine." Instrumental in securing this declaration was Chaim Weizmann, a British chemist and Zionist activist who became president of the World Zionist Organization and subsequently was the first President of Israel.

Despite its language regarding the rights of Palestine's non-Jewish communities, the Balfour Declaration offended Arab nationalists. They sought control over the entire Middle East, which at the time was still dominated by Turkey. Because of this, they objected to the Jewish immigration to Palestine which had begun in substantial numbers in the early 1880s.

The breakup of the Ottoman Empire after the First World War increased uncertainty and instability in the Middle East. As a result, the Allied Council in 1920 granted Great Britain a mandate over Palestine. The League of Nations approved the mandate (which included the Balfour Declaration) in 1922.

At the close of the Second World War, Nazi genocidal policies had so shattered the European Jewish community that it became apparent that Jewish resettlement was vital. Zionism presented an answer because the growing Jewish community in Palestine was willing to accept Jewish refugees, while no state would do so. The British had retained the mandate over Palestine and during the war years had virtually halted immigration because of Arab protest. At the same time, Zionists were demanding unlimited immigration. Britain in 1921 had divided the area administratively into two sections, separated by the Jordan River. Henceforth, only the section west of the Jordan was "Palestine," and it was this region that was in question.

Britain turned the issue over to the United Nations. After several months of study, the General Assembly on November 29, 1947, adopted Resolution 181 (II) which called for the partition of western Palestine into two states, one Arab and the other Jewish. On May 14, 1948, the State of Israel came into being.

For years there had been turmoil and violence in the region. Now, there was actual war. Israel's neighboring Arab states—Egypt, Iraq, Lebanon, Saudi Arabia, Syria, Transjordan, and Yemen—invaded, and in the ensuing conflict, Israel retained its territory. The combatants seized the area that the U.N. Resolution set aside as Arab Palestine. Transjordan annexed most of it, despite protests from Egypt and Syria. Subsequently, in 1949 the country ceased to use the name "Transjordan" preferring "The Hashemite Kingdom of Jordan," or simply "Jordan." Both Israel and Egypt also acquired additional territory. Many Arabs left the region, although some stayed and became citizens of Israel. The armistice agreements made no provision for refugees.

Violence has been a way of life in the Middle East, and much of it revolves around the question of the Palestinians. The Palestinian Liberation Organization has come to speak for the displaced Arabs, and many other organizations exist to work against the interests of Israel. The situation is tragic, and the entire region remains incendiary. Again, nationalism—both Jewish and Arab—has proven the recipe for disaster.

OTHER MODERN MANIFESTATIONS OF NATIONALISM

In modern times the turmoil surrounding Israel's emergence as a Jewish homeland and the Palestinian struggle to achieve a state of their own is only one example of the effects of nationalism. In the Republic of South Africa, the minority white population is in control of a much larger group, and even within that minority, the Afrikaners politically dominate those of English heritage. In states such as Australia, the United States, and New Zealand the white majorities have overwhelmed native populations, as have the Chinese invaders who now control Taiwan.

The westward sweep of the United States across the Continent is an example of expansionist nationalism. The water's edge did not stop this movement, and it absorbed into the United States such additional nations as Puerto Rico and Hawaii. Following Indian independence, the new secular—yet very definitely Hindu—nation moved to absorb other territories and peoples, such as those in Hyderabad, Pondicherry, Goa, Sikkim, and elsewhere. The U.S.S.R. moved similarly to absorb neighboring populations into the Soviet state.

As for separatism, one of the most bloody modern instances is to be found in Nigeria. The Ibo attempted in the late 1960s to secure independence from the dominant Hausa and establish an independent state of Biafra. The protracted civil war that followed was especially brutal and brought mass starvation—as well as failure of the Ibo's cause. Other separatist examples include the attempt by militant Sikhs in India to obtain their own state, attempts by American black nationalists some years ago to separate from the rest of the country, and the activities in Canada on behalf of an independent Quebec. There are similar nationalistic movements of Puerto Ricans seeking independence from the United States, Basques from Spain, Hindu Tamils from Sri Lanka, and numerous others. In this regard, one also must note the creation of Pakistan from what previously had been India, and the creation of Bangladesh from what previously had been Pakistan.

The tendency today is for every nationality, however small, to aspire to a state of its own. At the same time the ideology of the state overwhelms national groupings and has reconstituted itself into a new and artificial nationalism. It would be difficult to design a system more likely to engender conflict.

NATIONALISM, THE NATION-STATE, AND WAR

As distinct from "nation," which refers to group awareness based on perceived common values and which may or may not have its own political organization or territory, a "state" is a political organization that is highly territorial. A state may include many nationalities, as is the case in Yugoslavia or the Soviet Union. It may exist with little regard to heritage, whether racial, religious, ethnic, cultural, or linguistic, as is the case in the United States. On the other hand, it may be solidly based upon a single nation of shared cultural values, as is essentially true with regard to China, The Netherlands, Iceland, France, and many others. Technically, the combination of a nation and a state is what is meant by the term "nation-state."

Some scholars, especially some German writers, have argued that states vary in character according to the extent to which they are built upon a nation. In their view, the true nation-state, the *Kulturnation*, reflects a common heritage of language, tradition, religion, and world view. The other kind of state, the *Staatnation*, based solely upon expedience or logical schemes, is purely political, not the result of historical evolution. They would argue that the United States and the Soviet Union, as well as many of the new African states, would fall within this category.

Regardless of how significant these categories may once have been, they no longer are sufficiently meaningful to be of concern. It is exceedingly rare to find an example of a state that would not

ALBERT J. BEVERIDGE

William McKinley is continuing the policy that Jefferson began, Monroe continued, Seward advanced, Grant promoted, Harrison championed, and the growth of the Republic has demanded. Hawaii is ours; Porto Rico is to be ours; at the prayer of its people Cuba will finally be ours; in the islands of the east, even to the gates of Asia, coaling stations are to be ours; at the very least the flag of a liberal government is to float over the Philippines, and it will be the stars and stripes of glory. And the burning question of this campaign is, whether the American people will accept the gifts of events; whether they will rise, as lifts their soaring destiny; whether they will proceed upon the lines of national development surveyed by the statesmen of our past, or whether, for the first time, the American people doubt their mission, question fate, prove apostate to the spirit of their race, and halt the ceaseless march of the Institutions?

The opposition tells us that we ought not to govern a people without their consent. I answer, the rule of liberty that all just government derives its authority from the consent of the governed, applies only to those who are capable of self-government. We govern the Indians without their consent; we govern our Territories without their consent; we govern our children without their consent.

From a speech, "The March of the Flag" (1898)

contain important exceptions to any generalizations that one might make in evaluating it as a *Kulturnation* or a *Staatnation*. It is now the state itself that is of concern, whatever its heritage. Nationalism's importance stems from its relation to the state. Nationalism is group identity so strong that it seeks to create a state, to separate from one (which would lead also to the creation of a state), to come to dominance within a state or to extend the control of one state over others.

Common usage recognizes this. Despite the technical distinction between "nation" and "state," the current tendency, as discussed earlier, is to use the terms almost interchangeably. The term "nationalism" now almost always refers to the actions of states, or, in the case of stateless groups, to actions directed toward obtaining a state for themselves. Similarly, the term "nation-state" now generally refers simply to any state, regardless of technical meanings. In some ways, this is appropriate because it reflects a complicated reality in which both nationalism and the state are vital but only because of their association with one another. They are now so entwined that it is difficult to separate them. For our purposes, it is not essential that we do so.

Nation-states themselves resulted from conflict. They emerged from internal struggles against outmoded systems of power and also from international competition, fear, and jealousy. The power of the nation-state quickly became the criterion of national prestige and worthiness. International relations were then a reflection of an "us versus them" mentality. The result was international anarchy, with each state acting as it chose, to pursue its own interests regardless of others, so long as it had the power to do so. However much nation-states may vary, none has been free from these tendencies.[2]

The rivalries that nationalism inspired led directly to imperialism, which is a form of expansionist nationalism. It may take a variety of forms, from the classic conquest of other lands for the purpose of creating colonies, to the more subtle pressures of economic or political exploitation. The common element of imperialism is exploitation and dominance of others. The motives, however, may not be so simple as they appear. As Barbara Ward has noted, "After 1880, all the major European powers believed that if they did not annex territory, someone else would be there before them. Thus the Western colonial system, in spite of being the largest imperial system in history, resembles the old empires very little. It was less a purposive act of conquest than a by-product of national rivalry in Europe, itself."[3] The effects of nationalism rarely remain confined within national borders.

Expansionist nationalism may also lead a nation-state to attempt to expand its territory or to seek to incorporate all whom it regards as bearing national kinship into its borders. In Canada, Australia, and the United States "westward movements" brought

---

[2]See Arieli, pp. 1–13.
[3]Barbara Ward, *Nationalism and Ideology* (New York: W. W. Norton, 1966), p. 53.

the conquest of enormous territories. With regard to the American takeover of Texas and California, much of the justification was that the majority of the residents were white, Protestant, and English-speaking. One should note, however, that expansionist nationalism will always find justifications for its tendencies, and that those justifications may vary according to the situation and even from time to time within the same situation.

Nazi Germany sought to expand throughout Europe to provide "living space" for the Volk. It also sought to incorporate Germans living outside Germany into the German state. The Chinese seek to incorporate Chinese living in Taiwan into the Peoples' Republic, India moved aggressively in the years following independence to incorporate Hindu areas into India, and in the nineteenth century Greek nationalism led to consolidation within Greece of areas in which Greeks had lived under Turkish rule. Similar claims can lead to attempts to reclaim territory perceived as previously held, such as India's seizure of Goa, China's negotiated settlements that will lead to Chinese possession of Macao and Hong Kong, and both the creation by the Jews of the State of Israel within Palestine and the attempts by Arabs to recapture that territory.

The manifestations of nationalism within states are similar to those projected into international relations. The prevailing ideology in the United States is illustrative in this regard. It has incorporated such a strong tendency toward exclusiveness that it frequently has been highly belligerent. The assumption has been that there is an "American Way of Life" that not only is unique but is superior to all others.

This assumption has frequently been accompanied by the belief that the social and political practices of the United States constituting that way of life are universally valid for all peoples. If one accepts this, then it is easy to assume that any rational person, if sufficiently informed, would agree. It could then follow that those who disagree either are irrational or malevolent. It is but a short step to the position that the United States has not only the right, but even the duty, to spread its institutions to other nations.

Such reasoning supported the westward movement that virtually exterminated native populations and spread across the

Continent in the nineteenth century, going even across oceans and great distances to seize Hawaii, acquire Alaska, and for a time to control the Philippines. In the mid-nineteenth century the name applied to this movement was "Manifest Destiny," as if there could be no question that expansive nationalism—conquest—was ordained as America's destiny. Such attitudes led the United States to interfere in the internal affairs of other countries, sometimes even to the extent of controlling their governments, especially in the Caribbean nations, until well into the twentieth century.

Certainly the United States was not unique in having practiced imperialism. In fact, its record regarding colonialism is mild when compared with those of major European nations. Ultimately, for example, America did grant independence voluntarily to the Philippines. It did withdraw voluntarily from direct control of the governments of Caribbean states. Although the United States was among the great powers that invaded and humiliated China early in this century and then demanded payment from the Chinese for damages that resulted when they attempted to assert their sovereignty, only America repaid China. It set aside the funds to be used for scholarships to educate Chinese students.

The point is not that the United States behaved more inappropriately than other nations. Rather, it is to illustrate that, regardless of how mild it may have been in a relative sense, America did engage in classic imperialism. That it did so demonstrates that even a humanitarian ideology—an ideology of freedom—when infected by the ideology of nationalism, can lead to violence, oppression, and exploitation.

Barbara Ward, in discussing what she termed the failures of nationalism, pointed out that it could not provide for complete cohesion even inside a state because of the difficulty of dealing with minorities. She described its essential nature as being "to leave other people out." This, she noted, was not necessarily fatal, since other institutions, including the family, do the same. They, however, are unlikely to claim "exclusive loyalty and authority. But nationalism has such pretensions. Moreover, it can back them with the ultimate choice of life or death." She pointed to the irrationality of which nationalism is capable, excluding from any association and goodwill fellow human beings simply because they live beyond a border. The most extreme example, of course, is nazism; the Nazis, in her words, "made the nation-state their god."[4]

Today, our very world view is shaped by ideologies of nationalism and the nation-state. Despite numerous attempts to form regional or world groupings, the nation-state remains supreme. No military organization such as the Warsaw Pact or NATO, no economic arrangement, such as the European Economic Community, and no world association such as the former League of Nations or the current United Nations has ever commanded the power over the human mind and imagination—over political ideology—that nationalism and its foremost expression, the nation-state, continue to exert. Nationalism's influence in world affairs far outweighs that of any other ideology, including liberalism, democracy, socialism, and—contrary to the expectations of Marx and the Marxists—even communism. Each of these, in fact, itself reflects nationalism's unmistakable influence.

NATIONALISM AND THE THIRD WORLD

In today's jargon, the industrialized West (dominated more or less by the United States) and the communist nations (dominated more or less by the U.S.S.R.) constitute the First and Second "Worlds" respectively, though one rarely hears them described in this manner. The less industrialized nations, whether termed "underdeveloped," "less developed," or "developing," constitute the "Third World." Both Marxist countries and Western democracies continually strive to gain the allegiance of such states. Marxists seek to gain influence in their governments, while Western nations, especially the United States, work to keep them from "going communist." Although there is no shortage of communists and capitalists in the Third World, it requires only rather brief exposure to recognize that the predominant attitude there is likely not to be "pro-Soviet" or "pro-American," but rather a sense of identity with their own nation-state and some resentment at the industrialized world, whether Marxist or Western. This reflects the strength of nationalism, which supersedes other ideologies in its appeal.

[4]Ward, pp. 56–57.

Thus it is dangerous to generalize too freely and to think of the "Third World" as an entity. Less industrialized nation-states differ from one another just as do highly industrialized nation-states. For that matter, communist states differ from one another as well. It is, for example, more complicated for Americans to obtain permission to visit the Peoples' Republic of China than East Berlin. Entering and leaving China, however, provide none of the tension that one may feel when proceeding through Checkpoint Charlie. In Germany, both East and West, armed officials are a common sight, as they are in most of Europe and elsewhere. In China, as in the United Kingdom, the police are unarmed. Nepal, India, Pakistan, Bangladesh, and Sri Lanka are all Third World nations in South Asia, yet they are quite different, just as France, the Federal Republic of Germany (West Germany), Belgium and The Netherlands are different from one another despite being industrialized Western European nations.

Nevertheless, the "Third World" framework can be helpful as an explanatory device if used with caution. Third World countries obviously do share certain characteristics. Many such states think of themselves as among the "Nonaligned Nations," that are allied with neither of the two great powers. Most of these nations reject capitalism but are non-communist as well. The most notable exception is Cuba, a member of the Nonaligned movement, yet explicitly a Marxist-Leninist state. "Non-aligned" therefore does not always mean what the words imply, because Cuba is openly allied with the Soviet Union and speaks out forcefully against the United States.

Some states in the Third World, such as Cuba, are Marxist-Leninist. Some are socialist. Some, such as Singapore, Chile, and Mexico are capitalist. Many have one-party governments yet generally profess to be democratic. Of course, the word "democracy" has gained such ideological force that virtually all of the world's governments make some such claim. A few, such as India, are democratic in a manner approximating that in the West. Many are ruled by dictatorships of the right, others of the left. Still others have governments unique unto themselves and do not fit well into the Right-Left spectrum. One thing that they all share is strong sentiments of nationalism, and a desire to handle their own affairs free of outside interference. This does not mean that they wish to be isolated from other nations or that they do not seek aid from the industrialized world. Such aid is essential. It does mean that they wish to have their independence as expressed through their own nation-states.

NATIONALISM AND THE NATION-STATE IN PERSPECTIVE

Some form of state organization has existed since the beginnings of civilization. For better or worse, we tend in fact to assume that civilization presupposes some kind of formal political organization based upon territory. Similarly, human beings are social animals and throughout history have generally had strongly developed awareness of group identity. Nationalism, however, did not develop fully until the turmoil associated with the French Revolution produced mass politics and concentrated national attention upon the state, producing the nation-state.

No phenomenon in history has had greater effect upon the lives of human beings than the nation-state. It obviously meets some strongly perceived human needs, emerging as it did to become universal in a relatively brief period. It has produced concentrated political and economic power unequalled in history. This power has created widespread—though far from universal—material well-being, and it has made great progress in protecting public health and welfare, bridging geographical distances, and exploring even beyond the confines of the planet. It has also provided a sense of identity for the people and inspired sacrifice for the benefit of the whole.

The other side of the picture is all too evident. The nation-state's positive power is overshadowed by its negative potential. It has institutionalized violence and now certainly has made mass destruction—and very likely even total annihilation—possible. Its existence encourages international struggle, which becomes ever more dangerous. It has the power to bend human beings to its service and to manipulate their minds and perceptions.

It is this power over the human mind that is at once the nation-state's greatest promise and its greatest threat. So pervasive is the state, and so strong is nationalism, that their combined presence creates a new political ideology that is the culmination of centuries of predecessors, and permeates virtually all the ideologies of politics now existing.

Attitude Toward Change

Nationalism is almost a "generic" political ideology, reacting to change according to conditions. Whether it favors change—and, if so, what kind of change—or whether it advocates maintenance of the status quo depends essentially upon power relationships. Nationalism leads groups to seek or resist change according to their position in relation to other groups.

Attitude Toward Human Nature

Nationalism is compatible with a variety of other ideologies, regardless of whether they are optimistic or pessimistic about human nature.

Attitude Toward the Potential of Human Reason

As with the attitude toward human nature, nationalism is compatible with ideologies regardless of their assumptions about the potential of human reason.

Attitude Toward Human Progress

Nationalism implies little with regard to human progress. It does, however, lead one to tend to identify human progress with the fortunes of one's own group. In seeking to advance the group, therefore, there is some implication that human progress at least is possible.

Attitude Toward the Relationship of the Individual to the Community

Nationalism may coexist with, or as a part of, nearly any other political ideology, regardless of that ideology's approach to individual relationship with the group. Strictly speaking, therefore, nationalism itself implies nothing about individual-community relationships. Nevertheless, nationalism does have a strong tendency to suppress individualism and to place the good of the group

[Among] the Purposes of the United Nations are

- To develop friendly relations among nations based on respect for the principle of equal rights and self-determination of peoples, and to take other appropriate measures to strengthen universal peace;

- To achieve international cooperation in solving international problems of an economic, social, cultural, or humanitarian character, and in promoting and encouraging respect for human rights and for fundamental freedoms for all without distinction as to race, sex, language, or religion. . . .

From the Charter of the United Nations (1945)

ahead of that of the individual. It honors the person who sacrifices for the group and in authoritarian situations requires the sacrifice; at best, even in the most democratic of situations, it places strong psychological pressures upon individuals to value the community's welfare ahead of their own.

PROSPECTS FOR THE FUTURE

One may as well criticize the weather as to criticize nationalism and the nation-state. Assuming that we avoid war and mass annihilation, there is no likelihood for change in the near future. Nationalism is among the strongest human sentiments in the world today, and the nation-state dominates the planet. It is easy to wish for something better—for something with less potential for harm—but wishing accomplishes nothing.

Understanding, however, may lead to some accomplishment. Although nationalism will remain with us, and although the nation-state will not wither away, an awareness of the limitations and dangers of nationalism can bring about policies that will lessen the likelihood of violence and destruction. If one recognizes that the national interest cannot be completely separate from the interests of others and that what harms others ultimately harms one's own nation, it may be possible to develop an enlightened self-interest that transcends the more narrow considerations of nationalism.

In any case, education can develop commitment to the community, for the nation, without diminishing the role and status of others. It can also produce an understanding of the nation-state, its benefits, its powers, and its dangers. Rational societies can produce rational systems with rational leaders. Such societies can produce nation-states that behave rationally in dealing with their own populations and with the rest of the world as well. To accomplish this requires an understanding of the effects of nationalistic ideology; it also requires an ability to see as far as possible beyond the restricted boundaries of one's own nationalism.

Violence, Nonviolence, and Political Ideologies

10

*I*t requires no great degree of perception to recognize that ideologies, especially political ideologies, may be related to violence. The argument here goes considerably further. Sociologists, psychologists, journalists, and novelists understand that violence often becomes a consuming passion that transcends its origins. It begins as a tactic to achieve a certain goal, but frequently supersedes everything else and becomes its own justification. Political writers who deal with violence, however, generally ignore some of its most fundamental implications and treat it only as a tactic or as an effect.

Military analysts in considering strategy and tactics will discuss the "proper" functions of violence and how it may be used.

Such discussions may include ethical dimensions that deal with which uses of violence are permissible and which not. Of uppermost concern will be results. What are the desired effects? What level of violence is necessary to produce them? What level will produce an undesirable effect? Should one use the minimum amount of force and violence compatible with the desired outcome, or the maximum?

Other political writers may ask questions dealing more fundamentally with the nature of violence itself. If the use of violence is proper, how may it be controlled so as to keep it within accepted limits? Are there situations in which violence is completely improper? Is it possible that violence is improper in all situations and that any use of violence is counterproductive? Rather than achieving peace and stability—if those are the goals—could it be that violence under any circumstances only engenders more violence?

The effect of political ideology upon violence has been a matter of obvious concern since the rise of fascism and nazism. Students of ideologies may conclude that some, such as certain kinds of anarchism or communism, are more likely than others to encourage violence. Some analysts, while certainly not arguing that all ideologies are equally violent, might conclude that for one reason or another virtually all have at least some violent potential. What they rarely if ever do is to look at it from the other side, considering not only the effects of ideology upon violence but also the effects of violence upon ideology.

Viewed in this fashion—and from the perspective of our broad definition of political ideology—it is clear that the seductive potential and addictive power of violence are so great that at times they can overwhelm other considerations. When this happens, it can itself actually become a political ideology of violence for its own sake. Nazism is the most obvious example. In national socialism, violence was not merely a tactic of the ideology but became in fact its substance and justification. Nearly the same phenomenon occurred under Stalin and in Cambodia under the bloodthirsty Pol Pot regime. Similarly, the power of violence to cause revulsion is also sufficiently great that political ideologies of nonviolence have emerged as counterforces. To be sure, violence throughout history has dominated, and it is at its most powerful when it becomes an ideology. Nonviolence, too, is strengthened

---

BENITO MUSSOLINI

. . . Fascism, in so far as it considers and observes the future and the development of humanity quite apart from the political considerations of the moment, believes neither in the possibility nor in the utility of perpetual peace. It thus repudiates the doctrine of Pacifism. . . . War alone brings up to their highest tension all human energies and puts the stamp of nobility upon the peoples who have the courage to meet it.

From "Fascism" (1932)

---

when it rises to the status of an ideology, and like violence, it thrives upon organization. When it has emerged as an organized force, it has been remarkably effective. It is possible that only organized nonviolence can counter violence in today's world. When violence combats violence, whatever else the outcome, violence always wins. It is the enormous consequences that violence now threatens that have encouraged many of the nonviolent to turn away from passivity and toward active and organized efforts. Because to some extent the advocates of violence have allies from the adherents of nearly all other political ideologies, nonviolent activists find themselves facing tremendous odds. If nonviolence survives, it will only be because its advocates have succeeded in appealing to imaginations and convincing others that their approach can be successful. Whether others can be convinced, or whether this would constitute "changing human nature" has yet to be demonstrated.

ADOLF HITLER

The first fundamental of any rational *Weltanschauung* is the fact that on earth and in the universe force alone is decisive. Whatever goal man has reached is due to his originality plus his brutality.

From a speech on April 2, 1928

DEFINITIONS

It is interesting to note that definitions of violence generally stem from discussions of nonviolence. Judith Stiehm has outlined the terms common in the literature and noted that "violence" and "nonviolence" cannot be defined simply as opposites. A physical assault, for example, is an act of violence. A question in private regarding the wisdom of an act is not, yet it also is not an act of nonviolence.[1]

Stiehm suggested that definitions must arise from consideration of coercion, which involves attempts to change behavior without necessarily altering attitudes or beliefs. She noted that some advocates of nonviolence rule out any use of coercion, arguing that violence includes any act that causes discomfort, whether physical or mental. Others, especially some Christian writers, assert that the character of an act results from the intention of the actor, the "spirit" of the act. This could mean that highly destructive acts committed in a "spirit of love" could be nonviolent—bringing to mind, for example, the Spanish Inquisition—while

---

STRATEGY BOARD
AMERICAN SECURITY COUNCIL FOUNDATION

The argument against the value of military superiority is especially pernicious because it is always used to justify reducing U.S. military strength. It is never applied against Soviet military power. It is worth remembering that the world was a safer place and Soviet aggression more muted when the U.S. enjoyed overwhelming strategic superiority, because we had a monopoly of nuclear weapons and strategic delivery systems. With a rough U.S.-Soviet parity of numbers and quality of both weapons and means of delivery, the best that can be achieved is some politically useful margin of military superiority.

From *A Strategy for Peace Through Strength* (1984)

---

[1] Judith Stiehm, *Nonviolent Power: Active and Passive Resistance in America* (Boston: D. C. Heath, 1972), pp. 19–24.

harmless acts could be violent if committed with evil intent. She pointed out that most theorists of nonviolence in assessing an act concentrate on the act itself, not the intentions of the actor, and that most permit some coercion.

Stiehm arrived at a definition of violence by distilling common elements from the writings of nonviolent theory. They "unanimously reject . . . the threat or use of physical restraint, injury, or destruction of persons or their property. If physical restraint, injury, or destruction (or the threat of these) is accepted as an appropriate definition for the term *violence*, then it follows that *nonviolence* is left to encompass a wide range of coercive behavior; it stops short only at the physical. On the other hand, not all acts that have no physical consequences are properly referred to as nonviolent, for to be nonviolent, an act must also occur in a context where violent action would generally be considered either legitimate or normal, as in the biblical admonition to "turn the other cheek" when struck, rather than hit back. Nonviolent action, then, implies restraint; it suggests that one deliberately refrains from expected violence."[2]

These are the definitions with which we will operate. Violence involves physical restraint, injury, destruction, or threats of such action. Nonviolence applies to deliberate acts that exhibit self-control to avoid violence, but may include coercion. It may also, of course, include noncoercive acts such as persuasion.

Stiehm also discussed other relevant terms.[3] "Nonviolence" no longer is so likely to be equated with "pacifism" or "passive resistance," because many nonviolent actions are far from passive or pacific. Because much nonviolent action seeks often very assertively to bring about social and political change, one now often sees the term "nonviolent resistance." She therefore has distinguished "resistance" from "nonresistance," and "passive resistance." "Nonresistance" is unwilling compliance. "Passive resistance" is simply refusal to comply, whether publicized or not, and it may be a purely individual act. "Resistance" seeks to change policy or behavior to benefit others, not merely oneself.

"Nonviolent resistance," therefore, is "restrained action calculated to change another's behavior for a social purpose without

[2]Ibid., pp. 20–21.
[3]Ibid., pp. 21–22.

MULFORD Q. SIBLEY

Those who insist that it is possible to resist non-violently external aggression as well as internal social injustice are often asked, "But what would you do about enemies like the Nazis? Could they really be opposed effectively by non-violent means?" The answer is that there *was* considerable experience with exactly this problem during World War II. Denmark and Norway, in varying degrees and contexts, did utilize the techniques of non-violent resistance with rather notable results. To be sure, there was violent resistance also; and even where non-violent resistance was employed, it was not because principles like Gandhi's were consciously adopted but rather because other methods were not available. When all this has been admitted, however, the record—particularly in Norway—is not unimpressive.

From *The Quiet Battle* (1963)

---

use or threat of physical restraint, injury, or destruction of one's opponent or his property." Stiehm added two "commonsense" additions to her definition, the first being that in order to be considered nonviolent, an act must occur in a situation in which violence might be expected or understandable. The second addition was that in order to be considered resistance, an act must be outside the normal channels provided for action by the society. A strike, for example, is now considered in the United States to be a normal part of the collective bargaining process, and therefore is not to be considered "resistance" although "the identical action could accurately have been described as resistance in the 1920s."[4]

Finally, we will consider Stiehm's discussion of the term "civil disobedience" which "may be defined as the deliberate and public infringement of a law recognized by the actor as legal (that is, as constituted and enforced in accordance with accepted governmental procedures) for the purpose of producing social change."[5] For civil disobedience to occur, one must disobey the government. At the same time, the person practicing civil disobedience continues to consider himself or herself a loyal citizen. The idea

[4]Ibid., p. 22.
[5]Ibid., p. 23.

is that it serves the state better to practice civil disobedience, when warranted, than to comply with unwise or unjust laws. The person who does so, does so openly, with maximum publicity, and generally, he or she will accept any penalty.

Some who protest may seek to use the legal system to avoid punishment. The goal may be to discredit the legal system, or to clog the courts so that punishment may become impossible. It may simply be that the defendant believes that he or she has done all that is possible, and that going to prison would accomplish nothing more or might harm the cause by removing an actor from the scene.

THE IDEOLOGY OF VIOLENCE

No doubt there will be some who will question whether it is appropriate to consider violence as an ideology, rather than as a tool or a method. I would argue that in some circumstances it is appropriate. If the situation is somewhat unclear there remains no doubt that violence has a pervasive influence upon politics, and that upon occasion it does escalate to become an end in itself. Speaking specifically of terror, David Rapoport wrote that "by definition terror entails extranormal violence, and as such is almost guaranteed to evoke wild and uncontrollable emotions. Indeed," he said, "the people attracted to it may be so intrigued by the experience of perpetrating terror that everything else is incidental."[6] Even H. L. Nieburg, who has written of the need for violence—indeed for its utility—in a political system (discussed below) admitted that "it is true that domestic violence, no less than international violence, may become a self-generating vortex which destroys all values, inducing anarchy and chaos."[7]

As in discussing the political effects of religious ideologies, our broad definition of "political ideology" makes it possible to see the political effects of belief systems that might generally be

---

[6]David C. Rapoport, "Fear and Trembling: Terrorism in Three Religious Traditions," *American Political Science Review*, 78:3 (September 1984), pp. 658–77; quotation on p. 675.
[7]H. L. Nieburg, "The Threat of Violence and Social Change," *American Political Science Review*, 56 (1962), pp. 865–73; reprinted in Joan V. Bondurant, ed., *Conflict: Violence and Nonviolence* (Chicago: Aldine/Atherton, 1971), pp. 73–88.

GENERAL DAVID M. SHOUP

Somewhat like a religion, the basic appeals of anti-Communism, national defense, and patriotism provide the foundation for a powerful creed upon which the defense establishment can build, grow, and justify its cost. More so than many large bureaucratic organizations, the defense establishment now devotes a large share of its efforts to self-perpetuation, to justifying its organizations, to preaching its doctrines, and to self-maintenance and management. Warfare becomes an extension of war games and field tests. War justifies the existence of the establishment, provides experience for the military novice and challenges for the senior officer. Wars and emergencies put the military and their leaders on the front pages and give status and prestige to the professionals. Wars add to the military traditions, the self-nourishment of heroic deeds, and provide a new crop of military leaders who become the rededicated disciples of the code of service and military action.

From "The New American Militarism" (1969)

considered nonpolitical. As noted in that discussion, this definition "can apply to ideologies with primary orientations that are other than political." Similarly, it can reveal the ideological implications of actions and orientations, however unsystematic they may be.

It would, however, be fruitless to engage in debate over whether this does or does not cause violence "truly" to rise to the status of an ideology. Surely all can agree that the effects of violence are important not only upon politics, but also upon political ideology. It follows that a study of the role of violence can assist in developing a better understanding of political ideologies, and should therefore be considered in any comprehensive attempt to do so.

This is especially so in the modern world. With the rise of the nation-state, violence has become an integral part of politics, both domestic and international. Although armies have existed throughout history, only since the development of the nation-state has the presence of huge standing military forces become virtually universal as the basis of the political process. Nearly the whole of the earth's population now accepts this as routine. There are, of course, enormous differences among states as to the integrity of their institutions and practices. Nevertheless, with regard to the willingness to use or at least to threaten the use of force, there is little difference among them. Both Marxist-Leninist countries and Western-style democracies "resort to threats of mass annihilation and both seem to be willing to shatter the whole structure of civilized society in the name of some abstraction which neither can define with precision. Each claims it is 'defending' itself when it resorts to the most horrible preparations for mass slaughter."[8] Despite the easing of tensions between the Soviet Union and the United States since Mulford Q. Sibley wrote this statement, his essential point remains worthy of consideration.

Certainly ideological violence existed long before the rise of the nation-state. Rapoport's discussion of religious terrorist traditions demonstrates that it is not a new phenomenon. Of the three groups that he considers—the Thugs (Hindu), the Assassins (Muslim), and the Zealots-Sicarii (Jewish)—all are ancient, and except for the Thugs, they had explicit political purposes. He noted that other religions, including Christianity, have had their own violent and terrorist traditions.

What is new is the organization of violence as an integral part of nations and nation-states. "Before the nineteenth century," Rapoport noted, "religion provided the only acceptable justifications for terror. . . . We see terrorists as free to seek different political ends in this world by whatever means of terror they consider most appropriate."[9] Although Rapoport spoke specifically of terrorists, his comments are applicable also to institutional violence, which in the twentieth century has far exceeded any that could have been imagined previously.

It is true that modern terrorists bear considerable kinship to their antecedents far back into history. It is nothing new for terrorist groups to become so preoccupied with violence that it becomes a major part of their ideology. It happened with the groups that Rapoport cited as well as with many others from that time to

---

[8]Mulford Q. Sibley, *The Quiet Battle* (Garden City, N.Y.: Doubleday & Co., Anchor Books, 1963), pp. 371–72.
[9]Rapoport, p. 659.

this. Many modern groups offer examples, such as the Provisional Wing of the Irish Republican Army, factions of the Palestine Liberation Organization and certain other Islamic fundamentalist movements, some adherents of the Jewish Defense League, various paramilitary associations, neo-Nazi organizations in Europe and the United States, many racist bands such as the Ku Klux Klan and The Order in America, leftist terrorist groups in recent years such as the Baader-Meinhof Gang and the Red Brigades in Europe, and the Weather Underground and numerous others in the United States. The list is endless and includes countless examples from the right, the left, and the simply confused.

Groups such as these are the ones that command the headlines. Within hours, news and pictures of the bombing of an airport or a department store or the hijacking of a cruise ship or an airliner will be flashed around the world. Their power is the power of publicity. Their actual importance, however, is tiny, relative to the formal actions of nation-states.

Totalitarian rulers tend explicitly to use the power of the state to direct violence and terror against their own peoples. In many totalitarian states violence to the point of terror becomes a matter of public policy. They thus incorporate fear as an explicit principle of governing. Hitler, Stalin, and more recently Pol Pot in Cambodia are the most obvious examples.

Although the totalitarians may be the first to spring to mind when one considers violence and the state, they certainly have no monopoly upon violence as a matter of policy, or even upon terror. To cite only two of the many possible examples, the regimes of Idi Amin in Uganda and the late "Papa Doc" Duvalier in Haiti were not sufficiently systematic to be truly totalitarian, yet they were solidly grounded in violence and terror against their own people. E. V. Walter has remarked that "it is true that the study of totalitarianism has been one of the few paths to recent theories of terrorism, but it has led to an incorrect identification of organized terror with systems of total power."[10] The smallest modern war vastly overshadows the actions of most terrorist rulers, and Western democracies participate as avidly as do dictatorships.

[10] E. V. Walter, *Terror and Resistance: A Study of Political Violence* (New York: Oxford University Press, 1969), p. 4.

The tendency of warfare since the French Revolution has been toward involvement of more and more of the population, until now it includes the whole. During a modern war, no longer is the contest merely one between opposing armies. Rather the combatants include entire societies, and entire societies become the targets. No one should be permitted without challenge to claim that nuclear weapons may be directed solely against military targets. Their prey is the city, and all its inhabitants, military, civilian, old, young, strong, weak, men, women, and children. The only two nuclear weapons ever detonated in warfare, those that the United States exploded, devastating two Japanese cities at the close of the Second World War, demonstrate this.

Violence and the devices to inflict violence seem always to find their justifications. World War I was the first in which armies made extensive use of the new technological device, the machine gun, or as we now would say, the "automatic weapon." It was also the first to use conscription successfully on a wide scale. At first, it seemed as if the new weapon was so terrible that it would make war unthinkable. Then, coupled with the new techniques of trench warfare, the war settled down into a long period of near stalemate in which the only effect was constant death. This could never have happened without the nation-state, and the commitment, loyalty, and reverence that the nation-state demanded from the entire population. It was this exaltation of the state that made conscription possible, and it was conscription that made possible the constant flow of young men to be sent to their death, which alone could permit such conditions to continue. The nation-states devised many rationalizations for the violence. It was not senseless, not a blunder; it was the result of explicit strategy, that of a "war of attrition."

Similarly, in World War II, the new technological marvel, the B-29 bomber, was designed to attack industrial targets in Japan and eliminate the Japanese capacity to continue the war. When the American commanders discovered that such bombing did not have the desired effect, they did not consider halting bombing raids on Japan. Rather, they expanded them. What previously had been strategic bombing of industrial centers became indiscriminate fire bombing of Japanese cities, with no pretense that civilians were safe from attack.

Devices for violence, once employed in war, continue to be employed regardless of their effect until the war ends. Once such devices are seriously proposed, they gather a momentum of their own until they are funded and produced, regardless of any potential effect or military benefit. The neutron bomb is a device that kills through intense radiation but has relatively little blast effect so that it does minimal damage to buildings, bridges, and other structures. The initial justification for proceeding to develop the bomb was that it could be used to halt masses of armored Soviet troops on the move to prevent them from overwhelming Europe. Despite the fact that such radiation would be unlikely to kill invaders quickly enough to prevent them from achieving their objective, the plans proceeded. New justifications for constructing the MX missile changed whenever objections to previous justifications demonstrated them to be faulty. The only constant was that the plans proceeded and the missiles were constructed.

One may note the pervasiveness of an ideology of violence in the reaction to the Reykjavik Summit Conference in October 1986. Ever since the public first became aware of the atom bomb, the dream had been for the achievement someday of nuclear disarmament. For the first time there had been serious, official discussion of just that, the dismantling of nuclear weapons. The nuclear-free dream evaporated as soon as there was the slightest possibility, however remote, that the Soviet Union and the United States would arrive at some such agreement. Immediately the official public relations machines in America and Europe began protesting. First, they said, it cannot be done. Second, and more to the point, they argued that it should not be done, saying that only the presence of a nuclear threat could avoid war.

These comments are not intended as indictments of policy or as condemnation of public officials. Their purpose is to illustrate the effects of violence in connection with the nation-state. States have demonstrated ample willingness to turn to violence for countless reasons, some vitally important, some—at least in hindsight—trivial. More important for our purposes is the effect of violence upon thought and action, the manner in which violence encourages yet more violence, and the influence that violence has upon the political ideologies that justify the actions of states. It is thus that violence becomes its own ideology.

H. L. Nieburg has provided an illustration. He has written of the *need* for violence, not only official violence practiced by a state or for self-defense, but even for "private individual or group violence, whether purposive or futile, deliberate or desperate," because "this induces flexibility and stability in democratic institutions." The threat of violence, and even "the occasional outbreak of real violence," he argued, are "essential elements in peaceful social change not only in international but also in national communities."[11]

The substance of his argument is that "the risk of violence is necessary and useful in preserving national societies and that real violence must now and then occur in order to make threats of violence credible.[12] His definition of government is the agency capable of exerting the greatest amount of violence. If a private force comes to exceed the government's power to commit violence, then that force becomes "the highest authority" and therefore "the new government."[13] Law cannot be a substitute for violence, he maintained, because law is based upon violence. "Law always rests on force," he wrote, "a legitimate monopoly in the hands of the state, and it can be changed by the threat of private violence," so that threats of violence "operate to moderate demands and positions."[14]

Nieburg's definition of violence is essentially the same one that we have adopted. It is "direct or indirect action applied to restrain, injure, or destroy persons or property."[15] His argument is identical to the one that undergirds military preparations for national defense, the argument that peace comes only through strength. He cited numerous benefits resulting from violence. "The credible threat of violence in the hands of nations has a . . . stabilizing effect. . . . In international politics also the threat of violence tends to create stability and maintain peace. . . . If the reputation of a nation's military power is allowed to tarnish, future bargaining power will be weakened."[16] The threat of domestic violence restrains all governments, even those of totalitarian states.[17]

[11] Nieburg, p. 73.
[12] Ibid., p. 74.
[13] Ibid., p. 80.
[14] Ibid., p. 82.
[15] Ibid., p. 87, fn 1.
[16] Ibid., p. 83.
[17] Ibid., pp. 84–85.

Nieburg's essay is one of the few that explicitly proclaim an ideology of violence. Its assumptions, however, are not unusual. What is unusual is that he presented them clearly and consistently, without surrounding them with language that tends to soften their implications. His essay documents the existence of an ideology of violence and makes plain not only the connection between violence and the nation-state but also between the nation-state and violence as a *political ideology*. He has therefore performed a service.

Rarely has violence in the United States been as explicitly advocated as among certain extremist groups in the 1960s and early 1970s. The historian Richard Hofstadter in 1970 identified what he termed a "rising mystique of violence on the left." He noted the long history of violence on the right in America and pointed to the leftist phenomenon as something new and as reflecting a "decline of the commitment to nonviolence on the Left."[18] He pointed to the dropping of "Nonviolent" from the name of the Student Nonviolent Coordinating Committee, the prevalence of articles dealing with such things as the construction of Molotov Cocktails, and the popularity of the writings of Frantz Fanon, the Martinique-born, French-educated psychiatrist who provided a "full-throated defense of the therapeutic and liberating effects of violence."

Hofstadter described various approaches to violence. Some may merely enjoy its use, while others hope that it will bring a beneficial result. One frequent theme was that violence would provoke counter-violence and reveal the true nature of the establishment and the system. The constant, however the justifications varied, was the praise for violence. He wrote that "violence has come to have the promise of redemption. 'Violence alone,' writes Franz (sic) Fanon in *The Wretched of the Earth*, one of the canonical works of the new politics, 'violence committed by the people, violence organized and educated by its leaders, makes it possible for the masses to understand social truths and gives the key to them.' "[19]

[18]Richard Hofstadter, "The Future of American Violence," *Harper's Magazine* (April 1970), pp. 17, 48–53; reprinted in John Livingston and Robert Thompson, eds., *The Dissent of the Governed* (New York: Macmillan, 1972), pp. 294–305. For an extensive compilation of documents pertaining to violence in American history, see Richard Hofstadter and Michael Wallace, eds., *American Violence* (New York: Vintage, 1971).
[19]Hofstadter, p. 297.

DWIGHT D. EISENHOWER

Until the latest of our world conflicts, the United States had no armaments industry. American makers of plowshares could, with time and as required, make swords as well.

But we can no longer risk emergency improvisation of national defense. We have been compelled to create a permanent armaments industry of vast proportions. Added to this, three and a half million men and women are directly engaged in the defense establishment. We annually spend on military security alone more than the net income of all United States corporations.

Now this conjunction of an immense military establishment and a large arms industry is new in the American experience. The total influence—economic, political, even spiritual—is felt in every city, every state house, every office of the Federal Government. We recognize the imperative need for this development. Yet we must not fail to comprehend its grave implications. Our toil, resources and livelihood are all involved; so is the very structure of our society.

In the councils of government, we must guard against the acquisition of unwarranted influence, whether sought or unsought, by the military-industrial complex. The potential for the disastrous rise of misplaced power exists and will persist.

We must never let the weight of this combination endanger our liberties or democratic processes. We should take nothing for granted. Only an alert and knowledgeable citizenry can compel the proper meshing of the huge industrial and military machinery of defense with our peaceful methods and goals, so that security and liberty may prosper together.

From his Farewell Address (January, 1961)

Hofstadter argued that such a reverence for violence flowed from the "hideous and gratuitous official violence in Vietnam. . . . after having created and made heroes of such a special tactical force as the Green Berets," he said, Americans should not have been astonished at the result.[20] Moreover, he contended, violence has not only been a part of American culture, but has been "pervasive in human experience."[21] He granted the necessity for

[20] Ibid., p. 295.
[21] Ibid., p. 299.

violence, at least upon occasion, but argued that it must be limited and controlled—always the most difficult consideration where violence is involved—and that in order to be at all justifiable, it must be successful.

E. V. Walter is one of the most careful students of political violence. In examining traditions of violence in various cultures, he noted that it serves several functions. Of course it can be an instrument of control, but it may serve other purposes as well, such as being "a privilege of social rank."[22] He cited African examples, but there are many others. Hinduism long taught that a Brahmin could kill an untouchable who permitted his shadow to fall across the Brahmin's path. In feudal Japan, a Samurai had the authority to kill a commoner on the basis of nothing other than whim. Even in the West, at least until recently, low-ranking military personnel were subject to physical punishment to the point of injury—sometimes death—by those of higher rank.

It is true, Hofstadter said, that "violence can succeed in a political environment like that of the United States under certain conditions. Those who use it must be able to localize it and limit its duration." Certainly all advocates of violence, and even many who oppose it for a variety of reasons, would agree, however reluctantly. Hofstadter proceeded to call attention to a fact that such persons generally overlook. "If violence sometimes works," he wrote, "it does not follow that nothing but violence works."[23] It is this insight that motivates the theorists and practitioners of nonviolence.

THE IDEOLOGY OF NONVIOLENCE

Few subjects are so misunderstood in the popular mind as pacifism and nonviolence. The stereotype that equates the avoidance of violence with mere passivity, or even more erroneously, with cowardice, is largely an unconscious acceptance of the ideology of violence. As we have seen, the ideology of nonviolence involves self-discipline and courage, and its orientation is decidedly activist. Joan Bondurant quotes Mohandas Gandhi, the architect of Indian independence and one of the most prominent advocates of nonviolence in history, as writing "I do believe, that

[22]Walter, p. 12.
[23]Hofstadter, p. 301.

where there is only a choice between cowardice and violence, I would advise violence." She added that Gandhi "insisted that nonviolent conduct is never demoralizing whereas cowardice always is."[24]

As remarked at the beginning of this discussion, nonviolence is considerably more than the absence of, or even the opposite of, violence. Just as violence is often a method that human beings employ to achieve their goals, so too is nonviolence. Moreover, nonviolent tactics are no more limited than those of violence, as regards the kinds of goals to which they may be applied. Advocates of nonviolence may well seek the same ends as others, and have much the same concerns. A person's wish to avoid war and other violence, for example, does not imply that he or she is less concerned with the country, or is uninterested in national defense. There are elaborate schemes of nonviolent national defense that pacifists suggest as actually being more effective and presenting vastly less danger to humanity and the world than military measures.

As an interesting aside, those who remain unconvinced that nonviolence has anything to offer other than passivity or even cowardice should examine the Japanese martial art of aikido. The existence of a "nonviolent martial art" illustrates the great variety of possibilities available within the framework of nonviolence. I use the term "martial art" here in a generic sense, of course. A more literal description of aikido would be a nonviolent art of self-defense.

Aikido requires extraordinary training and discipline, both physical and mental. It involves turns, dodging techniques, and wrist twists; most styles have no aggressive moves. Therefore, there can be no matches between practitioners; it is not a sport. The rule is to avoid pain and cause no injury. Moreover, aikido teaches that one should smile while avoiding an attack, with the intention being not only to remain free from injury, but also to prevent the attacker from committing a wrong, and if at all possible even to win his friendship.[25]

[24]Joan V. Bondurant, ed., *Conflict: Violence and Nonviolence* (Chicago: Aldine/Atherton, 1971), p. 9.
[25]See Jay Gluck, *Zen Combat* (New York: Ballantine, 1962), pp. 179–84; Jearl Walker, "The Amateur Scientist: In Judo and Aikido Application of the Physics of Forces Makes the Weak Equal to the Strong," *Scientific American*, 243:1 (July 1980), pp. 150–62; Yoshimitsu Yamada, *Aikido: Complete* (Secaucus, N.J.: Citidel Press, 1969); and George Leonard, "The Nonviolent Martial Art," *Esquire* (July 1983), p. 132.

Obviously, aikido is not political, although it shares many of its principles with theories of nonviolent national defense, which definitely is relevant to political ideology. Many, in fact most, of the Oriental martial arts incorporate some principles of pacifism, or nonviolence, but resort quickly to violence if the situation is sufficiently threatening. Aikido is unique in that it is thoroughly consistent, both in theory and in practice. I mention it to illustrate the vigor and diversity within theories of nonviolence, a richness that is too little known, which explains the general lack of understanding.

Theories of nonviolence are hardly new. They go back to the teachings of Jesus, and considerably beyond. America has had an especially active tradition of nonviolent activists beginning as early as the Quakers of the 1600s, and it has contributed greatly to the world literature of nonviolence. Of the two most prominent twentieth-century advocates of nonviolence, one, Dr. Martin Luther King, Jr., was an American. The other, Mohandas Gandhi, acknowledged his debt to another American, Henry David Thoreau.

As Staughton Lynd has written, "it is often supposed that nonviolence is a philosophy conceived by Gandhi and Tolstoy and recently imported into the United States by Martin Luther King, Jr. The fact is that a distinctive American tradition of nonviolence runs back to the seventeenth century. Thoreau's influence on Gandhi is well-known. Tolstoy, too was indebted to American predecessors. In 'A Message to the American People,' written in 1901, Tolstoy stated that 'Garrison, Parker, Emerson, Ballou, and Thoreau . . . specially influenced me'."[26] Garrison, of course, was the militant abolitionist William Lloyd Garrison (see below). The other Americans Tolstoy mentioned were mostly transcendentalists: Theodore Parker, Ralph Waldo Emerson, and Henry David Thoreau. The remaining figure whom Tolstoy credits as an influence was Adin Ballou, the author in 1839 of *Nonresistance and Government.*[27] Ballou formulated a Christian anarchism based upon "nonresistance," a term that may today seem somewhat confusing. It refers to a form of nonviolence in which groups "passively obey the State so long as it does not require them to perform

---

[26] Staughton Lynd, ed., *Nonviolence in America: A Documentary History* (New York: Bobbs–Merrill, 1966), p. xv.
[27] For a selection, see Leonard Krimerman and Lewis Perry, eds., *Patterns of Anarchy* (Garden City, N.Y.: Doubleday/Anchor, 1966), pp. 140–49.

positive acts that run counter to their non-violent professions. Taxes may be paid, but there can be no active participation in office and no entering of the army—both of which are regarded as participations in violence."[28] In 1841 Ballou founded a utopian community, Hopedale, that endured, based upon his principles, for some fifteen years.

Lynd proceeded to say that "there is good ground for arguing that the Christian pacifism of the radical Reformation was kept alive from about 1650 to 1850 primarily by Americans; and that, in view of the cumulative impact of [William] Penn and [John] Woolman [Penn, the leader of the Pennsylvania Colony, and Woolman were both Quaker activists], Garrison, and Thoreau, William James [the American philosopher and psychologist], and Jane Addams [the pioneer social worker and founder of Hull-House], and now Martin Luther King, Jr., America has more often been teacher than student in the history of the nonviolent idea."[29]

We have mentioned Tolstoy's philosophy in the chapter on anarchism and noted his advocacy of noncooperation based upon his reading of Christianity. His Christian anarchism incorporated nonresistance to evil as a fundamental tenet, along with complete reliance upon the individual conscience. His withdrawal from the state was complete. His ideas to some degree influenced such American intellectuals as presidential candidate and Secretary of State William Jennings Bryan, the prominent lawyer Clarence Darrow, and Jane Addams. His major influence, however, was upon Gandhi, and this became the source of Tolstoy's political significance.[30]

Judith Stiehm has pointed out that in "pre-Constitutional America," it generally was "Christian and not secular nonviolent resistance that was practiced."[31] The story of the Quakers and their antislavery activity is well-known, as is their excellent relations with the Indians. "It remains an undisputed fact that so long as seventeenth-century Quaker views predominated and a large proportion of the population adhered to that faith, the community was never menaced by Indians. During the same period

---

[28] Sibley, *Quiet Battle*, p. 7.
[29] Lynd, p. xvi.
[30] See Peter Brock, *Twentieth-Century Pacifism* (New York: Van Nostrand Reinhold, 1970), p. 4.
[31] Stiehm, p. 4.

most of the other colonies had many difficulties with the tribes and some suffered cruel wars."[32] In addition to tireless and gentle Quaker activity in opposition to slavery, those Quakers who had been slaveholders in virtually all instances chose principle over profit and freed their slaves. Quakers were almost unique in such consistent adherence to the tenets of their religion even when it damaged them economically.

The Quaker religion began in England in the middle of the seventh century. Its founder, George Fox, taught that human beings should adhere to Christ's "Inner Light" and that to resort to violence would be to deny that indwelling spirit. Few groups in history have been more dedicated to their beliefs and more willing to act accordingly. In contrast with many other religious groups, Quakers have tended to be active politically and to participate in the political system with reform as their goal. As pacifists, however, they have refused to serve in the military and frequently have suffered as a result. Their gentle activism has supported the cause of nonviolence and has worked to alleviate misery and want. Their official name, the Society of Friends, seems to be especially appropriate.

Both Quakers and Mennonites have produced large numbers of conscientious objectors to military service in the United States and to some extent in Europe as well. Each group has contributed significantly to traditions of nonviolence, but their differences are notable. The Mennonites tend to be rural, to adopt distinctive dress, and to set themselves apart from matters of this world—including matters of politics. Their history dates from Anabaptist activity in Holland, Switzerland, and Germany in the sixteenth century. The name "Mennonite" comes from Menno Simons, who in 1536 founded the denomination and based it upon strictly pacifistic principles. Although many Mennonites have moderated their separatism and passivity, many others, especially in the United States, retain their traditional ways and their hostility to government and the state. Their passive stance and willingness to pay taxes and fines according to the doctrine "render unto Caesar," have enabled them to escape some of the difficulties that the assertive Quakers have faced.

[32] Sibley, *Quiet Battle*, p. 207.

Prior to the Civil War, peace groups were among the most active reform organizations in America, but their efforts and those of other reformers tended to be absorbed by the antislavery movement as the War approached.[33] The abolitionists had their own pacifist wing, typified by William Lloyd Garrison, founder of the passionately abolitionist newspaper *The Liberator*. Garrison's rhetoric was fiery, but nonviolent. He preached fervently that one must avoid all participation in politics, even voting, to avoid compromising principles of militant nonviolence. Not only was he active in the American Anti-Slavery Society, but in 1838 he also wrote the declaration of the New England Non-Resistance Society. Garrison, however, ranks as one of the American nonviolence movement's greatest failures.[34] When the Civil War began, his commitment to abolitionism remained strong, but his dedication to nonviolence crumbled. He not only supported the war, but—it is doubtful that Garrison ever did anything halfway, or without total commitment—he supported it with great enthusiasm. As Stiehm put it, his change was "dramatic and complete." He "joyfully proclaimed" the war to be "the best possible way of 'exorcising' the South of its 'deadliest curse'."[35] Some former pacifists, such as Wendell Phillips, joined Garrison in supporting the war, but others, such as Adin Ballou, maintained their principles, as did Quakers and Mennonites.

Despite Garrison's change of heart, he appears to have had an influence upon the tradition of nonviolence. "Today's students of nonviolence almost inevitably drink long at the springs of Gandhi's thought. Gandhi in turn credited his inspiration to three sources: the New Testament, John Ruskin, and especially Leo Tolstoy. To complete the circle, Tolstoy asserted that it was William Lloyd Garrison who first proclaimed the principle of nonresistance to evil as the basic principle for the organization of man's life. Thus, the doctrine of nonviolence might be said to have been on a one-hundred-year leave of absence from the United States. During that period it visited both in Europe (Tolstoy's Russia) and Asia (Gandhi's India); now it has returned home only to be

[33] Alice Felt Tyler, *Freedom's Ferment* (New York: Harper Torchbooks, 1962).
[34] Lynd, p. xxviii.
[35] Stiehm, p. 5.

confronted with many of the same problems as those that confronted Garrison."[36]

Stiehm had ample justification for saying that nonviolence had
taken a leave of absence from the United States for a century, but
as she herself admitted this is not entirely correct. No one, however, could take issue with her implication that pacifism is certainly a much more difficult doctrine to advocate when at war, or
with her observation that "peacetime pacifism is not an unusual
phenomenon."[37] The First World War virtually destroyed the peace
movement, but there were those, however few, who remained
committed to their principles, and new organizations advocating
nonviolence emerged even during the conflict.

It is noteworthy that "all during the war a number of clergymen steadfastly maintained their opposition to the military, and
to violence. Among these were John Haynes Holmes, Norman
Thomas, and A. J. Muste. These individuals and others with similar beliefs were among the founders of the Fellowship of Reconciliation (FOR), organized in England in 1914 and in the United
States in 1915. This group has provided advocates of nonviolence
and social justice with an effectively functioning organization
from that day to this." It has also encouraged the formation
of other reform organizations, including, among others, the American Civil Liberties Union (ACLU) and CORE, the Congress of
Racial Equality.[38]

There are many instances of the use of nonviolent political
techniques in twentieth-century America, many of them successful. Many advocates of women's suffrage aided their cause by
mass demonstrations, civil disobedience, and other nonviolent
protest. The Nineteenth Amendment to the Constitution was the
ultimate result. The First World War brought about the first large-
scale and relatively successful use of military conscription in the
United States. Protests did not succeed in eliminating the draft,
but arguments on behalf of nonviolence did bring about provisions for conscientious objection then, in World War II, and in
the "Cold War" decades that followed.

It is possible that the labor movement in many ways reflects
resounding success for nonviolent action, although the situation

[36] Ibid., p. 6.
[37] Ibid., p. 8 fn 13.
[38] Ibid., p. 13.

is not an obvious one. As a rule, labor achieved its advances through nonviolent techniques, but as Stiehm put it, "its struggle was not advertised as nonviolent, nor is it usually classified that way. The crucial question is whether labor's success was achieved because it did not renounce the possibility of using violence (it did make its potential for violence clearly evident)."[39] It is impossible to answer the question definitively, but the movement brought about tactics that were innovative techniques of nonviolence. The most apparent was the "sit down" strike, in which workers sat on the job, refusing to work. They also refused to leave, thus preventing the employer from bringing in non-strikers to replace them. This strategy first appeared in 1936 in the automobile industry.

It is the cause of civil rights that has brought about the most dramatic instances of nonviolent action in recent American history. In fact, the American Civil Rights movement includes some of the most outstanding examples of nonviolence of all time. It would be impractical to repeat here the history of civil rights in the United States or even to provide a thorough discussion of the movement's nonviolent aspects. There are many works dealing in depth with these subjects. It nevertheless is important to an understanding of the ideology of nonviolence to examine some of the high points of the Civil Rights movement as it developed after the Second World War and to give some attention to the ideology's greatest exponent within that movement, a young Baptist minister, Dr. Martin Luther King, Jr.

There were attempts in the 1940s to achieve civil rights through the use of nonviolent techniques, even during the war. As early as 1942, members of CORE, including James Peck and Bayard Rustin, chose Stoner's Restaurant in Chicago to conduct a sit-in demonstration.[40] As the years progressed, there were several attempts to integrate lunch counters, amusement parks, theaters, and other places of public accommodation. Finally, in 1954, the political system began to respond when the U.S. Supreme Court ruled in the case of *Brown* v. *Board of Education of Topeka* that racial segregation in public schools was unconstitutional.

It was in the following year, 1955, that an incident occurred that was so dramatic as to capture the nation's attention. It was

[39] Ibid., p. 10.
[40] Ibid., p. 14.

the Montgomery, Alabama bus boycott, which came to signify, for many people, the beginning of the Civil Rights movement. It began when Rosa Parks, a black seamstress who had studied nonviolence, refused to give up her bus seat to a white man. In the conflict that resulted, the city's blacks boycotted the buses. They walked, organized carpools, shared taxi rides, and otherwise arranged for their own transportation. After a year-long campaign, the transit system was almost bankrupt, and the city agreed that it would no longer segregate the buses.

It was the bus boycott that brought prominence to Martin Luther King, its organizer. It also served as an example to other civil rights advocates of the potential of nonviolent direct action. The techniques were not new. Gandhi had used similar tactics with considerable success in his struggle for Indian independence, and there were precedents even in the United States, as mentioned earlier. King's success in Montgomery, however, was the first substantial victory for civil rights entirely from within the black community, and it inspired others to action at the same time that it seized the imagination of white America.

In 1960 a group of black students sat at a "whites only" lunch counter in Greensboro, North Carolina, insisting that they would remain until served. They remained firm in their refusal to depart, but they also steadfastly refused to fight. Their action began a wave of "sit-in demonstrations" throughout the South. Regardless of how they were abused, whether verbally assaulted or physically beaten, the demonstrators refused to resort to violence.

In 1957, under the leadership of Senate Majority Leader Lyndon Johnson, a civil rights act creating the Civil Rights Commission and making it a crime to prevent a qualified citizen from voting in a federal election became law. Although it was a mild act, it was the first national legislation dealing with black civil rights since the days of Reconstruction following the Civil War nearly a century earlier. In 1960, in response to bomb attacks intended to intimidate blacks and civil rights organizations, another law made it a crime to use interstate commerce or cross a state line to contribute to or threaten a bombing. It also authorized the Attorney General to investigate to determine whether citizens were being denied their right to vote. Members of Congress from the

South worked vigorously against this bill, and Majority Leader Johnson kept the Senate in session all night to defeat a filibuster and secure Senate approval.

The next year, 1961, saw the massive use of yet other nonviolent tactics. It was the year that the "freedom rides" began. Black and white civil rights workers from outside the South joined the southern activists to ride in interstate buses, sitting in "whites only" sections. Sit-in demonstrations continued, and huge marches began.

Sporadic violence directed at blacks in America had never been limited to the South, but had always been a feature of southern life. After the 1954 Court decision and the Montgomery bus boycott, such violence began to escalate. Beginning in the late 1950s and continuing well into the 1960s, there were numerous bombings and murders of civil rights workers, both white and black. The Governor of Virginia had called for "massive resistance" to black civil rights, the Governor of Arkansas attempted to use National Guard troops to prevent the integration of Central High School in Little Rock, and the Governor of Alabama "stood in the schoolhouse door" in a symbolic "attempt" to keep black students out of the University of Alabama. It later became apparent that Governor Wallace's show at the University of Alabama was just that, a show. He had agreed with federal authorities that he would step aside peacefully when ordered to do so. Such efforts (however real or symbolic) by state officials greatly encouraged the violent elements in their societies. The demonstrators, however, under the leadership of Dr. King and many others, consistently remained nonviolent.

In 1963 one of the greatest demonstrations in American history occurred. Some 300,000 persons, black and white, converged upon Washington, D.C. to listen to Dr. King's "I Have a Dream" address from the steps of the Lincoln Memorial. Despite the tensions and fears that such a demonstration is likely to cause—illustrated by the presence everywhere of law enforcement officers including military troops, police, and deputized officials—the atmosphere was uniformly one of good will. The City of Washington did not record one crime for the entire twenty-four-hour period. The beautiful weather and the presence of so much force may be partial explanations, but the peaceful spirit that prevailed and the

MARTIN LUTHER KING, JR.

Then I was introduced to the life and teachings of Mahatma Gandhi. As I read his works I became deeply fascinated by his campaigns of nonviolent resistance. The whole Gandhian concept of *satyagraha* (*Satya* is truth which equals love and *graha* is force; *satyagraha* thus means truth-force or love-force) was profoundly significant to me. As I delved deeper into the philosophy of Gandhi, my skepticism concerning the power of love gradually diminished, and I came to see for the first time that the Christian doctrine of love, operating through the Gandhian method of nonviolence, is one of the most potent weapons available to an oppressed people in their struggle for freedom.

. . . This principle became the guiding light of our movement. Christ furnished the spirit and motivation and Gandhi furnished the method.

From *Strength to Love* (1964)

emphasis upon nonviolence that was unmistakable no doubt also played a part.

By 1964 Lyndon Johnson had become president, and he threw his considerable power behind the movement for black civil rights. "We shall overcome," he said, echoing in a speech before Congress the words of the Civil Rights movement. The result of the example that King and others set, together with the persistent nonviolent pressure of the demonstrators and Johnson's support, was the Civil Rights Act of 1964, by far the most significant civil rights legislation in a century.

Other advances followed, including the 1965 Voting Rights Act, the Twenty-Fourth Amendment that outlawed the payment of poll taxes as a prerequisite for voting in federal elections, and "affirmative action" programs designed to eliminate discrimination in employment. As the cause progressed, however, the commitment to nonviolence dwindled. Violence emerged from within the movement, as illustrated by the removal of "Nonviolent" from the name of SNCC, the Student Nonviolent Coordinating Committee. SNCC had been one of the most prominent of the civil rights organizations.

Following a period of considerable violence, including many urban riots in black areas, the mood of the country changed. Although most white Americans appeared to support the reforms that had brought greater civil rights, the impetus to institute additional reforms had ceased. By the 1980s, there no longer existed the national mood that in the 1960s had brought governmental pressure to bear on discrimination. The Reagan Administration, in fact, in many ways appeared to retreat from earlier reforms. Among the many examples of this were its minimizing of the role of the Civil Rights Commission and its support for tax-exempt status for a segregated college.

What does this say to a student of nonviolence? One might conclude that nonviolent techniques had been somewhat successful, but that their success was limited. After all, violence did continue, and finally infected even the movement that previously had been consistently nonviolent. It is possible to argue that nonviolence failed, that those who had been its advocates were forced to turn to violence by the failure of nonviolence to accomplish enough. Those who argue in this manner might advocate greater violence, in order to halt the retreat from civil rights that they perceive not only within the Reagan administration but throughout the political system.

The advocates of nonviolence, of course, would argue differently. They would point to the extraordinary successes of nonviolence, so long as the movement remained dedicated to it. They would point out that, as violence emerged to counter violence, the gains for civil rights tended to halt. They would add that the later retreat from the goals of civil rights came only when nonviolent tactics no longer were in evidence. Their conclusion would be, therefore, that the Civil Rights movement demonstrated the effectiveness of nonviolence, and that the failures were not the failures of nonviolence, but rather failures to remain steadfast and adhere to nonviolent principles.

As support for their argument, the advocates of nonviolence would point to one of the inspirations of the American Civil Rights movement, the nonviolence of Mohandas Gandhi (1869–1948) who worked aggressively for Indian independence. No figure in the twentieth century has contributed more to the theory of nonviolence, or to its practice. To be sure, his great successes were accompanied by great failures, but his influence demonstrates that even in a world of nation-states, it is possible for power to develop outside the boundaries of the official power structure.

The ability to develop and to use political ideology is not limited to government officials or to those who have wealth and occupy high positions within the system. Both Gandhi and Martin Luther King are examples of those who without official position have accomplishments on a scale generally reserved in the modern world for leaders of states. Their careers also illustrate the potential effectiveness of an ideology of nonviolence even when facing armed force.

A note of caution may be advisable at this point. One person may indeed develop the skill in utilizing political ideology that can enable him or her to challenge the might of a state, or an empire, as Gandhi and King did. As their examples illustrate, that ideology may be one of nonviolence. It is not ideologies of nonviolence alone, however, that have great potential. Certainly Hitler, no less than Gandhi and King, is an example of an outsider who manipulated political ideology to challenge a system—in fact, a world order—yet his ideology was one of violence and destruction. The power of nation-states is awesome, and it is somewhat comforting to recognize that there nevertheless remains at least some potential for individual action to accomplish significant change. One should keep in mind, however, that this creates the potential for harmful as well as beneficial change, depending to a large extent upon the motivating ideology.

Gandhi's central principle was his idea of "Satyagraha," which he defined as "the Force which is born of Truth and Love or nonviolence."[41] He referred to it as "soul force," or "truth force." Gandhi acknowledged his debt to Hindu writings, Tolstoy's works, Thoreau's "On Resistance to Civil Government," and the Christian New Testament, especially the Sermon on the Mount.

As his thought developed, he became confident that numbers were less important in a nonviolent conflict than, as Sibley put it, "an intense commitment to truth." Gandhi completely rejected the use of physical force, spurning an ethic that would lead to the injury of an opponent. Sibley dealt with the difficult question of whether it is possible to have any conflict without injury of some

---

[41] See the selection from Gandhi's "The Origins of Satyagraha Doctrine" in Sibley, *Quiet Battle*, pp. 32–45; definition on p. 36.

sort, without denying the "considerable validity to the conception of Satyagraha." He suggested that "some types of social struggle undoubtedly cause less injury to the opponent than others—particularly less irreparable injury. Perhaps," he wrote, "the line should be drawn between those forms of struggle likely to lead to irreparable injury and those that may result only in secondary or relatively minor inconveniences."[42]

Gandhi was a committed Hindu who left India to study law in England, then proceeded to the Union of South Africa to practice. In South Africa the severe discrimination that he and other Indians faced shocked him so greatly that he began to lead protests against the government. Over a period of time, he renounced his Western lifestyle and adopted practices that he believed combined traditional Hindu pre-industrial virtues with the universal truths that he perceived from Hinduism, Christianity, Islam, and all the world's great religions. Central to his belief was nonviolence in the active form of Satyagraha.

Gandhi remained in South Africa for more than twenty years and returned to India permanently in 1915. The history of his campaigns there is well-known and includes massive programs of civil disobedience and hunger strikes to the point of death to force the British to agree to his demands. Ultimately, the British withdrew, granting India and Pakistan their independence on August 15, 1947.

Gandhi's great moral force was an influence for peace and good will between the majority Hindus and the large minority of Muslims. Many of his followers were not committed to nonviolence as a principle, yet adhered to nonviolent tactics because of their intense respect for him personally. Despite Gandhi, however, there was enormous bloodshed in riots between the two groups both before and after Independence, causing him extreme anguish. His greatest sorrow was the violence, and his failure to prevent the partition of British India into Hindu India and Muslim Pakistan.

After Independence and partition, Gandhi continued his tireless efforts for good will among all groups and persons. It was his emphasis upon fair treatment for all that led to his death. On January 30, 1948, a few brief months following Independence, a

[42]Sibley, *Quiet Battle,* pp. 30–32.

Hindu fanatic who represented a right-wing Hindu group that found his efforts to prevent hostility between Hindus and Muslims offensive, stood up in a crowd and assassinated him with a handgun. Mohandas K. Gandhi, the "Mahatma," or "Great Soul," who had dedicated his life to nonviolence, met his end by the violence that he so deplored, and at the hands of an adherent of the religion to which he was so dedicated.

How effective was nonviolence in India? As Sibley remarked, "there is still a dispute as to precisely what factors were most important in leading Great Britain to give up the Indian Empire," but "there can be little doubt that the non-violent campaigns led by Gandhi from 1920–21 onward played a very important role."[43] Nonviolence was influential, but not completely successful. Many intellectuals in India believe that its techniques would have been useless against a more brutal enemy such as the Nazis. Perhaps (except on the part of Gandhi himself) Indians lacked adequate commitment, or perhaps the difficulties were simply too enormous for any completely successful outcome. Certainly, neither India nor Pakistan has adopted nonviolence as a principle of state. Each has committed aggression and fought wars, and each has even achieved the ability to develop those instruments of ultimate destruction, nuclear weapons. Gandhi would weep with tremendous grief, but one can make a powerful case that the situation would have been vastly worse without his benign influence and the memories of Satyagraha among Indian politicians, and even some in Pakistan.

More than four decades have passed since Indian Independence. Is there still a place in the world for Satyagraha or similar techniques? Was the American Civil Rights movement merely an aberration, or does a practical ideology of nonviolence continue to exist? Can it be effective under modern conditions? The existence of a number of organizations that work without government backing and maintain a steady record of successes indicates that nonviolent resistance may continue to have a significant place in world affairs. Advocates of nonviolence would go considerably further; they would argue that, especially in view of the incomprehensibly destructive power of modern violence, nonviolence not only is—and must be—significant, but is the only practical remaining method of settling human conflict.

[43] Sibley, *Quiet Battle*, p. 30.

One of the most outstanding examples of such an organization is Amnesty International. Amnesty International has as its purpose the elimination of torture and capital punishment and the release of political prisoners in every country. It defines political prisoners as those held because of their political, religious, or other beliefs, or because of their race, culture, or sex. The association is completely voluntary and has no official standing. In fact, it refuses to accept any government funds. It has existed since 1961 and as of mid-1987 reported that it had many thousands of members around the world, organized into more than 3,400 chapters in more than fifty countries.

Amnesty International does not describe itself as a group practicing nonviolent resistance and does not discuss politics at all. Its purposes are narrow and specific. It is completely nonpartisan and supports the release of all political prisoners in all countries, providing that they have committed no act of violence and do not advocate violence. Nevertheless, its approach is clearly within the nonviolent tradition. Rather than to attack its opponents or incite efforts to storm prisons to release inmates, it uses publicity as a tool. Regimes generally prefer to hide it when they torture prisoners, but Amnesty International publicizes what they do. The organization has documented official torture in more than sixty-five countries and has called the torture to world attention.

Amnesty International identifies cases, either individually or collectively, that it terms "prisoners of conscience." Local chapters "adopt" such persons, taking on no more than three at one time in order to avoid diluting their efforts. Members then send floods of letters and telegrams to heads of state and government and to officials whom they have identified as having jurisdiction over the prisoner or prisoners. They encourage others to do likewise and they seek maximum publicity for the case, writing letters to newspapers (where the press is free to print them), issuing newsletters and reports outlining the conditions in various countries, and otherwise mobilizing international pressure upon governments. They attempt to inspire public demonstrations on behalf of the prisoners, to provide help to their families, and to work for swift and fair trials. When possible, they write letters of encouragement to the prisoners themselves.

Many times the Amnesty International campaigns have contributed to domestic pressures within countries that have assisted in influencing governments to free the prisoner of conscience. The letter-writing efforts have been especially successful. Through the years Amnesty International has helped to win the release of thousands of prisoners in more than one hundred countries. Its goals and successes have gained it considerable respect. It is significant that in 1977 Amnesty International was awarded the Nobel Prize for Peace. As the Human Rights Handbook puts it, "by upholding the right of private individuals to question the behaviour of governments, bureaucracies and prison authorities, Amnesty International has largely succeeded in establishing the validity of this mode of action—through its relative success and its now widespread acceptance."[44]

Amnesty International acts in a gentle, intellectual manner. A more dramatic and physical example of group nonviolent action is the environmental organization Greenpeace. Greenpeace has sailed ships into atomic test areas in attempts to prevent nuclear explosions. In the early 1970s, for example, Greenpeace members sailed the "Phyllis Cormack" (which they renamed the "Greenpeace") repeatedly into waters near Amchitka Island, in the Aleutian Islands of Alaska, attempting to halt the explosion of a hydrogen bomb that officials of the United States planned as one of a series of tests there. The ship stayed in international waters, just outside American jurisdiction, yet near enough to be in danger.

Because of schedule shifts, accidents, and maneuvers by American officials, the U.S. Navy gained authority to tow the "Greenpeace" away. A subsequent effort with a converted minesweeper, the "Greenpeace Too," also failed, and Greenpeace was not present when the bomb detonated. Nevertheless, there had been great publicity, and the Atomic Energy Commission announced that although the test had been "safe and successful," there had been a change of plans and there were "no further tests required."[45]

Greenpeace did not originate this form of nuclear protest. As early as 1958, three other Americans accompanied Albert Bigelow, captain of the ketch "Golden Rule," in an attempt to sail into the hydrogen bomb test area in the Marshall Islands. Their purpose was to halt a scheduled test and to generate pressure to cease

---

[44]Marguerite Garling, *The Human Rights Handbook* (London: Macmillan, 1979), p. 8.
[45]Robert Keziere and Robert Hunter, *Greenpeace* (Toronto: McClelland and Steward Ltd., 1972), n.p.

testing altogether. They did not progress beyond Hawaii, where American officials imprisoned them, but their voyage did receive great publicity.[46] There were other similar attempts as well, including one by Earle Reynolds, who actually made it to the test site and was subsequently arrested.[47] Such actions may have contributed to the agreement among most world states in 1963 to halt atmospheric nuclear testing, culminating in the limited test ban treaty of that year.

Other nuclear protests have continued, in Europe, the United States, and elsewhere. Numerous organizations such as SANE, Women Strike for Peace, CNVA (the Committee for Nonviolent Action), Bertrand Russell's Campaign for Nuclear Disarmament, and a host of others have worked diligently to halt the arms race and to oppose nuclear weapons. There have been protests at launchings for nuclear submarines, and demonstrators have trespassed at missile sites in the United States. A group of trespassers at one such site near Kansas City in 1986 received prison sentences, some as long as eight years, an unusually harsh punishment. Press reports in April of 1987 indicated that one of these demonstrators had agreed to pledge future adherence to the law. The judge reduced the sentence by one-half, still an extremely heavy punishment for such a nonviolent act. In May another person made the same pledge and received a reduction to one year in prison.

Greenpeace has continued its activities in opposition to all nuclear tests, and it has repeatedly sailed into the French nuclear test zone in the South Pacific to disrupt tests there. New Zealand officials have vigorously protested the French tests, which they perceive as dangerous to their country. In 1986 a Greenpeace ship, the "Rainbow Warrior," was in a New Zealand harbor when French agents sabotaged and sank it, not only destroying the ship, but causing loss of life.

New Zealand protested vigorously to France; it captured and convicted the French agents, sending them to prison. French officials at first denied the incident, then admitted it and agreed to pay reparations to New Zealand, which released the prisoners to France. The episode brought great international attention to the question of French tests and adverse publicity to France—one of

---

[46] Albert Bigelow, *The Voyage of the Golden Rule* (Garden City, N.Y.: Doubleday, 1959).
[47] Earle Reynolds, *The Forbidden Voyage* (New York: D. McKay, 1961).

the few nations that refuses to accept the test ban treaty and therefore insists on conducting tests that send radioactive debris into the atmosphere and around the world. It also demonstrated the importance that France attached to Greenpeace's nonviolent campaign against nuclear testing.

Among the many activities that Greenpeace adopts to preserve the environment is its attack upon whaling. Because of the threat to whales as an endangered species, all nations had ceased to kill them except for Japan and the U.S.S.R. Greenpeace is an avid foe of whalers of both countries, sending its ships to follow their ships, and putting small boats directly into the paths of the whaling vessels when they near schools of whales. They endanger their own lives, offering their boats and their bodies as targets between the whales and the harpooners.

Such nonviolent activism receives maximum publicity—as the members of Greenpeace are careful to ensure—including movies and videotapes of the most dramatic moments. The bravery of the Greenpeace sailors is obvious, as is the frustration and irritation of the whalers. Not only has Greenpeace succeeded in saving many individual whales, but in mid-1987, both Japan and the Soviet Union announced that they would cease all whaling activities, a clear victory for nonviolent resistance.

CONSIDERATIONS

The purpose here is not to provide a history of nonviolence, nor is it to present a comprehensive list or discussion of the many organizations that are important. There are many in-depth treatments of pacifism, nonviolent theory, and the history of nonviolent resistance.[48]

---

[48] Those interested in pacifism in the twentieth century should turn to Brock; for conversations with noted figures of the 1960s, to James Finn, ed., *Protest: Pacifism and Politics* (New York: Vintage, 1968); for the best general treatments of nonviolence, to Sibley's writings, esp. *The Quiet Battle*; to Stiehm for an excellent brief treatment of nonviolence in America; for essays on civil disobedience, to Hugo Adam Bedau, ed., *Civil Disobedience: Theory and Practice* (New York: Pegasus, 1969); and for nonviolent alternatives to military national defense, to Sibley's *Quiet Battle*, to Adam Roberts, ed., *Civilian Resistance as a National Defence: Non-Violent Action Against Aggression* (Baltimore: Penguin, 1969), and to various publications of the American Friends Service Committee, esp. *In Place of War: An Inquiry into Nonviolent National Defense* (New York: Grossman Publishers, 1967).

Our focus, however, is political ideology; specifically, the ideologies of violence and nonviolence. Every ideology provides some sort of goal toward which to work. In the case of nonviolence, it is to achieve a certain kind of world. This goal is not well-defined but "would appear to imply one in which social and political organizations are not used to manipulate men for the glory and gain of other men; in which the employment of physical force is always discriminate and never deliberately injurious—or disappears altogether; and in which conflict, assuming its inevitablility in the life of man, takes place without resort to violence and increasingly at the level of ideas."[49]

The goal of nonviolence includes human rights in general, and individual social and political freedom in particular. Groups, including nations as we have defined them, would have the right within broad limitations to self-determination and autonomy. "But the war-making, sovereign nation-State of modern times could have no place within a non-violent society." It would be difficult to imagine "a world without military bureaucracies, conscription, bemedaled generals, twenty-one gun salutes, budgets dominated by the call to mass violence, and the centralization of power engendered in considerable measure by the war-State. At the very least, the nature of the historical 'State' would be radically transformed as one of its major functions ceased to be preparation for war."[50]

A nonviolent society would be one with considerable decentralization. It would recognize the need for some overall planning and for some central structure, but decisions would be as close to the people as possible. Thomas Jefferson's "ward republics" come to mind here (see pp. 46–48). It would provide for the "will of the people" to prevail, yet that is only one of its values. It also would provide for individual conscience and individual autonomy, as do Quaker procedures within their meetings.

The advocates of nonviolence would argue that this is more practical than it may sound. Many nonviolent traditions already exist. We have courts, legislatures, and restrictions upon the use of violence by government forces, all consistent with nonviolent principles. Modern society is a mixture of patterns, violent and nonviolent. Either could be expanded.

[49] Sibley, *Quiet Battle*, pp. 359–60.
[50] Ibid., p. 360.

Could a nonviolent society prevail against the violence of foreign countries? The advocates of nonviolence contend that there can be effective nonviolent national defense. Such a defense would depend upon the dedication of every citizen and the commitment both to the society and to the principle of nonviolence. There would be no violent resistance even in the case of invasion—which, they argue, would be highly unlikely to occur because a nonviolent nation would threaten no one. The defense would come in the form of nonviolent resistance; ultimately, of a general strike. It would cause suffering, they admit, but certainly less so than war. No country has the resources to rule another without the cooperation of those who are to be ruled. One country could destroy a nonviolent nation with nuclear weapons out of spite, but there then would be nothing left to rule, and the attacking country itself would be severely damaged, if not destroyed, by the effect of the annihilation that it wrought.

Sibley has remarked that even if a nonviolent nation has to suffer injustice, it does not commit it. But are societies too violent ever to change? Most major religions, including those adhered to by a vast majority of humanity, include strong pacifist strains. As remarked above, nonviolent traditions exist alongside those of violence. Studies of the American soldier in the Second World War indicated that some two-thirds of them were unable to shoot enemy soldiers, even after military training, when the situation called for it.[51]

The basic questions of politics are the boundaries between human rights and property rights, the duties and rights of the individual and the community, and the obligations between the people, collectively, and their leadership structure. Nonviolent theory deals with all of these and encourages a program of action. If there remains any doubt that nonviolence may truly become a political ideology, this should lay them to rest.

[51] See Sibley, *Quiet Battle*, pp. 361–77, from which I have taken much of the previous discussion.

Epilogue

By this time, the importance of political ideology should be clear. We have examined various ideologies, including many that have not previously been recognized as falling within that category. We also have observed how ideologies operate in the real world and how they affect the manner in which human beings live. In recognition of the most important feature of a political ideology—its action orientation—we have accepted a broad definition that includes all thought systems that have practical effects upon politics.

In so doing, we have expanded our concern beyond the narrowly political. Religion, administrative theory, violence, nonviolence, and a host of other considerations become relevant. It is difficult in many instances, for example, to distinguish between economic and political theory or ideology; at one time there were departments of "political economy." There is no doubt that Marxism should be classified as economics. The same holds true for socialism and to some extent for liberalism as well. But they are hardly less political than economic.

It is simple to recognize in such obvious cases that it may be helpful to classify an ideology in more than one discipline, but many other examples are anything but obvious. Some ideologies will be difficult to recognize as political because traditionally they have not been so considered. Our definition of political ideology permits us to avoid the limitations of rigid categories. We can apply categories or disciplines as we find them useful, and they need not be exclusive; we may feel free not only to classify an ideology in one or more categories, but to avoid applying any category at all when to do so would add no clarity. We therefore are able to concentrate upon effects rather than upon semantics and to apply whatever discipline may be relevant to our studies. In a real sense, then, our broad view of political ideology is based upon an interdisciplinary approach.

Political ideology joins thought and action. Thus, to understand politics and political developments it is essential to have an understanding of political ideology. This in turn requires at least some understanding of history, economics, sociology, philosophy, psychology, religion, and other fields in addition to political science. Similarly, it requires an awareness of other ideologies that may become political.

THE IDEOLOGUE

Although an understanding of politics requires a knowledge of various ideologies, it is not sufficient merely to understand ideological details. It is important also to be aware of the psychological effects of ideology upon political actors. The content of an ideology of course affects any political system in which it is significant, but the way in which political actors respond to the ideology is equally important.

All people respond to one or more ideologies whether they recognize it as such or not. Everyone turns to ideology in one way or another, usually as a guide, which is its proper function. Different persons, though, react in different ways. For some, the power of ideology is overwhelming, so that it becomes no longer merely a guide, but an all-consuming force that supersedes any critical abilities that they may have had. Such persons become ideologues.

There are examples on all sides and from all points on the political spectrum. A 1979 controversy surrounding folk singer Joan Baez is a pertinent illustration. Ms. Baez had been a prominent protester against the war in Vietnam and had been severely critical of American policy. Following the war, there were numerous reports—some documented by Amnesty International—that the Vietnamese government was torturing political prisoners and that conditions in prison camps and "re-education centers" in Vietnam were extremely brutal. In response, she formed a new organization, a "Humanitas-International Human Rights Commission," to bring pressure upon the government of Vietnam to halt the human rights abuses and held a news conference to protest Vietnamese violations of prisoners' human rights.[1] She followed with an advertisement in five newspapers in which she and eighty-three other public figures who had been opposed to the war signed an open letter to the government of Vietnam, charging that "Thousands of innocent Vietnamese, whose only 'crimes' are those of conscience, are being arrested, detained and tortured in prisons and re-education camps."[2]

Then came the controversy that reflected the approach of the ideologue. Several others who also had been war protesters were outraged that Joan Baez would attack Vietnam publicly. The implication was that to criticize Vietnam in any way was to "sell out," *regardless of its policies!* Hans Konig, for instance, published a letter in the *New York Times*[3] in which he said that taking out such advertisements in opposition to the war had been appropriate because they were directed at ourselves. Ms. Baez's open letter, however, was *not* appropriate because it amounted to "lecturing" to the Vietnamese, which we had no business doing. Similarly, the activist lawyer William M. Kunstler engaged in an open dispute with Ms. Baez regarding her criticisms. Mr. Kunstler considered Ms. Baez's complaints to be out of line because Vietnam is a socialist country, and socialist countries should not be criticized for any reason. Such approaches identify the presence of ideologues. She responded quite reasonably that the war had been wrong, and she had spoken against it. Mistreating prisoners is also wrong, and she would speak against that too, regardless of which government might be responsible.

The ideologue permits the ideology to supersede all other considerations. This is the danger. Content is, to be sure, vitally

---

[1] *New York Times* (May 30, 1979), p. 14.
[2] Ibid. (May 31, 1979), p. 5.
[3] Ibid. (June 8, 1987), p. 30.

important, but even benign content can have pernicious consequences in the hands—or minds—of ideologues.

We do not have to refer to the extremes of history, the terror following the French Revolution, the horrors of Pol Pot, the insanity of the Third Reich, for examples of damage done by ideologues. An example that is closer to home and considerably less extreme—one, in fact, that is "All-American"—may be easier to comprehend.

THE IDEOLOGUE IN ACTION: ECONOMIC IDEOLOGY AS POLITICAL IDEOLOGY

An economic ideology that dominated much of the discussion of the American presidential election of 1980 was "supply-side economics," which, along with other policies of the newly-elected president, Ronald Reagan, quickly came to be called "Reaganomics." The essence of supply-side economic doctrine was that sharp tax cuts would so stimulate business activity that they actually would increase government revenue. The argument was that taxes in the United States were so high that they stifled the economy.

If there were no taxes, of course, the government would have no tax revenue; if taxes were 100% of income, the government also would have no tax revenue because no one would work simply to turn over everything earned to the government. The government would receive the greatest amount of tax revenue from tax levels set somewhere between zero and 100%. The supply-side advocates asserted that tax levels in 1980 were too high on the curve toward 100% and that therefore the government would receive increased revenues simply by lowering tax rates. The lower tax rates were supposed to increase the incentive to earn, which in turn would so stimulate the economy that it would generate the higher tax income.

Ideologies frequently have the power to persist in the face of facts that should raise questions regarding their validity. In the case of supply-side economics, there was no evidence that U.S. taxes were so high that they restricted incentive. Quite the contrary. Not only were there other countries in 1980 with higher taxes that were outperforming the U.S. economically, but there had been times in America's own history when its taxes had been higher, yet its economy more vigorous.

"Reaganomics" became something more than mere supply-side economics. Mr. Reagan campaigned upon a program calling for cuts in domestic spending, cuts in taxes, and increases in military spending. At the same time, he severely criticized deficit spending and criticized his opponents for having operated with deficits exceeding fifty billion dollars. He promised that his program would balance the budget, despite his military increases, saying that cuts elsewhere in the budget plus the extra revenue generated from tax cuts—the supply-side argument—would more than compensate for the higher military spending. The promise of a balanced budget by 1984 was a key component of Mr. Reagan's campaign, and for years he had been well-known as a dedicated foe of all deficit spending.

Rather than increasing government revenues, the tax cuts reduced them sharply. So great were the reductions in revenue, in fact, that the Reagan administration was forced the next year to support sharp tax increases, though the increased taxes still were much too small to generate the same amount of revenue as before the cuts. The result was a huge increase in the budget deficit, which each year amounts to more than three times what it had been before the tax cuts. The Reagan administration did make numerous cuts in the budget, but when they had cut it as much as feasible, the reductions were still far too small to compensate for the combination of increased military spending and reduced revenues.

The outcome made it clear that political ideology was stronger even than the economic ideology that had generated it. Within four years, the foes of deficit spending had succeeded in doubling the national debt that it had taken the United States more than two hundred years to accumulate. The desire to keep taxes low had overwhelmed the desire to avoid deficit spending, and not once did Mr. Reagan ever submit a budget proposal that was in balance. He did, however, lend his support to an amendment to the Constitution that would require balanced budgets, and he reiterated tirelessly his belief that the only way in which the budget could be balanced was by additional cuts—generally unspecified—in the budget.

The man who served as the Reagan administration's budget director during the time that it implemented its program was David

A. Stockman, Mr. Reagan's first Director of the Office of Management and Budget. More than any single person except perhaps for Mr. Reagan himself, Mr. Stockman was responsible for "Reaganomics." He has provided an unusually revealing picture of the economic and political ideology involved—and an astonishingly unflattering picture of himself as an ideologue at work—in a remarkable book, *The Triumph of Politics: The Inside Story of the Reagan Revolution.*[4]

Mr. Stockman describes his ideological fervor throughout the book, and how, early in the campaign, he concluded that to Mr. Reagan supply-side economics was only a set of vague symbols. He wrote that "the candidate had only the foggiest idea of what supply side was all about" and that "no one close to him had any more idea."[5] He pointed out that politicians, with their worldly wisdom, were suspicious of ideologues, but that he managed to secure the support of the conservatives by eventually coming up with "what appeared to be a balanced budget and a big tax cut, too." He admitted that "the irony was that the supply-side idea was properly suspect by the GOP politicians from the very beginning: they knew in their bones they couldn't live with massive tax and spending reductions."[6]

Much of the book is a catalogue of errors and an admission that ideology alone was the driving force. By his own admission, neither Stockman nor anyone else really knew what was happening. As an illustration, the proposed military budget was considerably greater even than the new administration had intended. Their campaign proposals had called for an increase of from five to nine percent, based on President Carter's 1980 military budget of $142 billion. Mr. Stockman said that because of his—hence the administration's—miscalculations, the increases had been based upon an inflated base of $222 billion, which led to growth twice that which "candidate Ronald Reagan had promised in his campaign budget plan." Stockman said that he "stormed about the office fuming" over his mistake, but that the budget figures already were public and it was too late to correct them.[7]

[4]David A. Stockman, *The Triumph of Politics: The Inside Story of the Reagan Revolution* (New York: Avon Books, 1987).
[5]Ibid., p. 50.
[6]Ibid., p. 59.
[7]Ibid., pp. 118–19.

Another illustration is what Mr. Stockman called his "magic asterisk." When it became apparent during the early phases of the budget planning that not even the most unrealistically optimistic forecasts could bring the budget proposal into balance, he simply provided an asterisk. The footnote to which it referred said "Future savings to be identified." He described the tactic as "bookkeeping invention" and remarked simply that "if we couldn't find the savings in time—and we couldn't—we would issue an IOU."[8] So awed were the politicians by Mr. Reagan's sweeping victory and so powerfully did ideology hold others in its grip, that no one noticed the fraud, or at least, no one questioned it. Stockman made his intentions clear. He said that "Future savings to be identified" was simply "a euphemism for 'We're going to go after Social Security'."[9] He soon had his illusions dispelled, however, and recognized that "the whole plan had been put together too quickly. The $44 billion magic asterisk was a time bomb."[10]

As the deficit increased and the national debt accumulated, the administration turned its attention to rationalizing the troubles. The president and his advisers maintained that they had "inherited this mess," and that things would have been considerably worse without Reaganomics. Stockman was instructed to "make the numbers prove all this. Well, you couldn't. No known method of accounting could." Even if the Congress had given Mr. Reagan exactly what he had requested, the deficit by 1986 would have been $150 billion, while under Mr. Carter's policies it would have been only $80 billion.[11] Keep in mind that these comments indicting the Reagan fiscal program came from the man who essentially designed it, and he has admitted his own blame.

Mr. Stockman said that fairly early in the planning he began to recognize the magnitude of the difficulties that the country was facing as a result of the policies he had designed for President Reagan. He attempted, he said, to convince others in the administration—up to and including the president—of the seriousness of the situation. No one would listen, and the numbers continued to get worse. He asked why this was permitted to happen, and he answered his own question. "Ronald Reagan is a terminal

[8] Ibid., p. 135.
[9] Ibid., p. 175.
[10] Ibid., p. 195.
[11] Ibid., pp. 388–89.

optimist," he wrote, and had "absolute faith that these massive deficits were simply going to vanish."[12] The president and his advisers were so caught up in their own ideology that they literally could not see the danger. The world was different from what their ideology told them that it *had* to be because their policies were in effect. They could not recognize the difference because that ideology blinded them to reality.

"What do you do," Mr. Stockman asked, "when your President ignores all the palpable, relevant facts and wanders in circles. I could not bear," he wrote, "to watch this good and decent man go on in this embarrassing way." He attempted to resign his office because of his disillusionment and his guilt at what he had done to the country, but stayed until after the 1984 elections to avoid harming the president. His book is a chronicle of misinformation, miscalculation, irresponsibility, illusion, and the "dreamland" in which he contended the Reagan policymakers lived. Its conclusion is that those policymakers would rather be responsible for "calamity" than admit their errors.[13] Mr. Stockman remarked upon the irony of the fact that his "Grand Doctrine for remaking the world," had, in only four years "turned, finally, into a dutiful loyalty to nonsense. That," he said, "was the worst lesson of all."[14]

Loyalty, judging even from what he has said of himself, is not a quality that David Stockman possesses in great abundance. He evidently is a man who does nothing halfway, and he seems to embark upon each project as if it were a crusade, with enormous enthusiasm, regardless of what or who may stand in his way. But he seems not to be capable of maintaining his fierce ideological commitments when they prove not to bring expected results. Although his ability in the end to rise above his ideology speaks well for his intelligence, it does nothing for his peace of mind. His book is a lament for his own life as an ideologue.

SOME CONCLUDING THOUGHTS

However one reacts to David Stockman and his revelations, his candid description of policies, deliberate and accidental, reveals

[12] Ibid., pp. 405–6.
[13] Ibid., p. 435.
[14] Ibid., pp. 406–7.

much about the role of ideology in society. He admits that after only about nine months into the first year of the Reagan administration, he ceased to ask what should be done, but rather what could be done. "It is the question politicians ask, not ideologues," he said.[15] He began to recognize the harm that ideologues cause and that "the politics of American democracy made a shambles of" his "anti-welfare state theory." That theory, he recognized belatedly, "rested on the illusion that the will of the people was at drastic variance with the actions of the politicians."[16] The man who designed much of the Reagan program said that "the Reagan Revolution was radical, imprudent, and arrogant. It defied the settled consensus of professional politicians and economists. . . . It mistakenly presumed that a handful of ideologues were right and all the politicians were wrong about what the American people wanted from government."[17] Coming from its designer, this is certainly an indictment of policy, but coming from one who should know, it is even more an indictment of ideology in the hands of the ideologue.

Many ideologies display their objectionable features openly. Those persons whose inclinations are toward liberal democracy or democratic socialism, when confronted with fascism, for example, would reject it immediately—if they are consistent. On the other hand, they might accept with little question those ideologies incorporating values compatible with their own.

Throughout this book we have warned of the dangers of ideology. Even the best of them can be warped to become different from what they were originally. In the hands of an ideologue, any ideology can be dangerous, whatever its character.

But it is not only ideologues who distort or misuse ideologies. All governments find them to be useful, and extremely effective, as methods of social control. It is the ideology of nationalism that has created the modern nation-state, and it is the nation-state that uses ideology to maintain itself, and to achieve its purposes.

This is not to say that we can escape ideology—nor even that we should. As remarked earlier, ideology provides a guide to thought and conduct, and it helps human beings relate to the world around them, to their fellows, and even to themselves. Most

[15] Ibid., p. 324.
[16] Ibid., p. 408.
[17] Ibid., p. 429.

of us can recognize the dangers of the ideologue. We can agree that it is essential to control ideology within ourselves so that it does not become an all-embracing passion leading to fanaticism, and we can recognize it when it reaches that stage in others.

The more subtle dangers are perhaps the greater. It is not necessary to become an ideologue to become a slave to ideology. Whenever an ideology achieves the state that it goes unquestioned, it becomes a danger to thought. There is much more to humanity, of course, than the power of thought. Nevertheless, human thought is one characteristic that is essential to human functioning. When humankind operates automatically and without reflection, it becomes mindless—and heartless. No ideology—however benign, however worthwhile, however exalted—should be permitted to become completely dominant over the human mind. Independent judgment is vital, and even an ideology of independence, if taken too literally, too fervently, can destroy independence of thought.

We all have ideologies; they are inevitable in the modern world. As guides they are invaluable. They may be especially helpful if we are aware of them and if we continually examine them. The one characteristic that must not be surrendered is independence of thought. Our ideologies will affect our thought—otherwise they would not be our ideologies—but we must retain the ability to reflect upon them and, above all, to protect fiercely that most fundamental of prerogatives—the right to change one's mind.

REFERENCES CITED

Abbott, Walter M., ed. *The Documents of Vatican II.* New York: Guild Press, 1966.

Adrian, Charles R. *Governing Our Fifty States and Their Communities.* New York: McGraw–Hill, 1978.

American Friends Service Committee. *In Place of War: An Inquiry into Nonviolent National Defense.* New York: Grossman Publishers, 1967.

Anderson, Walt. *Politics and the New Humanism.* Pacific Palisades, Calif.: Goodyear, 1973.

Arendt, Hannah. *On Revolution.* New York: Viking, 1965.

————. *The Origins of Totalitarianism.* New York: Harcourt, Brace & World, 1968.

Arieli, Yehoshua. *Individualism and Nationalism in American Ideology.* Baltimore: Penguin Books, 1966.

Bachrach, Peter. *The Theory of Democratic Elitism.* Boston: Little, Brown, 1967.

Baldwin, Stanley E. *Charles Kingsley.* Ithaca: Cornell University Press, 1934.

Baradat, Leon P. *Political Ideologies,* 2nd ed. Englewood Cliffs, N.J.: Prentice–Hall, 1984.

Barnes, James, Marshall Carter, and Max J. Skidmore. *The World of Politics,* 2nd ed. New York: St. Martin's Press, 1984.

Bedau, Hugo Adam, ed. *Civil Disobedience: Theory and Practice.* New York: Pegasus, 1969.

Bellah, Robert N. "Civil Religion in America." *Daedalus* 96:1 (Winter 1967): 1–21.

Bellamy, Edward. *Looking Backward: 2000–1887.* Boston: Houghton Mifflin, 1966; first published in 1888.

Benello, C. George, and Dimitrios Roussopoulos, eds. *The Case for Participatory Democracy.* New York: Viking, 1971.

Bigelow, Albert. *The Voyage of the Golden Rule.* Garden City, N.Y.: Doubleday, 1959.

Bluhm, William T. *Ideologies and Attitudes: Modern Political Culture.* Englewood Cliffs, N.J.: Prentice–Hall, 1974.

Boff, Leonardo. *Jesus Christ Liberator.* Maryknoll, N.Y.: Orbis Books, 1978.

Bondurant, Joan V., ed. *Conflict: Violence and Nonviolence.* Chicago: Aldine/Atherton, 1971.

327

Brock, Peter. *Twentieth-Century Pacifism.* New York: Van Nostrand Reinhold, 1970.

Brown, L. B. *Ideology.* Baltimore: Penguin, 1973.

Butler, Benjamin F. Untitled speech to the Senate. *Congressional Globe.* 42nd Congress, 2nd Session, April 18, 1872. Appendix 267–68.

Christenson, Reo M., Alan S. Engel, Dan N. Jacobs, Mostafa Rejai, and Herbert Waltzer. *Ideologies & Modern Politics.* New York: Dodd, Mead, 1971.

Cornevin, Marianne. *Apartheid: Power and Historical Falsification.* Paris: UNESCO, 1980.

Dickson, David. "Limiting Democracy: Technocrats and the Liberal State." *Democracy* 1:1 (January 1981): 61–79.

Dvorin, Eugene P., and Robert H. Simmons. *From Amoral to Humane Bureaucracy.* New York: Canfield Press of Harper & Row, 1972.

Finn, James. *Protest: Pacifism and Politics.* New York: Vintage, 1968.

Frankel, Charles. *The Democratic Prospect.* New York: Harper & Row, 1962.

Fremantle, Anne, ed. *The Papal Encyclicals in Their Historical Context* New York: G. P. Putnam's Sons, 1956.

Garling, Marguerite. *The Human Rights Handbook.* London: Macmillan, 1979.

Gentile, Giovanni. *The Genesis and Structure of Society.* Urbana: University of Illinois Press, 1960.

Gluck, Jay. *Zen Combat.* New York: Ballantine, 1962.

Goodall, Leonard E. *The American Metropolis.* Columbus, Ohio: Charles E. Merrill, 1968.

Goodsell, Charles T. *The Case for Bureaucracy: A Public Administration Polemic.* Chatham, N.J.: Chatham House Publishers, 1983.

Gutierrez, Gustavo. *A Theory of Liberation: History, Politics, and Salvation.* Maryknoll, N.Y.: Orbis Books, 1973.

Gyorgy, Andrew, and George D. Blackwood. *Ideologies in World Affairs.* Waltham, Mass.: Blaisdell, 1967.

Harrell, C. A., and D. G. Weiford. "The City Manager and the Policy Process." *Public Administration Review* XIX:2 (Spring 1959): 101–7.

Harrigan, John J. *Political Change in the Metropolis.* Boston: Little, Brown, 1976.

Hayek, Friedrich A. *The Road to Serfdom.* Chicago: University of Chicago Press, 1957.

———. "Why I Am Not a Conservative," in Hayek, *The Constitution of Liberty.* London: Routledge & Kegan Paul, 1960.

Hays, Samuel P. "The Politics of Reform in Municipal Government in the Progressive Era." *Pacific Northwest Quarterly* 55 (October 1964): 157–69.

Himmelfarb, Milton. "Secular Society? A Jewish Perspective." *Daedalus* 96:1 (Winter 1967): 220–36.

Hitler, Adolf. *Mein Kampf.* Boston: Houghton Mifflin, 1962; originally published in 1925.

Hobbes, Thomas. *Leviathan.* Oxford, England: Basil Blackwell, 1957; originally published in 1651.

Hobhouse, L. T. *The Metaphysical Theory of the State.* New York: Barnes & Noble, 1960.

Hofstadter, Richard. "The Future of American Violence." *Harper's Magazine* (April 1970): 17, 48–53; reprinted in *The Dissent of the Governed*, John Livingston and Robert Thompson, eds., 294–305. New York: Macmillan, 1972.

Hofstadter, Richard, and Michael Wallace, eds. *American Violence*. New York: Vintage, 1971.

Ingersoll, David E. *Communism, Fascism, and Democracy*. Columbus, Ohio: Merrill, 1971.

"Instruction on Certain Aspects of the Theology of Liberation." Second Congregation for the Doctrine of the Faith, The Vatican, September 1984.

James, William. *Pragmatism*. New York: Meridian Books, 1955.

Jenckes, Thomas A. Untitled speech to the House of Representatives. *Congressional Globe*. 39th Congress, 2nd Session, January 29, 1867, 837–41.

Kateb, George. "The Night Watchman State." *The American Scholar* 45, no. 1 (Winter 1975–76).

Keziere, Robert, and Robert Hunter, *Greenpeace*. Toronto: McClelland and Steward Ltd., 1972.

Koch, Adrienne. *The Philosophy of Thomas Jefferson*. New York: Columbia University Press, 1943.

Kramer, Jane. "Letter From the Elysian Fields." *The New Yorker* (March 2, 1987): 40–75.

Krimerman, Leonard, and Lewis Perry, eds. *Patterns of Anarchy*. Garden City, N.Y.: Doubleday/Anchor, 1966.

LaHaye, Tim. *The Battle for the Mind*. Old Tappan, N.J.: Fleming H. Revell Co., 1980.

Lenin, V. I. *What Is To Be Done?* New York: International Press, 1929.

Leonard, George. "The Nonviolent Martial Art." *Esquire* (July 1983): 132.

Lewis, Eugene. *The Urban Political System*. Hinsdale, N.Y.: Holt, Rinehart & Winston, 1973.

Littell, Franklin H. "The Churches and the Body Politic." *Daedalus* 96:1 (Winter 1967): 22–42.

McCormick, Richard L. *From Realignment to Reform: Political Change in New York State, 1893–1910*. Ithaca: Cornell University Press, 1981.

McGovern, William. *From Luther to Hitler*. New York: Houghton Mifflin, 1941.

McLoughlin, William G. "Is There a Third Force in Christendom?" *Daedalus* 96:1 (Winter 1967), 43–68.

Macridis, Roy C. *Contemporary Political Ideologies*, 3rd ed., Boston: Little, Brown, 1986.

Magubane, Bernard Makhosezwe. *The Political Economy of Race and Class in South Africa*. New York: Monthly Review Press, 1979.

Manning, D. J. *Liberalism*. New York: St. Martin's Press, 1976.

Martin, Robert B. *The Dust of Combat: The Life of Charles Kingsley*. New York: W. W. Norton, 1960.

Mark, Max. *Modern Ideologies*. New York: St. Martin's Press, 1973.

Marx, Karl. "Later Political Writings, 1864–82," in *Karl Marx: Selected Writings*, D. McLellan, ed. New York: Oxford University Press, 1977.

Mason, A. T. *Free Government in the Making*, 3rd ed. New York: Oxford University Press, 1965.

Mehta, Ved. "Letter From New Delhi." *The New Yorker* (January 19, 1987): 52–69.

Meisel, James H., ed. *Pareto and Mosca*. Englewood Cliffs, N.J.: Prentice–Hall, 1965.

Mills, C. Wright. *The Power Elite*. New York: Oxford University Press, 1959.

Mussolini, Benito. *Fascism: Doctrine and Institutions*. New York: Howard Fertig, 1968.

Nieburg, H. L. "The Threat of Violence and Social Change." *American Political Science Review* 56 (1962): 865–73; reprinted in *Conflict: Violence and Nonviolence*, Joan V. Bondurant, ed., 73–88. Chicago: Aldine/Atherton, 1971.

Nietzsche, Friedrich. *The Use and Abuse of History*, 2nd (revised) ed. New York: The Liberal Arts Press, Inc., 1957.

———. *The Will to Power*. New York: Random House, 1967.

Nozick, Robert. *Anarchy, State, and Utopia*. New York: Basic Books, 1974.

Peterson, Merrill D., ed. *The Portable Thomas Jefferson*. New York: Viking, 1975.

Petrie, John, ed. *The Worker Priests: A Collective Documentation*. London: Routledge & Kegan Paul, 1956.

Plamenatz, John. *Ideology*. New York: Praeger, 1970.

Pritchett, C. Herman. *The American Constitution*, 2nd ed. New York: McGraw–Hill, 1968.

Rapoport, David C. "Fear and Trembling: Terrorism in Three Religious Traditions." *American Political Science Review* 78:3 (September 1984): 658–77.

Rejai, Mostafa. *Comparative Political Ideologies*. New York: St. Martin' s Press, 1984.

Reynolds, Earle. *The Forbidden Voyage*. New York: D. McKay, 1961.

Roberts, Adam, ed. *Civilian Resistance as a National Defense: Non-Violent Action Against Aggression*. Baltimore: Penguin, 1969.

Rosenthal, A. M. "Direct Link Between Khomeini and Hitler." *Kansas City Times* (January 13, 1987): A7.

Russell, Bertrand. *Power: A New Social Analysis*. New York: Norton, 1938.

———. *Proposed Roads to Freedom: Socialism, Anarchism, and Syndicalism*. London: George Allen and Unwin Ltd., 1919.

Sapiro, Virginia. *The Political Integration of Women*. Urbana: University of Illinois Press, 1983.

Sargent, Lyman Tower. *Contemporary Political Ideologies*, 5th ed. Homewood, Ill.: Dorsey, 1981; 7th ed. Homewood, Ill.: Dorsey, 1987.

Schiesl, Martin J. *The Politics of Efficiency: Municipal Administration and Reform in America, 1880–1920*. Berkeley: University of California Press, 1977.

Schumpeter, Joseph. *Capitalism, Socialism, Democracy*. New York: Harper & Row, 1962.

Shaw, George Bernard, ed. *The Fabian Essays in Socialism*. London: Allen & Unwin, 1958.

———. "The Impossibilities of Anarchism." *Fabian Tract 45*. London: Fabian Society, 1893.

Shirer, William L. *The Rise and Fall of the Third Reich.* New York: Simon & Schuster, 1960.

Sibley, Mulford Q. *Political Ideas and Ideologies.* New York: Harper & Row, 1970.

———. *The Quiet Battle.* Garden City, N.Y.: Doubleday & Co. Anchor Books, 1963.

Skidmore, Max J. *American Political Thought.* New York: St. Martin's Press, 1978.

———. "Urban America," in *American Government and Politics,* B. K. Shrivastava and Thomas W. Casstevens, eds., 254–67. Atlantic Highlands, N.J.: Humanities Press, 1980.

———. *Word Politics: Essays on Language and Politics.* Palo Alto: James E. Freel and Associates, 1972.

Steiner, George. "The Hollow Miracle," in his *Language and Silence: Essays on Language, Literature and the Inhuman.* New York: Atheneum, 1960; originally published in *The Reporter Magazine* (February 18, 1960); also reprinted in Max J. Skidmore. *Word Politics: Essays on Language and Politics.* Palo Alto: James E. Freel and Associates, 1972.

Stiehm, Judith. *Nonviolent Power: Active and Passive Resistance in America.* Boston: D.C. Heath, 1972.

Stockman, David A. *The Triumph of Politics: The Inside Story of the Reagan Revolution.* New York: Avon Books, 1987.

Thompson, Leonard. *The Political Mythology of Apartheid.* New Haven: Yale University Press, 1985.

———. *The Republic of South Africa.* Boston: Little, Brown, 1966.

Tyler, Alice Felt. *Freedom's Ferment.* New York: Harper Torchbooks, 1962.

Viereck, Peter. *Conservatism: From Burke and John Adams Till Now: A History and an Anthology.* Baton Rouge: Louisiana State University Press, 1985.

———. *Conservatism Revisited and the New Conservatism: What Went Wrong?* Westport, Conn.: Greenwood Press, 1978.

———. *Meta-Politics: From the Romantics to Hitler,* rev. ed. Baton Rouge: Louisiana State University Press, 1985.

———. *The Unadjusted Man: Reflections on the Distinction Between Conserving and Conforming.* Westport, Conn.: Greenwood Press, 1973.

Walker, Jack L. "A Critique of the Elitist Theory of Democracy." *American Political Science Review* LX (June 1966): 285–95.

Walker, Jearl. "The Amateur Scientist: In Judo and Aikido Application of the Physics of Forces Makes the Weak Equal to the Strong." *Scientific American* 243:1 (July 1980): 150–62.

Walsh, William P. "The American City Manager and the Italian Podesta." *Public Management* 62 (July 1980).

Walter, E. V. *Terror and Resistance: A Study of Political Violence.* New York: Oxford University Press, 1969.

Ward, Barbara. *Nationalism and Ideology.* New York: W. W. Norton, 1966.

Watkins, Frederick M. *The Age of Ideology—Political Thought, 1750 to the Present.* Englewood Cliffs, N.J.: Prentice–Hall, 1964.

Wilson, James Q. "Politics and Reform in American Cities," in *Capitol, Courthouse, and City Hall,* 5th ed., Robert L. Morlan, ed., 295–302. Boston: Houghton Mifflin, 1977.

Wolff, Robert Paul. *In Defense of Anarchism.* New York: Harper Torchbooks, 1970.

Woodbridge, Frederick E., and Robert Schenck. Colloquy in the House of Representatives. *Congressional Globe.* 39th Congress, 2nd Session, February 6, 1867, 1034–36.

Yamada, Yoshimitsu. *Aikido: Complete.* Secaucus, N.J.: Citadel Press, 1969.

Yates, Douglas. *The Ungovernable City.* Cambridge: Yale University Press, 1978.

Young, Crawford. "Patterns of Social Conflict: State, Class, and Ethnicity." *Daedalus* 111 (Spring 1982).

Index